THE COMPLETE IDIOT'S GUIDE® TO

Microsoft® Access 2000

by Joe Habraken

A Division of Macmillan Computer Publishing
201 W. 103rd Street, Indianapolis, IN 46290

Trademarks

Warning and Disclaimer

Executive Editor
Rosemarie Graham

Acquisitions Editor
Neil Rowe

Development Editor
Kitty Jarrett

Managing Editor
Jodi Jensen

Project Editor
Tonya Simpson

Copy Editor
Kate Talbot

Indexer
Bruce Clingaman

Proofreader
Eddie Lushbaugh

Technical Editor
Barbara Ansley

Team Coordinator
Carol Ackerman

Illustrator
Judd Winick

Interior Design
Nathan Clement

Cover Design
Nathan Clement

Layout Technicians
Ayanna Lacey
Heather Miller
Amy Parker

Contents at a Glance

Table of Contents

About the Author

Joe Habraken is a computer technology professional and author with more than 12 years experience as an educator and consultant in the information technology field. Joe is a Microsoft Certified Professional and has taught computer software seminars across the country. He has a masters degree from the American University in Washington, D.C., and currently serves as the lead instructor for the Networking Technologies program at Globe College in St. Paul, Minnesota. Despite all his stuffy credentials, Joe has a wicked sense of humor and really enjoyed writing the Complete Idiot's Guide to Microsoft Access 2000. Joe's other recent book titles include The Microsoft Access 97 Exam Guide, Microsoft Office 2000 6 in 1, and Using Lotus SmartSuite Millennium Edition (all Macmillan Computer Publishing).

Dedication

To my incredible spouse, Kim; thanks for loving me even when I'm sitting in front of the computer. I love you too!

Acknowledgments

Creating books like this takes a real team effort. I would like to thank Neil Rowe, our acquisitions editor, who worked very hard to assemble the team that made this book a reality. He also did a great job managing all the players involved as the book moved from initial concept to finished product. I would also like to thank Kitty Jarrett, who served as the developmental editor for this book and who came up with many great ideas for improving the content of the book. Also a tip of the hat and a thanks to Barbara Ansley, technical editor for the project. She did a fantastic job making sure that everything was correct and suggested a number of additions that made the book even more technically sound. Finally, a great big thanks to our project editor, Tonya Simpson, who ran the last leg of the race and made sure the book made it to press on time—what a great team of professionals.

Tell Us What You Think!

As the reader of this book, *you* are our most important critic and commentator. We value your opinion and want to know what we're doing right, what we could do better, what areas you'd like to see us publish in, and any other words of wisdom you're willing to pass our way.

As an Associate Publisher at Que Corporation, I welcome your comments. You can fax, email, or write me directly to let me know what you did or didn't like about this book—as well as what we can do to make our books stronger.

Please note that I cannot help you with technical problems related to the topic of this book, and that due to the high volume of mail I receive, I might not be able to reply to every message.

When you write, please be sure to include this book's title and author, as well as your name and phone or fax number. I will carefully review your comments and share them with the author and editors who worked on the book.

Fax: 317-581-4666

Email: office_que@mcp.com

Mail: Greg Wiegand
            Associate Publisher
            Que Corporation
            201 West 103rd Street
            Indianapolis, IN 46290 USA

Introduction

Lights, Camera, Access: Introducing Microsoft Access 2000

In today's fast-paced business world, we are constantly bombarded with facts and figures. With electronic media as the rule, the Internet and World Wide Web bring massive amounts of data right into your office and home via the personal computer. There is no doubt that we are living in the information age.

How well you manage all this information—this data—will certainly have a bearing on your own success. Whether you judge success in professional terms, such as building an important corporate database, or in personal terms, such as managing your ever expanding compact disc collection, Microsoft Access is the database management tool to get you there.

Now, the preceding paragraphs might lead you to think that this book is very serious. In one respect, you would be right. This book takes its job—teaching you the ins and outs of Microsoft Access—very seriously (as I, your faithful servant and author, do). However, this book's approach to covering material that normally would give you a near-fatal migraine is one of clever (at least, my mother thinks so), yet controlled, humorous abandon. This means that we are going to have loads of fun and lots of laughs (at least, some giggles) as we tackle a very powerful database management software application and win!

But I'd Rather Walk on Hot Coals Than Work with Databases

Databases have had a bad rep since the advent of the personal computer. Early database software was quite arcane and very user-unfriendly. It was not uncommon to see a coworker run screaming from the office, a complete nervous wreck, after tussling with a poorly designed database that used an almost indecipherable interface.

Tackling Databases with Access

Microsoft Access 2000 is extremely powerful and very friendly. Its easy-to-use features can help you build very complex and very usable databases for both business and home. You certainly don't have to be a computer guru to dive right into this software application and start building your own databases. This book is here to help you, and you will quickly learn great things, such as

➤ How to plan a proper database that will really work for you

➤ How Access makes it easy for you to build a database

➤ Ways to make data entry easy in your database tables and forms

➤ How to quickly and easily manipulate the data in your database with clever features such as queries

➤ How to report and print the information that you have in your databases so that it looks nice

➤ Ways to protect and maintain the valuable information that you place in your databases

This book will get you up and running in Access almost immediately. In the first three chapters, you will learn how to work with Access, how to get help when you need it, and all about the niceties of designing a database. After that, you will dive right in and work with a number of the database objects and features that Microsoft Access has to offer. You will certainly get your chance to build and troubleshoot databases as you become familiar with this great database software package.

So What's New in Access 2000?

Access 2000 adds several new features that make creating and using databases even easier. These changes range from a new adaptive menu system to an integration feature that makes Access the front-end client for powerful SQL client/server databases.

➤ The new Access Help system provides you with a new look and feel. You can look through the contents of the Help system, ask the Help system questions, and search for help on a specific topic. Don't worry, the Office Assistant is still part of the Access Help system and can provide you with context-sensitive help as you work on your databases.

➤ Access Front End for SQL Databases provides a new object type called projects. These projects are actually links to SQL databases found in client/server network environments. The Access project objects look and act just like normal database objects but link you to data on a database server.

➤ For creating Web-based data forms, Access also adds another new object: data access pages. These pages can be created from existing tables and are used to add data input forms on your Web sites. Data entered into a data access page is automatically placed in the Access database table.

This Book's for You (and Why)

As I sat down to write this book, I was thinking about you, and I figured you were probably a lot like me. You've worked on a computer before, and when you have to learn a new software package (such as Access), you like to cut to the chase and get up and running quickly.

I'll admit that this book is a little bit of an enigma. Although it will serve the novice Access user very well, I also think that the intermediate Access user will find a lot of new information and useful tricks and tips in these pages.

Using (Not Abusing) This Book

Certain conventions have been followed in this book to make things easy for you. When you should select an item, it appears in bold (for example, "Click on the File menu"). When you should type some text, it appears in a monospace font ("Type Kim in the First Name field"). The various toolbar buttons that you are asked to select are represented by a graphic next to the text, which should help you locate the correct button.

Because I really do want you to feel good about Access and its features when you finish this book, you will find that the text remains quite focused when it discusses a particular subject. However, for those of you who crave more information or just enjoy pleasant asides, additional information on certain subjects is provided in special sidebars and notes in the margins.

Check This Out

These boxes include tips about the Access features and database concepts covered in this book. A few might even contain sarcastic remarks, but hey, nobody is perfect.

Techno Talk

These boxes contain higher-level information or additional background information on various subjects. It's stuff that you might find comforting to know. On the other hand, if you don't feel that you have to know everything in the world, you can skip these tasty morsels of information.

Note

Notes provide you with additional cautions or special information that you should remember.

SEE ALSO

Cross Reference—These boxes provide you with a quick and easy way to find cross-referenced material in the other chapters of the book.

Trademark Courtesy

Although you might think that I am being quite courteous by listing the software manufacturers who have created the programs referenced in this book, I am, in fact, putting together an enemy list for the National Luddite Foundation (just kidding—oh, and Luddites are folks who hate technology). The trademarks and service marks that were totally obvious to us all are listed here:

Microsoft Windows 98, Microsoft NT Workstation, Microsoft Access, Microsoft Word, Microsoft Excel, and Microsoft PowerPoint are all registered trademarks of Microsoft Corporation.

Microsoft ActiveX and Microsoft Internet Explorer are trademarks of Microsoft Corporation.

If any trademark or service mark appearing in this book does not appear on the list, it is probably the result of a small error or petty jealousy, so no big deal.

Part 1

Getting Your Feet Wet with Access

Details, details. We live on a planet of over-managed minutia, a world where experts focus on specifics, a place where most of us can't seem to see the forest for the trees. When you're learning something new, it's extremely difficult (and often frustrating) attempting to jump right into the specifics.

Never fear, you're in good hands. This part of the book helps you get a handle on the big picture concepts of database management, provides you with a test drive of Microsoft Access, a powerful and easy-to-use database software package (or minutia manager, if you prefer), and shows you how to get help when you get stuck. It's a world of database fun and excitement that awaits you. So go ahead, turn the page, and jump right in.

Chapter 1

Databases, Access, and You

In This Chapter

➤ Defining the term *database*

➤ Understanding relational databases

➤ Talking semi-intelligently about Access

➤ Understanding the object of database objects

➤ Introducing the Access data access page for online data entry

➤ Beginning to plan your own database

The Almost Unspeakable Question: What Is a Database?

What is a database? That's a question that strikes fear into the hearts of many people. Tomes have been written on the subject. Governments have fallen because of this question. In fact, in some countries, it is illegal to utter this question (when I want to get rid of houseguests who have stayed too long, I ask them this question).

All right, maybe I'm exaggerating a little. You will find, however, that most people view databases as horribly complex entities. Fortunately for you, Access makes database management a breeze. And as for the unutterable question? Well, I'm not afraid to answer it, and by the time you finish reading this book, you'll be able to stop people on the street and describe the makings of a database—whether anyone wants you to or not.

A *database* is simply a collection of organized information relating to a topic: a list of very important clients, a collection of classic vinyl records, or a group of friends who all owe you money. Databases don't have to be the Darth Vaders of the personal computer software world; you can set up a database to be just as user friendly as anything you create in a word processing or spreadsheet software package.

Selling You on Databases

Databases are all around you—the phone book, the dictionary, even your home filing cabinet. Although some of these databases are more organized than others (let's not even start on my filing cabinet), each is a repository of information. You will also find that just about everyone around you uses databases.

The checkout clerks at the grocery store rely on a product database to give them a price every time they scan an item. The mechanic at the service station uses a parts database to see whether he can find a supplier that carries that thing that just fell off your car as you drove past the Lexus dealership (or was that the Saturn dealer?). You probably even use a computerized database when you look up books at your local library (see, databases aren't scary, although the Dewy Decimal system can be).

The main reason to use a database is to keep track of information. But there is much more to database management than putting information in the database; you also want to be able to retrieve, sort, collate, edit, and report the information. Access can do all this and more. Setting up, for example, a database of important clients requires that you input all the information relating to the clients. This sounds like a lot of work, especially if you have hundreds of clients. Eventually, though, you can manipulate and track the information easily and thoroughly—this is what makes Access (and a database, in general) an incredibly useful business or personal tool.

I hope that the panic-ridden urge to drop this book and run screaming from the room has subsided and you are feeling more comfortable with the whole concept of the database. You might even be thinking about all the things you can organize by using a database.

Relating to Access

Microsoft Access is a special kind of database software package, and it can help you build a special kind of database: a *relational database*. Yeah, I know, this book isn't supposed to be supertechnical. Besides, most people don't need a database to keep track of their relations. Bright red T-shirts at the family picnic usually do the trick. Don't worry, relational databases are not that hard to understand, and they are extremely useful when you want to manipulate data (and they won't manipulate you like your in-laws in Idaho).

A relational database divides information into discrete groups that can then be related to each other. For example, one grouping could contain customers, another grouping could show products, a third grouping could consist of suppliers, and a fourth grouping could contain orders. A relational database enables you to set up relationships between these groups and then create reports and forms that tie and display the information in the groups together.

A relational database is like a fisherman's net; each discrete group potentially relates to another discrete group so that all the information can be pulled together when you go fishing for it (this metaphor is making me seasick).

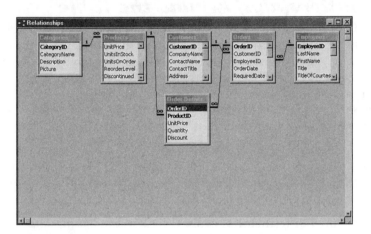

The relationships between the tables in an Access relational database give you incredible powers of manipulation over your data.

It's All in the Table

The core component of a relational database is a *table*. Each table holds the data relating to a particular area of information, such as your customers or suppliers.

Database tables look very much like a spreadsheet; you arrange the information in rows and columns. Each row holds all the information for a particular person, place, or thing. Each column contains a different piece of information pertaining to that person, place, or thing.

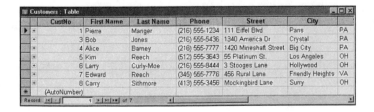

A typical database table.

9

In database terms, each row in the table is a *record*, so each person in a customer table has his own discrete record. Each discrete piece of information in the record is a *field*. For example, a person's first name is a field. You will learn much more about tables and records in Chapter 5, "Turning the Tables: Table Design," and Chapter 6, "Going On Record: Adding and Editing Data," and how to design a relational database in Chapter 8, "Between You and Me and Access: Table Relationships." At this point, just try embracing the concept of the relational database, which groups your information in discrete tables.

Gathering Your Relations(hips) Around the Table

As I said before, it's the tables in your database that you relate. This is done by a field or piece of information that is common to the tables. Later in this book, you'll actually (gasp) create your own databases. First, you'll create a Customers table, where you can assign a customer number to each of your clients. Then, you'll create an Orders table. When you place a new order in your Orders table, you can type in the customer number of the person placing the order. See how the data in the two tables is tied together—by a common piece of information, the customer number.

An example of how you can use this type of relationship between tables would be to create a report for a hardware store, showing how a particular hand tool is selling and who is buying it. This type of report requires related information from your Customers table, Orders table, and probably Products table.

Relational databases are far superior to their less-evolved cousin, the *flat-file database*. A good example of a flat-file database is a spreadsheet program such as Microsoft Excel. If you use a worksheet to track your customer orders, you must repeat all the customer information (his address, phone number, and so on) each time that customer places a new order. In Access, you must repeat the customer's number in the Orders table only; all the related information for the customer resides in the Customers table. Voilà! It all makes sense. Now you see how a relational database works!

A Database with a View: Access Objects

Access does not limit your database work to tables; it provides several ways to view and manipulate your data. Access categorizes each of these viewing and manipulating containers as *objects*.

Macros and Modules

Two of the most complex objects that you can create for your databases are *macros* and *modules*. You can create macros simply by using some Visual Basic code to automate certain repetitive tasks, such as the steps for printing a certain form. A module is a little more complicated; it can contain a great deal of code that invokes a particular complex procedure. Both these objects are complex productivity tools that might not suit the average user. (For more about macros, see Chapter 21, "The Little Engines That Can—Making Macros").

You will probably find that you will use most of the common objects in your databases, especially tables, queries, forms, and reports.

Access Queries, Forms, and Reports

A *query* is the way in which you ask your database questions, such as how many left-handed can openers do you have in stock, and do you have any regular customers who are left-handed and whom you can sell them to. The answer to a query can sort and select data in a particular table or tables. You learn all about queries in Chapter 10, "Reforming Your Forms," and Chapter 11, "Not a Stupid Question—Designing Simple Queries."

A *form* is an excellent way to view, enter, and edit the data in your table. It enables you to look at each record individually—a record-by-record view. Forms are the topic of discussion in Chapter 9, "It's All in Your Form," and Chapter 10, "Reforming Your Forms."

You can use a *report* to pull and summarize information from one or more tables in the database. Reports are a great way to present information in a very readable and attractive format. You will get your feet wet with reports in Chapter 13, "From Soup to Nuts—Creating Delicious Reports." Then you will expand your reporting techniques in Chapter 14, "No Need for a Calculator—Doing Math in Reports," and Chapter 15, "Pride of Ownership—Enhancing Your Reports."

In essence, each of these objects gives you a different view of your data. You will find that after you finish this book, you will want to have several objects set up for each database. After the various objects are in place, most of your database work will consist of either data input or reporting.

A New Access Object—Data Access Pages

Access 2000 also introduces a new Access database object: the *data access page*. Access data access pages are Web-ready data entry forms that can easily be created using the Data Access Page Wizard. These access pages can then be placed on personal or corporate Web sites and used as online data entry forms. The data entered on these pages on the Web is then placed in the associated Access database. Access data pages make it easy for you to build a customer list from the Web or design a Web site for online ordering of products or services. For more information about data access pages, see Chapter 23, "Surf's Up, Dude—Access on the Internet."

Access data access pages provide you with a fast way to create online order or questionnaire forms for your Web site.

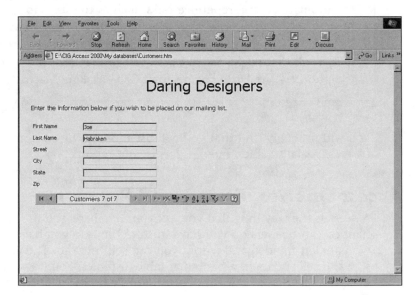

Access Projects Provide the Front End for SQL Databases

Access also provides a new file format called the *project*. Projects are actually front-end elements (menus, icons, objects, and so on) for powerful SQL databases that reside on a special network server. In an Access project, you will find that all the objects provided in the Project window are actually links to processes that happen on the database server. Access, in effect, provides you with an easy-to-use interface window that looks into a very complex database service on a network.

Planning Your Database

Rome wasn't built in a day, and neither were the sets for most of Cecil B. DeMille's film epics (You remember Charlton Heston flying around the Roman amphitheater in his chariot in *Ben Hur,* don't you?). Taking a little time to plan your database will pay off the very first time you print a successful report for your boss. You must keep in mind that you must set up the database data so that it is easy to manipulate. The following are a few tried and true rules that will help you design your database (I'm not saying, "Don't ever break the rules," but at least they will help you start):

➤ Grab a piece of paper and think through the database design; decide what tables, forms, and reports your database will most likely need. You can then build on this foundation.

➤ Set up the first table for the database. Make sure it provides all the information you will need for that particular category of data. If you design the table for customer data, make sure you include a column for Zip codes and phone numbers.

➤ Use forms for data entry. Forms enable you to concentrate on one record at a time and see each piece of information that must be input into the record. Incomplete records can be a real drag.

➤ Remember that Access is a relational database. Each table should contain information that relates directly back to the table's purpose. For example, a Customers table should hold information on customers, not on products. If you want product data listed, design another table for your products.

➤ Reports are the icing on the cake. They present your data in a positive and clear format. Design them carefully. They are probably the only thing related to your database that other people will see.

➤ Save your work and save it often. Don't even turn on the computer if you are going to spend hours inputting data and then not save the information. A power failure can happen at any moment. Protect your data!

The Least You Need to Know

➤ Access stores the data that you put in your database in tables. Each row in the table contains all the information for one particular person, place, or thing.

➤ Access is a relational database. You will have multiple tables in your database that connect the various groups of information.

➤ Database objects—queries, forms, and reports—let you manipulate and view your data. Queries enable you to sort and order your data by asking the table questions. Forms are very useful for data input. Reports enable you to show off your data in a desktop-published format.

➤ Access 2000 provides a brand new database object: the data access page. These pages provide a way to receive input from a Web page and have it saved to a particular database.

➤ Take the time to design your database up front. It will save you many headaches and database problems in the long run.

Chapter 2

Putting Access Through Its Paces

In This Chapter

➤ Starting Microsoft Access

➤ Opening a sample database

➤ Making your way around the Access workspace

➤ Viewing the database objects (from both sides now)

➤ Closing your database

➤ Exiting Microsoft Access

Now that I've discussed the tough stuff, such as relational databases and database objects, we can begin having fun! You will find that after you learn the basics, Access is a pleasure to work with.

Let's start our exploration of Access and its database capabilities by viewing one of the sample databases that Microsoft ships with Access: the Northwind Trading Company database. Before you can start perusing this database, however, you must start Access.

One Giant Step for Humankind (Launching Microsoft Access)

Access has almost as much built-in redundancy as you would find on a NASA spacecraft. However, because you want to start the Access software and build a database before they put an astronaut on Pluto (and before you reach retirement age), you can skip some of the more esoteric possibilities and go with the **Start** button on the Windows taskbar.

Location Is Everything

The Start menu displays folders that contain program icons (such as the one for Access). Program icons can also appear directly on the menu. Unless you did some weird custom installation, the Access icon should appear right on the Applications Start menu. Be aware that every computer can have a slightly different Start menu configuration.

Click the **Start** button on the Windows taskbar. Place the mouse pointer on the **Programs** group icon. A Start menu for all your applications appears.

Locate your Access program icon and place the mouse pointer on it. Click the left mouse button to start the application. If you have the Office toolbar showing on your desktop, you have yet another way to launch Access. Just click the **Access** icon on the Office toolbar.

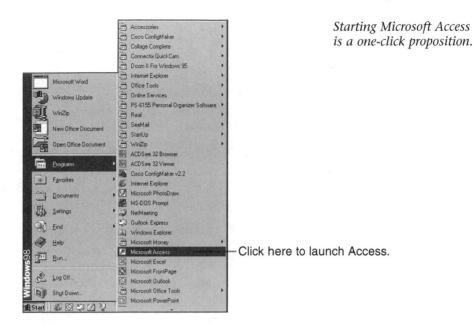

Starting Microsoft Access is a one-click proposition.

—Click here to launch Access.

Opening a Database File

When you launch Access, the first thing you see when the application opens is the Database dialog box. This dialog box enables you to create a new blank database, use the Database Wizard to create a new database, or open an existing database.

The Microsoft Access opening dialog box lets you choose what to do next.

Your Databases up in Lights

After you have used Access for a while, you will also find that the Microsoft Access opening dialog box displays a list of your most recently opened databases. To open a database on the list, select it and then click **OK**. You can also get to database files not on your most-used list by selecting the **More Files** choice.

Take a look at one of the sample databases that comes—ready for your enjoyment and edification—with Access 2000. First, you must open an existing database. By default, the **Open an Existing File** option button appears selected, but if it's not, click it now. Then click the **OK** button.

A Northwind Database Sampling

An Open dialog box appears. Locate the directory that holds the sample database files; the default location for the sample database files like those for the Northwind database is Program Files\Microsoft Office\Office\Samples.

You will find the sample databases in the Samples folder.

After you locate the **Samples** folder and click it, a list of the sample databases appears. Notice that the Files of Type box at the bottom of the dialog box contains the file type Data Files. Access databases are saved in the data file format (an extension of .mdb is placed on the filename). When you work with the Open, Save, and Export dialog boxes in Access, you will find that data file is the file type used.

Now on to our exploration of an Access database. Double-click the **Northwind** database file (in the Open dialog box) to open it.

When you open the Northwind database, a rather annoying and somewhat flamboyant screen appears, with information regarding this sample database. This screen is little more than an announcement and serves no real purpose. Click the screen's **OK** button, and it will go away (if it really annoys you, click the **Don't Show This Screen Again** check box, and it will disappear forever). You will find yourself face to face with the Northwind Database window and many great tools that will help you as you work with your databases. Welcome to the Access application window!

Taking a Look Through the Access Window

Take a moment to look around the Access workspace. Access resides in a typical application window; in this window, you will do your database thing. At the top of the window is the *title bar*. On the far right of the title bar are the *minimize*, *maximize/restore*, and *close* (×) buttons; these buttons enable you to manipulate the size of your application window. Below the title bar is the *menu bar*. The menu bar gives you access to all your software commands and features.

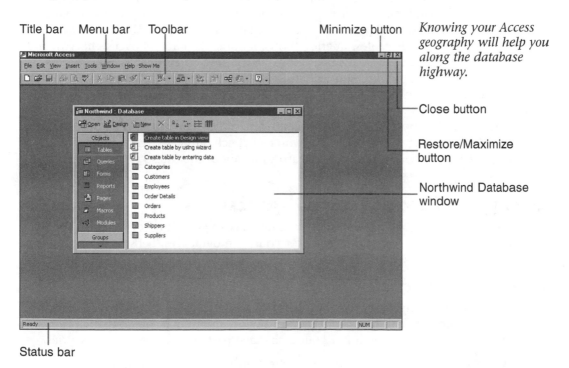

Title bar   Menu bar   Toolbar

Minimize button

Knowing your Access geography will help you along the database highway.

Close button

Restore/Maximize button

Northwind Database window

Status bar

19

Below the menu bar is the *toolbar*. Toolbars hold command buttons that give you one-click entry to powerful software features. Access has several toolbars, each with a different general purpose. When you open a database, the Database toolbar appears. This particular toolbar enables you to quickly initiate commands and features related to the creation and maintenance of databases.

When you work with the various objects that make up databases, such as tables, forms, or reports, you will find that each has a toolbar that gives you quick access to features related to that particular object.

At the bottom of the Access window (above the Windows taskbar) is the *status bar*. The status bar tells you what you have going on in the Application window. For example, when you work with a particular feature or command, this activity appears on the status bar. The status bar will also let you know whether you have your Caps Lock on or whether you have activated the Number Lock (the status bar will show CAPS and NUM, respectively).

The Database Window

One of the most important (if not *the* most important) items in the Access workspace is the Database window. The tabs on this window enable you to view, manipulate, create, delete, and format all the objects that make up databases. Of course you remember their names: tables, queries, forms, reports, data access pages, macros, and modules. The following sections take a look at all these objects except data access pages, macros, and modules. You will create data access pages in Chapter 23, "Surf's Up, Dude—Access on the Internet," and create macros in Chapter 21, "The Little Engines That Can: Making Macros." Modules require a little too much programming knowledge, and I don't want you to become a total PC gear-head, so I won't cover this particular object in the book. (But you can check out *Sams Teach Yourself Access 2000 in 21 Days* if you really want to learn more about modules.)

Getting to Know Your Objects

The Northwind database provides an excellent way to get your feet wet with the objects that you will eventually create for your own databases. Let's start with tables.

Get Your Feet off the Table

As I've stated more than once already and will no doubt state several more times before you complete this handsomely bound book (my middle name is *Superfluity*), database tables are where you put your data. Each particular piece of data is a *field*.

Click the **Tables** icon on the left side of the Northwind Database window, if necessary (that is, if you were playing around in the Database window when you should have been reading this book). All the tables in the database are listed on the right pane of the Database window, and each is represented by a table icon. Double-click the **Orders** table icon.

Where are the object tabs? Access 2000 has done away with the various object tabs found on the Database window in earlier versions of Access. To see a list of a particular object type, click the **Object** icon on the left side of the Database window. To view a particular object in the list, double-click the object's icon on the right side of the Database window.

Table Datasheet
toolbar

Fields

The Orders table in Datasheet view shows all the Access bells and whistles you use to create great tables.

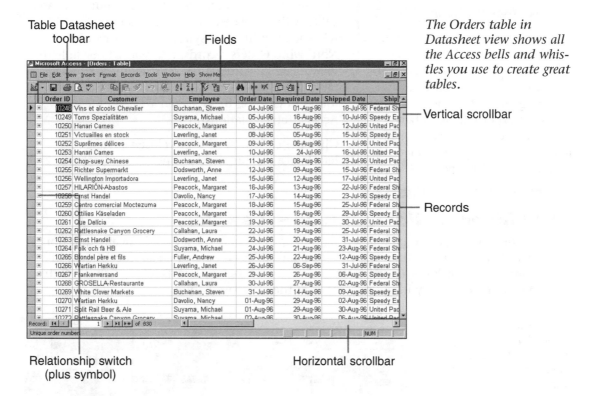

Vertical scrollbar

Records

Relationship switch
(plus symbol)

Horizontal scrollbar

Wow! This thing is big. It kind of looks like a spreadsheet (if you're familiar with Excel, you *know* that it looks like an Excel worksheet), doesn't it? This particular view of a table is the *Datasheet view*. Use the vertical and the horizontal scrollbars to peruse the data in the table. Notice that the datasheet divides into columns of information; these are your fields. Each row is a *record*. It's all pretty simple stuff, actually.

A Toolbar for Every Object

When you opened the Customers table, Access pulled a switch on you. It changed the Database toolbar to the Table Datasheet toolbar, which gives you buttons for features and commands unique to table maintenance. Take a look at how the toolbar changes each time you open a new object type.

What are those plus symbols on the left of each record? Access 2000 provides a quick way to look at records in other tables that are related to the records in the currently open table. Remember that Access is a relational database, and small tables containing discrete subsets of data will make up your database. Tables will be related, which means records will be related. Click the plus symbol (+) on one of the Northwind Orders records, and you will be able to view related records in the Northwind Products table. More about database relationships can be found in Chapter 8, "Between You and Me and Access: Table Relationships."

Click the close (×) button to close the table. Now let's take a look at another one of the database objects.

The Million-Dollar Question—The Query

Queries enable you to pull data from one or more tables; they are basically questions that you ask the database. Queries look like tables and are often subsets of data in your tables. Click the **Queries** icon in the Database window. Double-click the **Sales by Category** query in the right pane of the Database window.

Queries look much like tables but are actually a great way to select and summarize data from your tables.

Query fields   Query toolbar

Category ID	Category Name	Product Name	Product Sales
6	Meat/Poultry	Alice Mutton	$17,604.60
2	Condiments	Aniseed Syrup	$1,724.00
8	Seafood	Boston Crab Meat	$9,814.73
4	Dairy Products	Camembert Pierrot	$20,505.40
8	Seafood	Carnarvon Tigers	$15,950.00
1	Beverages	Chai	$4,887.00
1	Beverages	Chang	$7,038.55
1	Beverages	Chartreuse verte	$4,475.70
2	Condiments	Chef Anton's Cajun Seasoning	$5,214.88
2	Condiments	Chef Anton's Gumbo Mix	$373.62
3	Confections	Chocolade	$1,282.01
1	Beverages	Côte de Blaye	$49,198.08
8	Seafood	Escargots de Bourgogne	$2,076.28
5	Grains/Cereals	Filo Mix	$2,124.15
4	Dairy Products	Fløtemysost	$8,438.74
4	Dairy Products	Geitost	$786.00
2	Condiments	Genen Shouyu	$1,474.82
5	Grains/Cereals	Gnocchi di nonna Alice	$32,604.00
4	Dairy Products	Gorgonzola Telino	$7,300.74
2	Condiments	Grandma's Boysenberry Spread	$2,500.00
8	Seafood	Gravad lax	$629.20
1	Beverages	Guaraná Fantástica	$1,630.12
4	Dairy Products	Gudbrandsdalsost	$13,062.60
2	Condiments	Gula Malacca	$6,737.93
3	Confections	Gumbär Gummibärchen	$10,443.06

Record: 1 of 77

Number automatically assigned to a new category.

This query pulls information from the Orders table (the actual sales) and the Products table (take a look at the Products table; that's where the various products are listed), and a Categories table that groups products by category. This query also does some math and totals the dollar amounts of the orders for each product category. Pretty cool, huh? Although you might be a little intimidated now, you will be designing queries like this one in no time.

Close the query by clicking its close (×) button. Click the **Forms** icon in the Database window, and we'll take a look at the next object on our list.

Forming Your Own Opinion About Forms

Forms are great for entering and editing data. You can design forms for use with one table, or you can build them to service more than one table at a time. Double-click the **Customers** form.

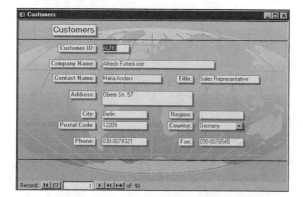

Forms are a great way to look at one record at a time.

This form takes advantage of one of several layouts that you can use to build attractive forms. Notice that the form shows you one record. A set of buttons at the bottom of the form window enables you to move forward and backward through the records. Try out the buttons. When you finish viewing the form, click the close (×) button.

Let's Have Your Report

Another one of the database objects that you will encounter is the report—a great way to summarize, list, and publish your data. Click the **Reports** icon to view the list of reports in this database. Double-click the **Sales by Category** report.

Reports are interesting in that they have some of the capabilities typically associated with queries. Reports are excellent at summarizing your data and making it look spiffy. Not only can a report show your data as text, it can also provide you with a graphical representation of your information—a chart.

Reports are the culmination of all your data gathering and input. You build your tables, queries, and forms, and when you have your data in the database just as you want it, you print out a great report and *shazaam*! You're promoted to middle management. Click the close (×) button to close the report.

Relationships Are Where It's At

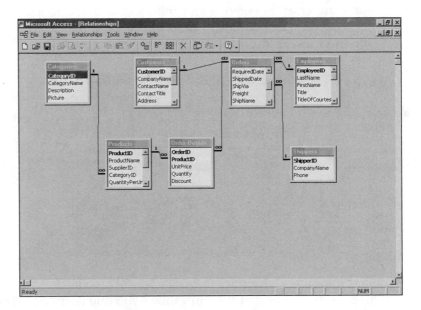

The bottom line in working with Access is understanding how different tables in the database relate; Access builds (with your help) relational databases, remember? For a preview of how the various tables in a complex database can be related, click the **Relationships** button on the Database toolbar.

The Relationships window is the place to relate those tables.

Access shows you how each of the tables links and by what field. (You will read about the possible types of relationships in Chapter 8, "Between You and Me and Access: Table Relationships.") For now, concentrate on the type of fields used to relate the tables. When you finish checking out the relationships (sounds like a guy with no date at the prom), click the close (×) button to shut down the Relationships window.

A Plea from Your Author—Spend Quality Time with Your Sample Database

Please take the time to peruse the other objects in this database when you have the chance. The Northwind database is very well designed and should give you excellent insight into how you can build your own databases. If it doesn't, no harm done—and you've looked as though you were busy. While you're at it, remember to treat this book with respect. Never let it leave your side. I don't want to find it on a table in a used book store.

Closing a Database

When you finish with a database, it's easy to get rid of it. Click the close (×) button on the Database window. So get rid of the Northwind database already!

Other Great Sample Databases

Access comes with other sample databases: an address book, a contacts database, and a sample inventory database. All these databases give good examples of typical database objects and some advanced database objects such as macros and modules.

After you close a database, not a whole lot goes on in the Access workspace. But there's no problem staying busy. You can open an already existing database by using the **Open** button on the Database toolbar, or if you would rather create a new database, you can click the **New** button.

There is a third alternative, of course. You can always exit Access.

Signing Off—Exiting Access

There will be times, I'm sad to say, when you're going to want to shut down Access completely and go off and neglect your database duties. But, hey, I guess it's not worth shedding tears over. I'll even show you how. Simply click the **File** menu and then choose **Exit**. If that's too much clicking for you, just click the Access window's close (×) button.

As you can plainly see (and you hopefully saw in this chapter), Access is a powerful yet easy-to-use relational database package. And those sample databases—wow!—they can really help you understand what kind of foundation a well-built database rests on.

The Least You Need to Know

➤ Launch Access via the Start button and the Programs group.

➤ All your database objects will reside in the Database window.

➤ Click the tab for the object type you want to work with.

➤ The Access toolbars are specific to the object type that you're currently working on.

➤ You can close a database, open an already existing database, or start a new database; you can find all the buttons necessary on the Database toolbar.

➤ Exiting Access by using the File menu or the close (×) button shuts down the application.

Chapter 3

Help, I Need Somebody...

In This Chapter

➤ Using the Office Assistant for help when you get in a jam

➤ Looking up information by using the Access Help Contents, Answer Wizard, and Index

➤ Getting context-sensitive help with the What's This? pointer

---

Sometimes things just don't seem to work the way they are supposed to, and computer software is no exception. No matter how hard you try, there are going to be times when you throw your hands up in the air and holler for help, especially if you misplace this fantastic book under a pile of dirty laundry. Access is great about throwing you the help lifeline when you're going down for the third time. And you'll find that there is more than one approach that you can use to get help in Access. It's all up to you.

Your Faithful Servant—The Office Assistant

You might be asking, "Who or what is the Office Assistant?" Well, whether it's a who or a what depends on you. The Office Assistant is a fantastic Help feature that provides great tips, context-sensitive help, and the capability to search for help on a particular topic.

The Office Assistant uses Microsoft's IntelliSense technology, giving it the capability to almost anticipate your problems and help you out when you are stuck. It really makes other ways of getting help obsolete. The Assistant was first available in Office 97, and Microsoft has improved the Assistant's capability to anticipate your needs in the latest Office 2000 version, which includes Access (which is great for you because you're trying to learn this superb database software application).

The Office Assistant appears as soon as you open Microsoft Access, and it sits in the Application window. You can drag the Assistant to any place in the Access workspace. If you don't see the Assistant, click the **Microsoft Access Help** button on the Database toolbar (or the current toolbar).

The Office Assistant is always ready to help you.

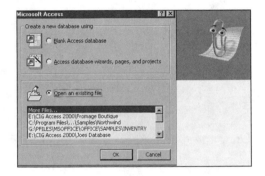

The Office Assistant is kind of like the Shell Answer Man (sorry, *Person*), but dresses better (boy, did I date myself with that one). The great thing about the Assistant is that you can find help in a couple of different ways. You can get *Suggested Help*, which gives you info on the task you're currently tackling (a little light bulb appears over the Assistant's head, letting you know that help is available), or you can search for help by typing a question or topic in the What Would You Like to Do? box.

The Assistant is even smart enough to move out of your way if it is too close to where you are currently working. To take a look at all these great possibilities, click the **Microsoft Access Help**, and the Assistant's balloon will appear. (If you inadvertently click the Office Assistant while you are working in Access, click the assistant a second time to close the assistant balloon.)

The Assistant's balloon is where you find the help you need.

Options button

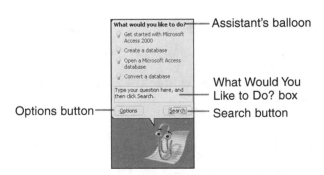

Assistant's balloon

What Would You Like to Do? box

Search button

Take a Guess—Suggested Help

The Assistant's balloon gives you two ways to get help. First, it provides a list of suggested Help topics that are germane (no, not Michael Jackson's brother—I mean *pertinent*) to the activity that you are currently dealing with in Access. For example, when you start Access, you will want to open, create, or import a database; the list of Help topics that the Assistant provides addresses these database issues.

This type of help—Suggested Help—can be very timely; if you work on a table and become stuck, the Assistant provides a list of suggestions that help you troubleshoot your problem with tables—exactly what you're doing at the time. This type of immediate help can be, well, very helpful!

Whenever you have difficulty with a particular feature, keep an eye on the Assistant. If a light bulb appears over the Assistant's head, you know that you can click the Assistant to receive a list of help related to the current task.

What Would You Like to Do?

"Nothing." That's the answer you always get from children under the age of 11; five minutes later, they're screaming that they are bored (offspring older than 16 won't even bother to answer...but I digress). Another great way to get help using the Assistant is the **What Would You Like to Do?** box in the Assistant's balloon. All you have to do is click in the box and type a question. You can even type the question in English—no geekspeak necessary.

What's All This Nonsense About IntelliSense?

IntelliSense technology is the programming genius behind the capability of certain Access features such as the menu system and the Office Assistant to anticipate your needs and provide you with a certain amount of personal accommodation on-the-fly. The new adaptive menus show only the menu choices that you've recently used—they adapt to your use of the commands. The Office Assistant, on the other hand, is programmed to detect the features you are currently working with and to provide you with context-sensitive help.

Say that you want information on creating a form. A question you might pose to the Assistant would be **"How do I create a form?"** After you type in your question, click the **Search** button.

The Assistant will search the Help database for you and return a list of Suggested Help topics such as Create a Form, Create a Form with Multiple Pages or Tabs, and other topics of this particular ilk. Click the topic that best fits your need. As soon as you click the topic, the Access Help window will appear with help related to the question you asked the Assistant.

*Type your question and then click the **Search** button. The Help window will come to your rescue!*

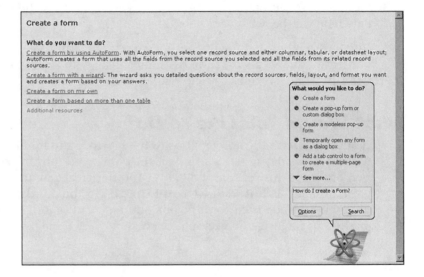

After the Assistant has helped you find your way to the appropriate Help topics, all you must do is a little additional clicking in the Help window to find the information that you need. You will find that the various Help topics in the Help window take the form of hyperlinks (yeah, just like on the World Wide Web). All you have to do is click the appropriate highlighted text, and you will be taken to the appropriate help section.

Appearances Are Important

The Assistant can take on several different personalities, including Clippit, an animated paper clip (which is the default Assistant); Rocky, a happy dog; Links, a purring kitty; F1, a helpful little robot; and the Genius, an Albert Einstein lookalike. Choosing a particular assistant is quite easy. Click the **Options** button in the assistant's balloon, and you are well on your way to customizing both how the Assistant looks and the kind of help the Assistant offers.

The Office Assistant's dialog box has two tabs: Gallery and Options. Use the **Gallery** tab to select the Assistant you want to work with. There are nine Assistants, and I'm sure one will suit your personality and frame of mind. A set of Back and Next buttons makes it easy for you to peruse the different possibilities. After you make your selection, click **OK**.

What Are My Options?

The Options tab of the Office Assistant's dialog box enables you to decide how the Assistant will interact with you. You can decide on several options, including whether the F1 function key (the usual key for Help) makes the Assistant appear, whether the Assistant will help you when you work with the various Access wizards, or whether the Assistant will guess at a list of Help topics when you run into trouble. All these features and several others are controlled by check boxes in this particular tab. After you make your selections, click **OK**. If you find that you don't understand a particular option or part of the dialog box, click the Help button (the **?**) in the upper-right corner of the dialog box. The mouse pointer becomes a question mark; when you click this help pointer on a part of any dialog box, you are given specific help on the item.

Cheap Thrills!

If you are ever totally bored and your coworkers won't talk to you, put the mouse pointer on the **Assistant** and right-click. A shortcut menu appears. Click **Animate**, and the Assistant will provide you with some cheap entertainment.

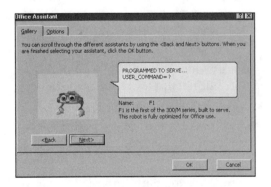

A ready and willing group of Assistants awaits your call.

When You've Had Enough of the Assistant

There might be times when you don't want the Assistant in the Access workspace. Don't worry, the Assistant is well adjusted enough to handle a little rejection. All you have to do is point at the Assistant with the mouse and right-click. A shortcut menu appears, and you can click **Hide** to remove the Assistant from view.

Feeling a little lonely? No problem. To bring the Assistant back onscreen, click the **Microsoft Access Help** button that resides on all the Access toolbars. You won't find a more loyal friend or anyone so willing to roll up her sleeves and give you a hand (unless you win the lottery, and then you will have many friends, whether you want them or not).

If you are totally sick of the Assistant, you can easily turn it off completely. Click the **Assistant** and then on the Assistant balloon, click **Options**. On the **Options** tab, deselect the check box that says **Use the Office Assistant**. It's that simple.

Getting Help Without the Assistant

Although the Office Assistant might seem to be the answer to everyone's Access problems, you can obtain help in other, more conventional ways. One of these is to go directly to the Access Help system and look up information in a table of contents and index; another is to ask questions of the Help system by using the Answer Wizard. First make sure that you've turned off the Office Assistant on the Assistant's Options tab.

Now you're ready to get help Assistant-free. Click the **Help** menu, then select **Microsoft Access Help**. The Help window appears and explains different ways to find help in Access.

On the left pane of the Help window are buttons that assist you in navigating the various help screens. The first button is the **Hide** button. This closes the entire left pane of the Help window (when you click the **Hide** button it becomes a **Show** button, which can be used to reopen the left pane of the Help window). The next two buttons allow you to move backward (**Back**) or forward (**Forward**) through the Help screens that you've already worked with during your help session. If you want to actually print a Help topic, click the **Print** button.

The left pane of the Help window also provides three tabs—**Contents**, **Answer Wizard**, and **Index**—each giving you a different way to look up the help or information that you need.

The **Contents** tab supplies a list that will take you to major groupings of information such as what's new in Access, an introduction to Access, and how to do specific tasks such as create a database or table.

Take a look at how the **Contents** tab supplies you with information on working with tables. Scroll down through the alphabetical Contents listing. Each main topic is represented by a book icon. Because you want to learn about tables, scroll down and double-click the **Creating and Designing Tables** book. The Help book icon opens up and displays a sublist of more specific topics—some in the form of books, others in the form of chapters. Double-click the **Creating and Opening Tables** book to get to more specific levels of information. Then click the **Create a Table** topic in the sublist.

On the right pane of the Help window, you are provided with some general information on creating a table, and then several hyperlinks to topics specifically related to creating a table appear under the heading "What Do You Want to Do?"

Hide Back Forward Print

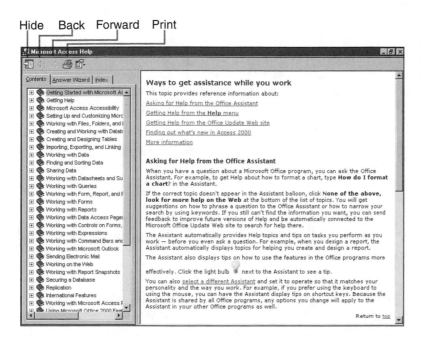

The Help window enables you to look up information in the Access Help file.

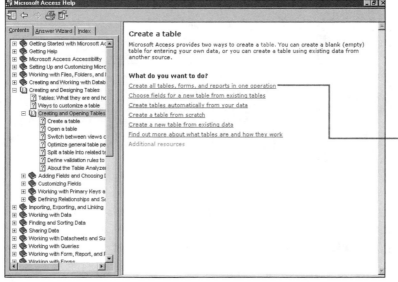

Click one of the topic hyperlinks provided in the right pane of the Help window to view specific instructions.

Glossary term

Say you want information on creating a table from scratch. Click the hyperlink **Create a Table from Scratch**. The Access Help system jumps to a series of steps and additional informational hyperlinks related to creating a table on your own. To get information specifically on creating a table from scratch, click the **Create a Table from Scratch Using Design View** link. If you find that you want to return to the previous window and click a different link, click the **Back** button at the top of the Help window.

Besides hyperlinks to different Help topics, you will find that certain key words are also highlighted in a different color. For example, on the Create a Table from Scratch in Design View help screen, the words `primary key` are in a different color than the text around it. Words presented in this fashion are *glossary terms*. Clicking them gives you a definition of the word or words.

Give it a try. Click the words `primary key`. A definition box appears and defines *primary key* for you. When you finish viewing the definition, click anywhere in the Help window, and the definition disappears (isn't this cool?).

Glossary terms are a great way to find a quick definition of a specific item in the Help system.

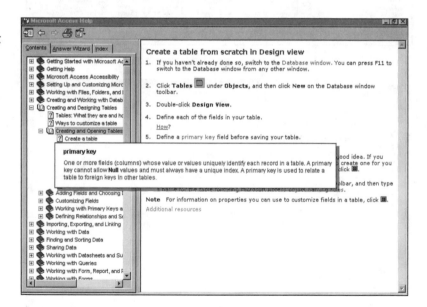

Using the Answer Wizard

Another way to get help in the Help window is to use the Answer Wizard. The Answer Wizard works almost exactly the same way as the Office Assistant does; you ask the Wizard questions, and it supplies you with a list of topics that relate to your question. You click one of the choices provided to view help in the Help window.

To use the Answer Wizard, click the **Answer Wizard** tab in the Help window. Type your question in the **What Would You Like to Do?** box. For example, you might type the question `How do I create a form?`

After typing your question, click the **Search** button. A list of topics will appear in the **Select Topic to Display** box. Select a particular topic, and its information will appear in the right pane of the Help window.

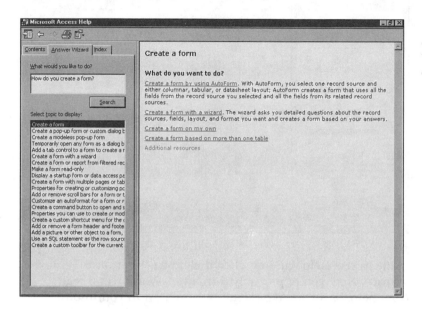

The Answer Wizard answers your question with a list of topics. Click a topic to see specific help in the Help window.

Using the Index

Another way to get help from the Access Help Topics window is to do keyword searches in the Help system's Index. To access the Index system, click the **Index** tab in the Help window. The Index enables you to type in a keyword or keywords, select from a list of existing keywords, or select from a list of topics that appear, based on your keywords or keywords you choose from the keyword list.

For example, suppose you want to find information on forms. Type `forms` in the **Type Keywords** box. Notice that the Index immediately starts moving down through the list of keywords in the **Or Choose Keywords** box and even attempts to complete the keyword you are typing. As you type `f`, the Help system automatically adds `acing` to make the keyword `facing`. As you continue to type `form`, other possibilities also pop up in the keyword box. After you have completed typing your index terms, click the **Search** button to find topics related to your index term.

You can view different Help screens by selecting different topics from the **Choose a Topic** box. If you decide you want to start the search from scratch, click the **Clear** button and type a new index term in the keyword box.

*Type keywords in the **Type Keywords** box and then click **Search** to view related Help topics in the topic list.*

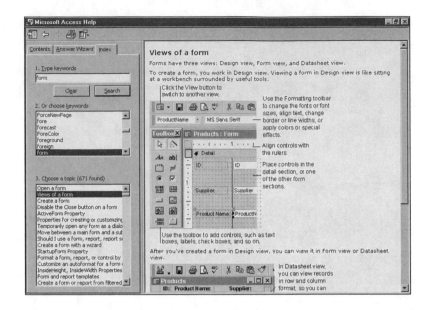

When you finish using the Access Help window, click the close (×) button to remove it from the Access workspace. Now you're probably thinking, "Wow, Access really gives me great ways to get help." And you'd be right. But hold on to your mouse, Access newbie, because there's more!

What You See Is What Gets You Help

You might be one of those visually oriented people who like to pick up their cues from what they see around them. Well, this is your lucky day. You can actually use the mouse to click a part of the Access window and get help. All you have to do is click the **Help** menu and then select **What's This?**

The What's This? menu selection turns your mouse into an informational help probe, sort of like those satellites NASA is always throwing at Mars and Venus; when they touch down, they gather information and beam it back to Earth. Well, that's how the mouse works when you activate the **Help** button. Boldly click where you've never clicked before (pretty much anywhere in the window), and Access provides you with some help on the item you selected.

Give it a try. After you arm your mouse pointer with the **What's This?** question mark, click the Office Assistant. A box pops up and provides you with a sentence or two of help on the item you clicked. In this case, Access tells you that the Assistant provides you with help and tips to accomplish your Access tasks.

You can also use this little trick on the parts of the various windows that you work with in Access and on the buttons of the various toolbars found in Access. Click the **Help** menu. Select **What's This?** and then click the **Spelling** button on the toolbar. Access gives you information on what the Spelling button does.

Hey, this is great—a quick way to find simple information on a specific area of the Access workspace. You will find that these mouse-click Cliff notes are often just what you need to stay productive in Access.

Okay, take a deep breath because you're still not finished exploring all the help possibilities in Access. Join me now in an exploration of Microsoft on the Web.

Getting Help on the Web

The Internet, and particularly the World Wide Web, have drastically changed the way everyone works using computers. The days of the isolated personal computer are over; users are now hooked into a giant network that spans the globe. You can take advantage of this by going directly to Microsoft for help, tips, and information on its software products.

Access and all the components of Microsoft Office 2000 can directly connect you to help on the Web. The great thing about using the Web pages related to Access and the other Office applications is that you can continue to work in Access while you check out the information on the Web. The fact that Microsoft keeps these Web pages full of information means that with Access, you get in-depth help that is regularly updated.

Access on the Web

When you install Access and any of the other Office 2000 applications from compact disc, you also have the option of installing Internet Explorer 5.0. You should definitely install this powerful Web browser because it has been fully integrated with the Office applications.

Connecting to Microsoft's Web pages is easy. Click the **Help** menu; then choose **Office on the Web**. The Internet Explorer window will open and take you to the Microsoft Office Update Web page. (If you want to visit this Web site when you are not working in Access, type the address `http://officeupdate.microsoft.com/default.htm` in the Internet Explorer Address box and then press Enter to go to the site.)

The Microsoft Office Update page offers you product assistance and links to product enhancements.

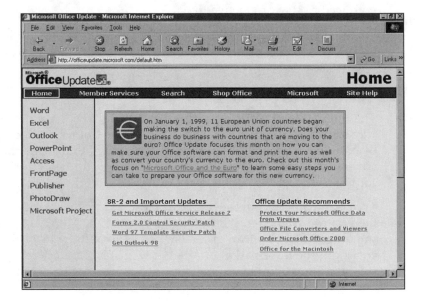

Surfing the Web with Bill Gates

When you're on the Office Update home page, you can easily connect to pages that can provide you with more specific help related to Access. The Office Update Page enables you to surf for information, program fixes, and additions. All the links that you need are provided on this one page.

If you want to get specific support on Access, click the **Access** link on the left side of the Office Update page.

All About Access

When you click the Access link, you are taken to a Welcome page that contains links to important software updates associated with Access. You will also find that four new links—Welcome, Updates, Downloads, and Assistance—now appear under the Access link on the left side of the browser window. You can click any of these links to view additional information related to Access:

➤ **Welcome**—This page opens as soon as you click the Access link. You are provided with the most important information about Access updates and other technical issues.

➤ **Updates**—This page gives you information and links to fact sheets that cover software updates and bug fixes for Microsoft Office. When updates specific to Access are available, they are also listed on this page.

➤ **Downloads**—This page contains links to all sorts of software goodies related to Access (and in some cases Microsoft Office). You can download additional sample databases, as well as more fonts and other tools that help you get more out of your Access installation.

➤ **Assistance**—This page provides links to white papers and other technical documents related to Access. It also includes a link to the most commonly related questions asked about Access.

Using these different Access online resources is really a snap—or should I say *click*? Just point to the link that you want to follow (such as **Assistance**), and then click. You will be taken to that particular page and can then peruse the various items that are provided.

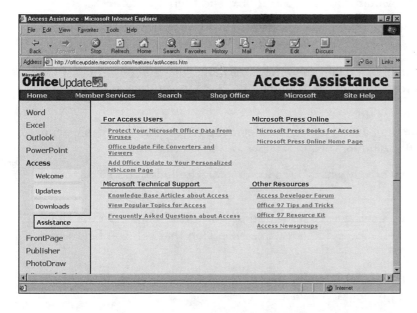

The Office Update page lets you follow links specifically for Microsoft Access.

When you have completed your Access research on the Web, click the Internet Explorer's close (×) button to close the application. If you plan on doing more Web browsing while you work in Access, click the Explorer's minimize button, and Explorer will be ready the next time you need it.

As you can probably see, you could nearly drown in all the information about Access that Microsoft provides on the Web. A good rule of thumb is to use the Help system and the Office Assistant first to solve problems and find answers on Access; then turn to the Web if you need more in-depth information.

There are really many ways to get help in Access. And don't be afraid or embarrassed to seek help; better to pause for a moment and get some help than to create a database that doesn't work for you. Besides, during those lonely nights when you are banging away at the keyboard entering data, Help can be just like having a conversation with a good friend.

The Least You Need to Know

➤ The Office Assistant provides a one-stop-shopping approach to finding help in Access. Simply click the Assistant, and you'll get help for what you are currently working on.

➤ When you need an answer to a simple, plain-English question, use the Assistant's What Would You Like to Do? box, and then click **Search**.

➤ The Help menu is a good place to go for help if you like browsing a table of contents or viewing an index for the Access Help file.

➤ Use the Contents tab when you're not totally sure what you need help with; it divides the information into broad categories and lets you look up information by subject.

➤ If you like the flexibility of asking the Help system questions, but can't stand using the Office Assistant, take advantage of the Answer Wizard.

➤ When you know exactly what you're looking for, the Index and Find tabs are the way to go.

➤ You can click up some quick help with the What's This? choice on the Help menu; it arms your mouse pointer with a Help icon that gets you help wherever you click.

➤ Surfing the various Microsoft Web pages involving Access is a great way to build up your own mental database.

Part 2

Catching the Brass Ring: Creating Databases

So you're feeling a little crazed. You've got the database theory stuff under your belt, and you're ready to take a crack at actually building a database. But you're not really sure what you might end up with. It's kind of like being one of those mad scientists in the B movies: You have the best intentions when you throw that switch, but your creation turns out to be a real monster.

Bringing your database into being in Microsoft Access is much simpler than it sounds. In fact, you'll find that there is plenty of help along the way. There are even wizards (a question-and-answer process for creating the various database elements) to help you build that ideal database. That's an advantage that Dr. Frankenstein could have used. Turn the page and create!

CHING

Chapter 4

Database Creation: More Fun, Less Filling

In This Chapter

➤ Using the Database Wizard to create great databases

➤ Naming a new database

➤ Specifying or creating a folder in which you can save your databases

➤ Viewing your new database and its objects

Now that you've taken Access out for a test drive and you have a good feel for what a database is and how to plan one, you can try your hand at building one. Remember, whenever you run into trouble, you can consult the Office Assistant for help.

Creating a New Database

For starters, you will create a simple database using the Access Database Wizard. The wizard will assist you in building the various objects—tables, queries, forms, and reports—that are found in a typical database. You can also create a blank database if you want to create all the Access objects from scratch.

Start Microsoft Access (a very important step). In the New Database window, click the **Access Database Wizard, Pages and Projects** option button (the little circle next to Database Wizard); then click **OK**. Hey, you're off to see the Wizard!

What's a Wizard?

Wizards are great productivity tools that guide you through a particular task (such as building a new database) via a set of screens. You are asked to respond to a question or make a particular choice from a list. The wizard will then move to the next step in the process, based on your response. What could be easier?

For those of you who already have the Access program window open, it's just a hop, skip, and a click to access the database templates that the new Database Wizard uses to create a new database. Click the **File** menu; then click **New**. When the New dialog box appears, click the **Databases** tab, and you're right where you need to be.

Working with the Wiz

Dorothy didn't get a whole lot out of her association with the Wizard; in fact, she found that everything she needed had been right in her own backyard. You will find, however, that the Access Database Wizard is no humbug hiding behind a curtain; it will help you quickly build extremely user-friendly databases. Now click your heals together and repeat after me, "There's no database like Access, there's no database like Access...."

The New dialog box you have just opened gives you access to several database templates. A *template* is nothing more than a blueprint for a database. It contains ready-made database objects such as tables, forms, and queries.

Access supplies you with many database templates.

Database templates

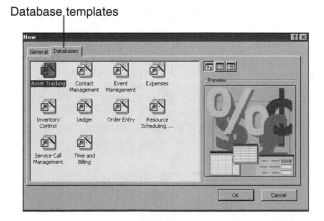

The New dialog box is divided into two tabs: General (where the blank database template, Data Access page template, and Project (SQL) template reside) and Databases (where a large group of different types of database templates lives.

SEE ALSO

> *SQL and Web Pages*—*Access 2000 has been designed so that you can easily work with client/server databases built into the SQL programming language. For more background on SQL, see Chapter 1, "Databases, Access, and You." Integrating Access with the World Wide Web and more information on Access Web pages can be found in Chapter 23, "Surf's Up, Dude—Access on the Internet."*

The Database Wizard makes sure that the Databases tab is selected and offers you many database possibilities; there are database templates for event management, contact management, even (gasp) a template for your expenses. (I hate expenses—they're, well, so expensive!)

Let's say that you want to put together a database that will help you track all your contacts—you know, all those people whom you talk to on the phone during the business day or meet at those sales conventions and whose names you can never remember (even though they wear those funny badges that say *Hi, I'm Al*). Because Access provides a database template for contact management (no, they don't mean those little pieces of plastic that you stick in your eyes each morning), you might as well take advantage of it (I'd rather take advantage of the Wine List template, but then I would probably never finish this book).

A great advantage of using a database template is that it will create several database objects (remember that in Access, objects are things such as tables, queries, forms, and reports). This means that you get ready-to-use tables, forms, and reports for your new database. All you must do is supply the data that will go into the database (meaning into the various tables created by the wizard).

Time to give this whole sample database thing a spin and see how a particular template can help you manage your business contacts. Click the **Contact Management** database icon and then click the **OK** button. The File New Database dialog box appears.

Check This Out

Fine-Tune Your Databases

You will find that the sample databases can get you started, but you might have to fine-tune them for the results that you need (meaning you might have to create additional objects or modify the fields in the tables created).

The File New Database dialog box lets you choose a name and location for your new database.

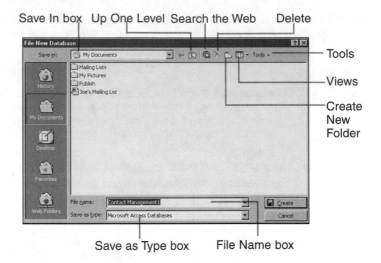

The File New Database dialog box is where you name your database and designate where you are going to keep it on your computer (such as in your computer's hard disk or on a local drive).

Pick Your Spot

You can save your files to drives other than your local drive or a floppy disk. The File New Database gives you access to all network drives (where you have been assigned rights), as well as any File Transfer Protocol (FTP) sites you might be attached to via the Internet or your company's intranet. For more about Access on the Internet, see Chapter 22, "Have It Your Way—Customizing Access."

Press a Button—Any Button!

We have all been conditioned from early childhood to keep our mitts off certain things—burning matches, nuclear isotopes, and buttons, especially red, blinking ones. You will find that Access and Windows 98 provide you with all sorts of great buttons. And you know what? You can push 'em and not destroy the world.

All you need to do now is specify a location for the database file that you want to create. You can use a currently existing folder on your local drive, or on your company's network drives, or you can use the File New Database dialog box to create a new folder.

This dialog box provides you with six buttons that make it easy to specify a location for your database file or view your file lists in different ways.

➤ Up One Level—Takes you to the parent directory of the directory that you are currently in.

➤ Search the Web—Opens your Web browser and takes you to a Web search page.

➤ Delete—Allows you to delete a selected file.

➤ Create New Folder—Lets you create a brand-new folder to hold your files.

➤ Views drop-down list—Allows you to change the current view of the files and folders shown in the dialog box. Five possibilities are provided on the View list:

  ➤ List—Displays the files in the window in alphabetical order, using small icons.

  ➤ Details—Shows a list of the files with additional information, such as when they were created or what type of file they are.

  ➤ Properties—Lists the files but also shows a property box that gives you information on the file size and when it was last modified.

  ➤ Preview—Allows you to view a preview of the selected file.

  ➤ Arrange icons—Click this selection, and a cascading menu allows you to sort the file icons shown in the dialog box by Name, Size, Type, or Date.

➤ Tools drop-down list—Use this button to delete, rename, add a file to the favorites list, or quickly map a network drive to a drive letter on your computer.

When you work with several buttons like those found in the Save As dialog box, remember that you can place the mouse pointer on them and get a ScreenTip that describes the button.

Other important areas in the File New Database dialog box provide you with places to type the filename and to designate where you want to save the file and what file type you want to create:

➤ Save In box—Where you designate the place on your local, network, or FTP drive where you want to keep the file

➤ File Name box—Where you type the filename

➤ Save as Type box—Where you specify the type of file that you want (because you are making a regular Access database, don't change the type)

Now you have to give your database a name. Type My Contacts in the File Name box. Okay, your database has a name, but it still needs a place to call its own on your local drive.

Now let's push the envelope a little and create a new folder on the local drive to use as a repository for the databases you create. This will help you keep your database files organized.

1. Click the **Save In** box drop-down arrow and select the **C:** drive (or if your computer's hard drive is not C:, choose the correct letter for your computer's drive).
2. Click the **Create New Folder** button.

It's very easy to create a new folder for your databases.

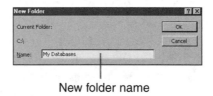

New folder name

3. Type My Databases in the New Folder Name box; then click **OK**. As soon as you click OK, the new folder is opened and is ready to receive your new file.
4. Click the **Create** button to begin the process of bringing your Contacts database into being.

Your computer will probably spin its wheels for a few moments as the Database Wizard loads. You will even see a database window being built for your particular database (more on database windows in a few minutes).

A Walk with the Wizard

Now the Database Wizard is in full stride. It consists of a series of screens that walk you through the database creation process. This enables you to control certain aspects of the database, which is nice. The wizard does limit your control, however, basing many of the components that you will end up with on the original database template you selected. It's like getting a haircut; you can tell the barber or stylist what you want, but when the scissors start to fly, the radical new do you wanted can end up looking like every other haircut that walks out of the shop.

Notice that the wizard tells you what type of information it expects you to store in this particular database:

➤ Contact information
➤ Call information

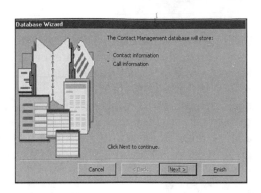

The Database Wizard walks you through the database creation process.

As you can see, this type of information would be perfect for a database that helps you track data related to your contacts and the calls that you make to them. Logging every call that you make can be a hassle, but this little gem of a database would help you do the job.

You will find that all the database templates provide database objects (tables, forms, reports, and so on). In some cases, you might find that objects have been created by the database template that you won't use. This is fine because Database Wizard is only the starting point. It's not that hard to manipulate your databases after you've laid the groundwork.

Perhaps you will delete several database objects created by some of the templates that you use. Others, such as the Contact Management template, will do a good job of providing you with a bare-bone database for a particular task. You will find that when you have a good feel for database creation, you can create most of your databases from scratch (the many maneuvers to do this are revealed later in this book).

Click the **Next** button to shift the Database Wizard into high gear.

Setting the Tables

On the next screen, you can view the tables that the wizard creates and the fields that these tables will contain. Again, remember that, depending on the template you have selected, some of these tables will be useful and others will not. Later you can delete the ones that are not.

Out in Left Field

At this point, you can also let Access know whether you want to include any optional fields in a specific database table. For example, select **Contact Information** in the **Tables in the database** list box.

No Deletions Without a Sales Slip

At this point in the database creation process, you can't delete any of the fields in the database tables. Later in this exciting text, you will learn how to delete fields, add fields, and do much, much more.

Scroll down through the **Fields in the table** box. Notice that there are several optional fields, such as marital status, spouse name, and contact's interest. Storing some information on what a particular contact is interested in might help you close that big deal with the contact, because they are so impressed by how much you remember about them. Knowing a few vital facts about any person is probably the greatest form of flattery (okay, I'm starting to sound like the slimiest used car salesperson).

To include the optional **Contact's Interests** field, click its check box.

You can peruse the fields in the other tables in this database if you want; simply select a particular table name. When you are ready to move to the next step, click the **Next** button.

You can select optional fields to be included in tables that are created by the wizard.

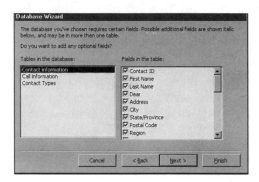

SEE ALSO

> *Creating Fields—You will be working with fields a lot when you create a table from scratch. You will experience field creation in Chapter 5, "Turning the Tables: Table Design."*

You Gotta Have Style

The Database Wizard now gives you several style options. Basically, it's up to you to choose what you want your different database screens to look like. This process is very much like wallpapering a room in your house. You are going to have to live with your choice for some time, so choose wisely.

Actually, Access is flexible about changing the style or look assigned to a particular database. In this case, because your database is your first foray into the world of database creation, choose **Expedition** by clicking it. The wizard gives you a preview of your new style.

Click **Next** to continue.

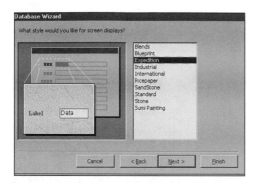

The Database Wizard lets you choose the look of your database screens.

You can also set up your reports using different styles. The wizard, a stickler for detail, wants to get a reading from you on how the reports you generate for this database should look. You have several choices. Because you are setting up a database for managing your multitude of contacts, why not choose the corporate style? This will make you feel like a big corporate wheel every time you view one of your database reports. Click **Corporate** in the style box and then click **Next** to continue.

What's in a Name?

Now that you've chosen the look for your database objects, the wizard wants you to give the database a name that it can put on all the reports that you create for the database. It makes sense to use a name that describes the database. You may use the same name that you gave to the database file when you saved it, but you don't have to.

Notice that in the title box, Access automatically sticks the name of the template—Contact Management—that you used to generate the databases. You, however, can let your creative juices flow and create a truly original name for this database; type My Contacts in the **Title** box.

Oh, well, I guess your creative abilities are just a little rusty—not unlike the Tin Man. "Oil can, oil can!"

Pictures Are Always Nice!

The Insert Picture dialog box is very much like the File New Database dialog box. To look in a particular folder, double-click it.

Picture This

Access provides several ways to create visually rich databases. In fact, you can even decide to include a graphic (a company logo or photo) on your reports.

To include a picture, click the **Yes, I'd Like to Include a Picture** check box. Then click the **Picture** button. The Picture button enables you to peruse your local drive, network, or Internet FTP sites for graphic files. You can use several picture formats. Several pictures come with the Access software, and an entire collection of clip art comes with

Microsoft Office. You can even scan in Mick Jagger's pic if you want to. Navigate to where your picture is located and make sure you select the picture; then click OK. The picture will appear on the wizard screen.

You can select a picture that will appear on your database reports—a great way to include a company logo.

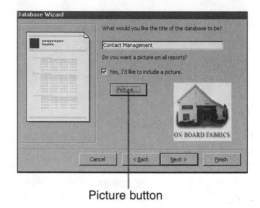

Picture button

The Checkered Flag

You are nearing the finish line; your database creation race is almost over. Let's recap the high points: You have chosen a sample database—Contact Management—that provides you with preset tables, forms, and reports. You have also selected a database style and a report style. You even opted to include a picture on your reports. Click **Next** to move to the final step in the database creation process.

The wizard wants to know whether you'd like to start the database; a check box provides this yes or no possibility, with yes being the default answer. You also have the option of displaying help while you work on this database. Starting the database means taking a look at your database. Of course you want to look at the database—that's why you created it! Click the **Finish** button.

The wizard lets you choose whether to look at your database right away.

The wizard now does its stuff and creates the various objects (table, forms, and reports) that are part of this sample database.

Psyching Out the Switchboard

When you create a new database with the Database Wizard, Access assigns a special form—the Switchboard—to your new database. You can use the Switchboard to view the various items in your database such as table, queries, and reports. The Switchboard is great for the novice user.

For example, say a friend who doesn't know Access wants to take a look at your Contacts database. No problem. A quick click in the right place and the Switchboard lets you take a look at your database tables and forms.

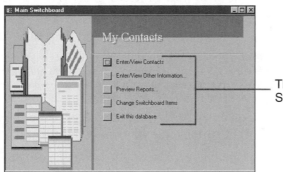

The Switchboard provides an easy way to add or view data in your new database.

The Database Switchboard

You are given a couple different choices concerning the type of information that you can view or edit. The first choice on the Switchboard enables you to view and enter new contacts into the database. For example, let's say you have a new contact that you want to enter into the database. Click the **Enter/View Contacts** button on the Switchboard.

A ready-made form appears. If you currently have records in the database, the first contact's record will appear in the form. If you haven't entered any records yet, you can enter your first contact directly into the form.

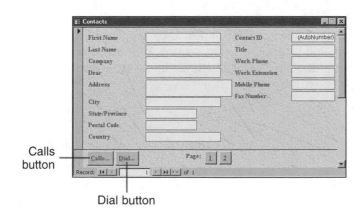

Calls button

Dial button

The Switchboard provides an easy way to add or view data in your new database. Just enter the contact's information into the form.

You will find that the objects created by the Database Wizard, such as the form shown, contain many extras. For example, this contact entry form supplies you with a **Calls** button in the lower-left corner, which takes you to a table of all the calls made to the contact shown in the current record. A **Dial** button is also present that will automatically dial the phone number of the currently shown contact, using your computer's modem.

Obviously, using the Database Wizard to create a new database provides you with database objects that are probably a little more sophisticated than you could create from scratch with your current Access knowledge base. These objects, such as the form we are currently discussing, take advantage of Access macros and other programming goodies that are discussed later in this book.

SEE ALSO

> *Using Forms—You might not totally appreciate how great forms are for data entry at this point in your Access journey. If you want to cut to the chase and read more about forms and their uses immediately, take a look at Chapter 9, "It's All in Your Form," and Chapter 10, "Reforming Your Forms." They'll give you the entire scoop on form design and use.*

When you have completed your data entry or viewing of records using the form, click the close button (×) in the upper-right corner, and you will be returned to the Switchboard.

Although it's hard to deny that the Switchboard can make data access and entry a very painless task, it does hide the actual nuts and bolts (meaning the objects that were created) of the database. So, you might want to do an end run on the Switchboard so that you can view the Database window and all the objects that it holds. This is easily accomplished because, remember, each object open in the Access window (including, in this case, the Switchboard and the hidden Database window) has a button on the Windows taskbar. To view the Database window for this database, click the **My Contacts** button (or the button for the database that you created) on the Windows taskbar.

A Database with a View

The Database window will appear and give you the opportunity to take a look at all the different objects that were created by the Database Wizard. When you first open the Database window, you will find that the forms in the database are currently listed. Notice that one of the forms is the Switchboard itself.

The Database window is a holding tank for the various objects that make up your database. Several views are available in the Database window, such as the small-icons list or the file details list that you can use as you view each group of objects in the database.

Notice that the Database window has an icon for each type of database object: tables, queries, forms, reports, macros, and modules. You can quickly take a look at another type of object by clicking the appropriate icon on the left of the Database window.

Take a look at the tables that are in this database. Click the **Tables** icon.

To take a look at a particular table, such as the Contact table, double-click the table's icon on the right of the Database window. You will find no surprises here; the table will consist of fields in columns, and each record will have its own row. If you haven't entered any data into the table yet, the table will appear as a blank row, with the appropriate field headings at the top of each field column.

See You Later, Switchboard

Rather than use the buttons on the taskbar to view the Database window, you can also close the Switchboard; click the Switchboard's close (×) button in its upper-right corner. The Database window will now appear alone in the Access window, and you can view the various objects that it contains.

The Database window holds all the objects in the database.

SEE ALSO

> ***Entering Data***—*For information on entering data into Access tables have a look at Chapter 6, "Going On Record: Adding and Editing Data."*

You can also view other objects—such as queries and reports—that have been created for the database. However, there will not be much to see until you enter data into the various tables found in the database.

The tables created by the wizard in the new database are ready and waiting for data entry.

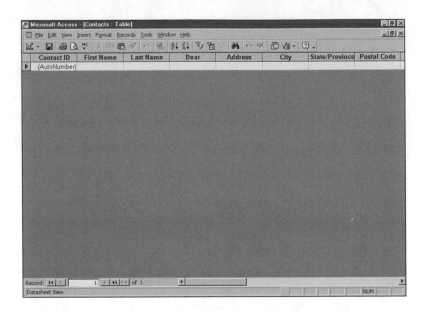

Getting the Big Picture

Obviously, the name of the game with databases is to enter data and then manipulate it. Normally, you will create a new database with the Database Wizard and then begin entering your data immediately. After you enter the data in your tables (either directly into the table datasheet view or into a form), you can manipulate the data and create objects such as reports.

Our work with the Database Wizard and our creation of the My Contacts database have served their purpose. They have shown how easily you can create a new database with the wizard and how various database objects can potentially give you different views of your data. Because we are finished with the database, you can close its window; click its close (×) button.

Give Yourself a Round of Applause

See, this database business isn't so tough. It's much better than trying to organize information on a bunch of dog-eared index cards or moldy file folders. Now that you have a feel for this whole database creation process and the different objects that go into a database, you can create a table of data in the next chapter.

The Least You Need to Know

➤ When you create a new database, you must give the file a name and a place to reside on your local drive or network.

➤ The Database Wizard creates your new database, based on a selected template.

➤ The database templates contain ready-made tables, forms, and reports that you can use for your data.

➤ You can use the Switchboard to add and view the data in your wizard-created database, or you can close the Switchboard and access the various objects in the database directly from the Database window.

Chapter 5

Turning the Tables: Table Design

In This Chapter

➤ Creating an Access table from scratch

➤ Designing fields of different data types

➤ Setting up a primary key for a table

➤ Using the Access Table toolbar

➤ Creating a mask for a field in the table

➤ Using the Table Wizard to make a new table

➤ Creating a table in Datasheet view

Okay, so you started Access, you used the Database Wizard, and you created a new database that holds sample data. In the My Contacts database that you created in Chapter 4, "Database Creation: More Fun, Less Filling," you had a chance to glimpse some of the various types of objects that are in a database—specifically tables, forms, and reports.

Of all the objects that you work with in Access, the most important is the table. It is the basic building block for all your databases.

Tabling the Discussion

Being an apprentice database wizard, you now know that the best place to enter data is in a table. Every row in the table is a discrete record. For example, each row in a customer database is information relating to a specific customer.

Every record in the table is divided into smaller, more precise bits of information. Yeah, you remember from earlier chapters that these items are called *fields*. Again, a field can be a customer's phone number or first name. Fields are a particular piece of information contained in the record for a particular person. The number of fields in the database table is up to you and depends on how many specific pieces of information you want in each record. The number of fields dictates the number of columns in your table.

SEE ALSO

> **The Look of the Table**—*If you need to refresh your memory on how a table that actually holds data will appear in the Access window, check out Chapter 2, "Putting Access Through Its Paces," and take a look at the sample databases discussed.*

It's the Wonder of New: New Tables for a New Database

Now that you know where the data needs to be, it's time to create a new table. You will first create a new database container based on the blank database template. When you have the new database, you can fill it with your own created objects, such as a new table.

To get in the swing of things, it's not a bad idea to set up a fictional business that you can build a sample database for. I suggest you create a database that will hold information relating to a cheese shop named The Fromage Boutique (*fromage* is the French word for cheese, get it?). When you have the cheese shop database up and ready to go, you can create a new object for it, namely, a table that will hold information on the shop's customers. The steps for creating the database and a Customers table are discussed in this chapter, so read on.

Bon, Allons! (I Mean, Let's Go!)

Now that I've pretty much exhausted all my high school French, we can concentrate on the database and table creation process. You will find that after you have created the new database file, the table creation process is a piece of cake, or actually cheese, in this case.

If you are already in Access, click the **New** button on the Database toolbar. The New Database dialog box appears. You've dealt with this particular dialog box before, when you created your new database based on the Contact Management template in Chapter 4. Make sure you select the **General** tab; then double-click the **Database** template.

Start Your Engines

If Access is not running, start the software by selecting the **Start** button on the taskbar and then the Access icon. When Access is up and running, the Access dialog box appears. Click the **Blank Access Database** radio button and then click **OK**. The File New Database will appear, as described below.

In the File New Database dialog box that appears, double-click the **File Name** box if the text in the box is not highlighted. Type Fromage Boutique as the database filename.

Use the **Save In** drop-down box to select a place on your local drive or on a network drive, if that's where you keep your information (you might want to save the database in the My Databases folder that you created earlier). Remember to click the **Create** button in the dialog box to conclude the database creation process.

Current directory

You can store your new database in a current folder or create a new folder.

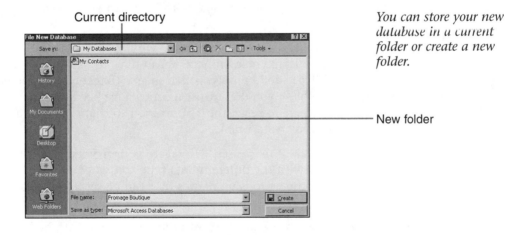

New folder

61

It's Alive, It's Alive!

Things are looking great. You are the proud owner of a brand spanking-new database. When you click the **Create** button, you return to the Access window; the Fromage Boutique database window sits right in front of you. This window, as you learned in Chapter 4, serves as a command center for adding and manipulating the objects in your database.

The Database window enables you to create and manipulate the objects in your database.

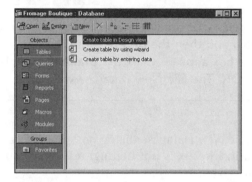

When you create a new database from scratch (using the Database template), like the Fromage Boutique database, it does not contain any database objects (although you do know that a new blank table will be opened automatically for you). This means that you must create all the objects that will be part of the database. Again, because tables serve as the building blocks of your databases and contain your database data, you will want to create a new table.

I'm sure you've noticed that on the left of the Database window are icons for each of the various object types that you can create in Access. You have to trust me on this one: Each category of object is currently empty, which means that the categories do not contain any database objects. If you don't trust me and have been clicking the object icons in disbelief, make sure to select the **Tables** icon so that your first action related to this new database is to create a table.

On the first time out, so to speak, it makes sense to create your new table in Design view. This enables you to work with the different data types provided for the fields in a table and allows you to view the various properties that can be set for a particular field.

Creating a table in Design view gives you the most immediate input into how the fields in your table will work. To enter Table Design view, double-click the **Create Table in Design View** icon in the middle of the Database window. The Table Design window will appear.

Insert Rows button

Indexes button

Primary Key button

Delete Rows button

Properties button

Build button

Database Window button

Table Design view enables you to build a table with custom fields.

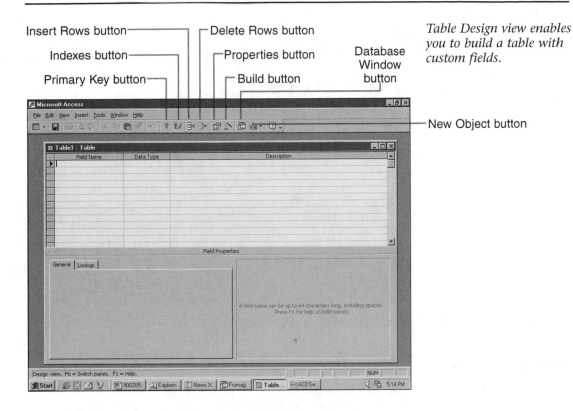

New Object button

The Table Design View Window

Table Design view is where you build a table from scratch; all the tools that you need in order to do the job are available. You already know that each database object has a unique toolbar with a special group of buttons to assist you when you create or work with them. The Table Design toolbar gives you one-click access to the features that you will use as you design your new table.

Fields of Dreams

Setting up the fields in Design view is pretty straightforward; all you have to do is give each field a name and let Access know what kind of information you plan on putting in that field. Access provides you with a description area that enables you to attach descriptive text to a field. This text appears on the Access status bar whenever you are in that particular field during data entry.

Because you plan to place customer information in this table, it makes sense to set up field names that request the type of data that you want for each person. Fields such as First Name, Last Name, and Address would be important to this type of table. Keep in mind that you have 64 characters (including spaces) for each field name that you create. It makes sense to keep your field names reasonably short and very descriptive. Then when you work with your table in Datasheet view, the field columns will not have to be super wide to accommodate stupendously long field names. Now, to create the fields.

63

Make sure the insertion point is in the first row of the field name column. Type First Name. Pretty easy so far; press Enter. This will move you to the Data Type column.

A drop-down list provides you with all the different data types.

Data type list

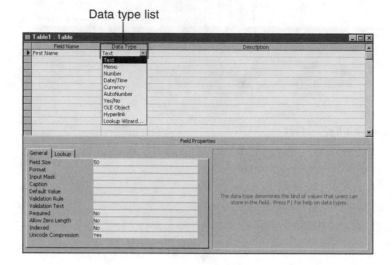

Not My Type

It was no big deal coming up with a name for your field, but what in the world does Access want now? What is a data type? Data types refer to the kind of information you plan to put in a particular field in the table. Letting Access know the data type makes it possible for special things to be done to that field, such as including the field data in a total sales figure or placing an employee picture in a field from another application.

Sounds complicated, but don't worry. Access doesn't leave your data types to chance. It gives you a list of acceptable formats. All you must do is step up to the plate (figuratively, of course), choose from the list, and crack, you're off to the next field.

Click the **Data Type** drop-down arrow. A list of data types appears. Access provides you with the following 10 data type settings.

➤ Text—Text and numbers up to 255 characters

➤ Memo—Lengthy text

➤ Number—Numbers used in mathematical calculations

➤ Date/Time—Date and time values

➤ Currency—Numeric data used in calculations

➤ AutoNumber—Sequentially numbered records

➤ Yes/No—Fields with true/false data

➤ OLE (object linking and embedding) Object—A picture, spreadsheet, or other item from another software program

➤ Hyperlink—A link to information in another file

➤ Lookup Wizard—A value chosen from another table

When you think about it, any fields that contain the names of people, places, or things will use the Text data type. After all, names are just a bunch of letters from the alphabet—text. Computer geeks like to call these things *alphanumeric characters*.

So, the best data type for your first name field is text. Select **Text** in the Data Type list. Text is placed in the Data Type box. Press Enter to advance to the next column.

Description (and Black Tie) Optional

The **Description** column is where you can place a descriptive tag to accompany your field. Then, whenever you enter the field during data entry, the description appears on the Access status bar.

The descriptions are totally optional. Their main purpose is to assist anyone who is doing data entry in a table and needs a reminder regarding what type of information should be placed in a particular field. The **First Name** field is self-descriptive; you put the first name in it. You can forgo the description on this particular field. Press Enter, and you can set up your next field.

Farther a Field

You already have a field for the customer's first name, so you'll probably need one for the last name. Make sure that the insertion point is in the second row of the field name column. Type Last Name and press Enter. The data type is correct—it's a text field (which is the default field type in Access)—so press Enter twice to advance to the next field (you can again skip the description).

You've Got the Moves

It's easy to move from column to column or row to row in Table Design view. The columns are the field name, data type, and description. Remember that each row in the Design View window is a different field. You can use Tab to move forward through the columns or Shift+Tab to move backward. The arrow keys on the keyboard can also be used to move in their respective direction (for example, the up arrow key moves up). If you are a mouse kind of person, place the mouse I-beam in a particular row or column and then click to place the insertion point.

Now you can polish off the particulars regarding the customers, fields that contain information on where they live. Add the following field names to your table: Street, City, State, and Zip. All the new fields will be text fields. You might wonder why the Zip code field is a text field instead of a numeric field. Zip codes are designations rather than numbers with mathematical significance. When you assign the number type to a field, you want to make sure that it has some mathematical significance, such as the number of cases in stock or the amount of money you have in the bank.

The (Primary) Key to Success

Database tables can be tricky if you don't have some sort of scheme that uniquely identifies each record in the table. The federal government (and, yes, the IRS) uses a unique social security number to identify each taxpayer. In a database table, a customer number field and a product catalog number field are both excellent ways to assign a unique number or designation that is particular to the record it contains. This special field is called the *primary key* or *key field*.

The key to understanding the key field is that it must uniquely identify each record. You might think that the Last Name field would do the job. But what if a bunch of Smiths and Joneses are in your database? When you determine the data that will go into your key field, remember that it must be different for every record; it can't repeat. This is why using a unique number such as a product code or social security number is your best bet when it comes to key field data.

Because you are working on a Customers table, you will create a customer number field that is designated as the primary key. Make sure that you are in the field name box below the Zip code. Type CustNo (abbreviated to keep the size of the field name manageable). Press Enter to move to the Data Type column.

Take a Number

You can handle how you determine the customer number for each of your customers in a couple ways. You can type a number for each of the customers during the data entry process, or you can let Access assign the numbers for you. Yes, that's right, Access will assign the numbers for you, which saves you a lot of typing and rules out the possibility of duplication.

So, where do you sign up for this automatic numbering option? You designate the Field type for the CustNo field as AutoNumber; it's that easy. Click the **Data Type** drop-down arrow and then click **AutoNumber**.

The CustNo field probably could use a description. That way, if you have someone doing data entry who isn't familiar with AutoNumber, she won't have a nervous breakdown when Access won't let her enter anything into the field. Press Enter and type This field gives each customer a unique number.

Super! You have the CustNo field set up. Now all you have to do is assign it the key field designation.

Access makes it very easy to designate the CustNo field (or any field) as the key for the table. Make sure that the insertion point is currently in the **CustNo** row. Click the **Primary Key** button on the Table Design toolbar. Notice that a key appears to the left of the CustNo field.

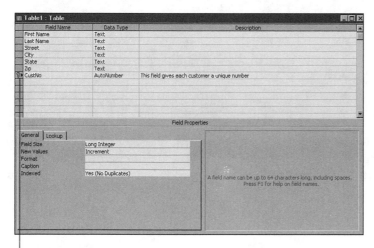

It's easy to assign primary key status to a field.

Primary Key button

Better Save Than Sorry

A fair amount of work has gone into the designing of this table, and you don't want to lose it. So save it already!

Click the **Save** button. The Save As dialog box appears, asking you for a name for the table. Type Customers in the **Name** box. Click **OK** to make the saving of your table a done deal. Notice that the name of your table, Customers, now appears in the upper left of the table design window.

Down in Front—Moving Your Field

As you set up your field names in each of the field rows, you might want to rearrange their order. For example, it would make sense to make the key field the first field in the new Customers table that you've been working with, so you must move the CustNo field. Access makes it very easy for you to move a particular field and its parameters in the Design window. All you must do is place the mouse pointer on the gray button (it looks like a box, but it's called a *selector*) just to the left of the field name. The mouse pointer becomes a right-pointing arrow. Clicking the row selector then selects the entire field row. To move the CustNo field, the first thing you want to do is select that field's row by clicking the row selector.

Click the Row Selector button to select a field row.

These gray boxes are row selectors.

To actually move the row and the field information in it, drag the selected field row to the new location (a small drag box appears next to the mouse pointer), which in your example would be the first row of the table. Good job—your dragging technique is quite impressive.

Check This Out

Drag and Drop: The Untold Story

Moving field rows in Table Design view and moving field columns in Table Datasheet view involve a common technique: drag and drop. To move a field row, select it by clicking its row selector. Then click the row and hold down the mouse button. Drag the row to its new location and then release the mouse button. This is called *dragging*. To move field columns in Datasheet view, click the column name and then drag the item to its new location. Then give your mouse a rest!

You're flying now. You've saved your table design, designated the primary key, and even moved a field. Now you can venture into a strange new world: the world of masked fields. (For greater effect, read that last sentence out loud in your best Rod Serling *Twilight Zone* voice.)

Who Is That Masked Field?

From out of the west, on a white horse, rode a masked man (okay, person) known as the Lone Data Arranger. Sorry, I couldn't resist the pun. The next step in designing a new table is to set up fields that make data entry really easy. This is done by putting an input mask on the field. An *input mask* is used to format the data you enter in the field (such as formatting numbers as currency) and to limit the number of characters that can be entered. Input masks are also great at placing items in the field for you, such as the parentheses around the area code in a phone number or the dashes in a social security number. The big question is, Where do you create input masks?

As you created the fields for your table, you might have noticed that the lower half of the Table Design window is taken up by a tabbed area titled Field Properties. Although you might think this area has something to do with agricultural real estate, the field properties are actually a set of parameters that you assign to a field to control how Access stores, handles, or displays the data.

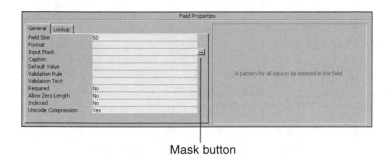

The Field Properties area in the Table Design window enables you to control how the data will appear and what kind of data can be entered in a particular field.

Mask button

It is in this Field Properties area that you define your input mask for a particular field. For example, you have a field that will hold the Zip code for each of the records in your table. It makes sense to set up the Zip code field so that it will allow the entry of five characters, automatically insert a dash, and then allow the entry of four more characters. (This is the format for the new Zip codes. Are these four new numbers the reason they keep raising the price of stamps?). Masking a field is quite easy; you merely invoke the Input Mask Wizard.

Riding with the Input Mask Wizard

Now we can get down to business and actually use an input mask to control how data is entered into the Zip Code field. In the Table Design window, click the **Zip** field row. The field properties that you set will now be assigned to this particular field. In the **Field Properties** box, click the **Input Mask** entry box. A button with an ellipsis appears in the far right of the **Input Mask** entry box. This button is the **Mask** button.

Click the **Mask** button. The Input Mask Wizard appears. This wizard contains a whole bunch of input masks for your data—Zip code, social security number, phone number, and so on—and even gives you an opportunity to try out a mask before you apply it to your data.

*The **Data Look** column shows you the pattern that your data will take as you enter it in the masked field.*

Input masks

Try It box

To apply an input mask to the Zip field, click the **Zip Code** input mask in the Input Mask dialog box if it isn't already selected. Before you do anything drastic, you'll want to test drive this mask. To do so, press the Tab key; the insertion point moves into the **Try It** box. Type **443405555** and watch what happens. The wizard inserts the dash after the first five characters. Try to enter additional characters; the wizard just beeps at you. The mask limits the number of characters to nine.

Looks to me like this mask thing is going to work out just fine. Click the **Next** button. The wizard even gives you the option of modifying the way the mask is set up. Click the **Next** button again. Now the wizard asks you whether you want the symbols in the mask (in this case, the dash) to be stored with the data; sure, a few stored symbols will not affect the size of your database file. (In the case of very complex masks that enter a large number of symbols, you might decide not to store them with the data.) Click the **Next** button to move to the last screen in the Input Mask Wizard.

Well, you made it. Just click the **Finish** button to assign this mask to your field. Now the mask pattern appears in the **Input Mask** box. Hi ho, Silver!

*The **Input Mask** box holds the input mask that you've created for your field.*

Input Mask box

Congratulations! Your Customers table looks great! You created several fields, set up an autonumbering customer number field, and masked the Zip field. Now you should make sure to save your work. Click the Save button on the toolbar.

Changing Your View Point

It makes sense to take a peek at this new table in Datasheet view—the view that you will actually be using for data entry. Again, the best place to go to change your view quickly and easily is the toolbar.

The very first button on the left side of the toolbar—the Datasheet View button—enables you to switch between Table Design and Datasheet views. Click the button. Shazam! You're in Datasheet view. The Datasheet is made up of rows and columns; each column has a heading that directly relates to the fields that you designed. When you start doing your data entry, you will find that each record appears in the datasheet as a separate row. Switching between Datasheet view and Design view will become second nature to you as you work with your Access tables. When you want to input or view data, go to Datasheet view. When you need to add or edit a field (such as put an input mask on a field), you use Design view. Let's return to Design view.

Click the Table View button again, and you are whisked back to Design view. Now, you could bounce back and forth between these two views all day and maybe even take the time to enter a little data, but your table design chores are not quite over. Remember, Access is a relational database, meaning that your database will be made up of more than one table. Each table will contain a discrete body of information.

For example, customer information will be in one table, product information in another, and order information in a third. The key fields in these tables will be used to relate the information. A record in the orders table will contain the number of the customer who ordered the product and a product number for the item that was ordered.

SEE ALSO

> *Relationships Explained*—All this talk about a number of tables related together in a database is explained in detail in Chapter 8, "Between You and Me and Access: Table Relationships."

You have a table that you can use for customer data, but you will also eventually need tables for your products, your orders or sales, and your suppliers. I mean, you are trying to run a cheese shop here, and you can't let poor database management curdle your profits.

Return to the Design view of your table and click the close (×) button to close the Design window. Notice that your Customers table now appears in the Database window for the Fromage Boutique database. Continue on your table design course and set up a table for your cheese products.

Using the Table Wizard to Design Your Database

You are probably starting to get a feel for the different routes that you can take in Access to design your databases and the objects they contain. To boil it all down to the simplest terms, you have a choice between using a wizard or not. The wizards are great if you must build a complex table and don't want to create all the fields from scratch and deal with a bunch of input masks. For simple tables, it's probably faster to design them from scratch. Using these two different paths wisely will enable you to build really great and very usable tables.

You already designed a table from scratch. Now see what the Table Wizard has to offer as you create a second table, the Products table, for your database.

A Little of This, a Little of That: Selecting Fields from the Sample Table

Make sure that you have selected the **Tables** icon in the Database window (on the left side of the window) and then double-click the **Create Table by Using Wizard** icon. The opening Table Wizard dialog box will appear in the Table Wizard window.

On the left side of the Table Wizard window, you see a list of sample tables. You can use one of these tables as the framework for the table you're building. The **Sample Fields** list box displays the fields available in the currently selected sample table. You use this wizard by selecting a sample table, selecting individual fields from that table, and inserting them into your new table. The sample fields you select for insertion into your table appear in the **Fields in My New Table** list box on the right side of the Table Wizard window. Many of these sample fields already contain input masks.

Let's build our new table using some of the fields from the sample database. In the **Sample Tables** list box (which can consist of business or personal sample tables, depending on the radio button selected), scroll down until you find the **Products** sample table; then click it. The **Sample Fields** list box changes to contain the names of all the fields available for that sample table.

In the **Sample Fields** list box, you can select the fields that you want to purloin from the sample table and include them in your own table. The first sample field available is ProductID, and it's a good one for you to put in your table. This field will serve the same purpose as the CustNo field that you put in your customer database. ProductID will autonumber each product you enter in the table, and the field will serve as the primary key for the table.

A set of buttons are available for inserting or removing sample fields from your table. Make sure to select the **ProductID** sample field and then click the **Add** button (the single, right-pointing chevron) to include the field in your table.

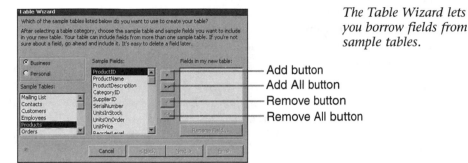

The Table Wizard lets you borrow fields from sample tables.

— Add button
— Add All button
— Remove button
— Remove All button

Put Them In or Take Them Out

Use the Add All button (the right-pointing double chevrons) to insert all the sample fields, the Remove button (the left-pointing single chevron) to remove unwanted fields, and the Remove All button (left-pointing double chevrons) to remove all the sample fields. Whether you are adding or removing fields, make sure that you click the field to select it before clicking Add or Remove. You can also rename a particular field by selecting it and then clicking the **Rename Field** button.

Use the **Add** button to place the following additional sample fields in your table in the order they appear (remember, you must select the field before clicking the **Add** button): ProductName, UnitPrice, UnitsInStock, UnitsOnOrder, and SupplierID.

And Now for Something Completely Different

Not really, but I didn't want your enthusiasm to wane. Now that you have selected the fields for your table, you can move to the next step. Click the **Next** button. The wizard wants to know what you want to name the table and whether you want it to automatically assign a primary key field to the table.

The wizard has already assigned a name for the table (Products) that is fine. It also makes sense to let the wizard assign the primary key. If you think back to the fields that you included in this table, the most likely key to assign as the primary key is the ProductID field. If the wizard doesn't choose the right key field, you can always change it later in Table Design view. Click the **Next** button.

The Table Wizard wants to know whether there is any kind of relationship between the existing tables in your database. For now, to keep things simple and to put off the discussion of table relations until later, just say that these tables are not related. Click the **Next** button.

The Table Wizard has completed the design of your new table and wants to know whether you want to start entering data in Datasheet view or take a look at the table in Design view. Because you worked in Design view before, take a look at how this thing is set up. Click the **Modify the Table Design** radio button. Click the **Finish** button.

Your finished table in Design view.

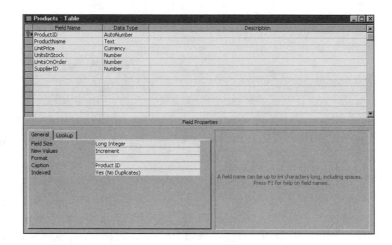

You have finished the table! As predicted, the ProductID field was designated the primary key. Peruse the other fields and notice that some are set up as text fields and others as number fields. If you ponder the purpose of each field, I think you will agree that the Table Wizard did a good job of setting up the fields and their properties. Click the **Save** button on the toolbar to make this whole thing a done deal. Click the close (×) button to close the Design window. You will now find two tables listed in your Fromage Boutique database window: Customers and Products.

Creating a Table in Datasheet View

If you like to dive right in and enter data, you can also create tables in Datasheet view. Creating tables this way immediately creates a table with 20 field columns and 30 record rows. This method still requires, however, that you enter Table Design view to specify the key field, field data types, field descriptions, and any field property changes. If you enjoy the immediate gratification of seeing your table in Datasheet view and would like to add the field names as column headings, this route will get you where you want to go—a new table!

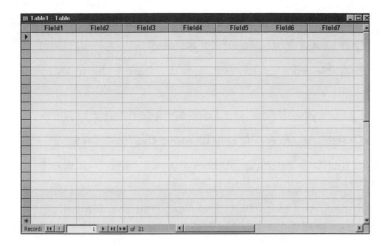

New tables can be quickly created in Datasheet view

To create a table in Datasheet view, double-click the **Create Table by Entering Data** icon on the right of the Database window. A new table in Datasheet view will appear. To enter the field names, double-click any of the field column headings (Field1, Field2, and so on). Simply type in your new field name.

After you've entered the field names, you can begin entering data. However, you will probably want to enter Design view and set the data types and other parameters (such as field masks) for the fields that you've created.

To switch between Datasheet and Design views of the table, click the View button on the Table Datasheet toolbar. Switching to Design view enables you to set up each field in the table as you did when you created a table from scratch in Design view. Remember to save the table when you have finished tweaking the various field properties.

You will probably find that creating tables in Datasheet view comes much easier after you have created several tables using either Design view or the Table Wizard. These two methods of creating tables make you much more conscious of how tables are set up and of what data types are used for particular fields of information.

So, now you've created some well-designed tables and are ready for the next step in building a database: data entry. Rest those fingers now. There's data input to do in Chapter 6, "Going On Record: Adding and Editing Data."

The Least You Need to Know

➤ You can create a new table from scratch and manually define the fields in the table.

➤ Table Design view is where you define your fields and their properties.

➤ Selecting a field in Design view makes it easy to move the field row.

➤ You can set up fields such as a customer number that will automatically number (autonumber) the records in the table.

➤ You can assign input masks to fields. These masks can limit the number of characters in an entry, as well as control the look of the entry in the field.

➤ You can also create tables using the Table Wizard. The wizard enables you to copy fields from sample tables; these fields have already been assigned appropriate field types and input masks.

➤ Tables can be created quickly by going directly to Datasheet view and entering the field names directly in the field columns. You will have to enter Design view, however, to enter the data types for these fields.

Chapter 6

Going On Record: Adding and Editing Data

In This Chapter

➤ Entering and editing data in the Table Datasheet view

➤ Moving your table with the greatest of ease

➤ Changing column widths

➤ Moving a field column from one place to another

➤ Adding and deleting fields in your table

➤ Using an AutoForm for easy data entry

You put your new data in, you take your old data out, you do the hokey pokey, and you shake it all about…oh, sorry, I was just killing time until you turned to this page. Now that you know how to construct databases and have worked through the table creation process, it's time to learn how you enter and manipulate data in a table.

Working in Datasheet View

In the last chapter, you saw that you can work on your tables in two different views: Design view and Datasheet view. The purpose of Design view is to set up the fields in the table, which determines the structure of the table.

It's Datasheet view that you use when you want to enter and edit the data that goes into the table. We will be spending most of this chapter in Datasheet view. So, get comfortable in your chair, place your hands on home row, and let's go for it.

Entering Your Data

Data, the information you put in your tables, is by far the most important component of this whole database thing. Empires are built and lost because of data, so it's important for you to get it in your database and get it organized.

Let's start by putting together a simple customer table. In fact, we can enter our data in the Customers table that you created for the Fromage Boutique database in the last chapter.

Make sure that you have the Database window for the Fromage Boutique database (or any other database) open on your desktop. Click the Tables icon to view the tables in the database and then double-click the Customers table (or any table) to open it.

When your table is open in Datasheet view, it's ready for data entry.

The first record you will enter

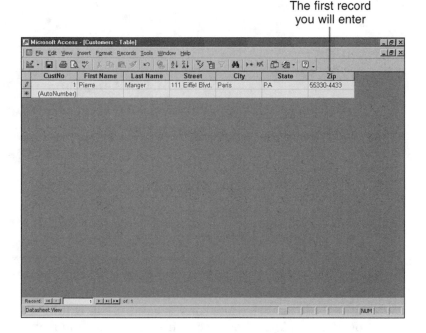

You have the Customers table open, and things appear as they should; the table is divided into rows (records) and columns (fields). You're probably thinking that a table in Datasheet view looks a lot like a spreadsheet (in Excel, for example). So that you can see as much of the data entry area as possible, click the Maximize button on the Table window.

Houdini Stole My Table!

If you inadvertently minimize the entire Table window and then click the Database button (in this case, for Fromage Boutique) on the Windows taskbar, you will find yourself staring at the current Database window. But there is no sign of your table. It seems to have disappeared. Not true—take a close look at the Windows taskbar, and you will find a button for the table (in our example, Customers). Click this button to restore the Table window to the desktop. Remember that Access 2000 opens separate windows for the database and objects that you have open. For more about the ins and outs of working with Access windows, see Chapter 2, "Putting Access Through Its Paces."

Time to type in our first customer's data. The First Name field is where you want to do your typing, so press the Enter key to move from the CustNo field (it's an autonumber field, so you don't have to type anything in it—just check the left side of the status bar to view comments related to a field.) to the First Name field. Type Pierre and then press the Enter key. Hurrah! You've entered data and advanced to the next field.

If you make a mistake when you are typing in a field, you can press the Backspace key to delete the typo. Then key in the appropriate text. What's that? you say. You've already moved to the next field, and now you see the typo? No problem, just use the mouse pointer (I-beam) to place the insertion point back into any of your fields with a quick click.

Fill in the rest of Pierre's record as follows (remember to press the Enter key at the end of each entry and remember that you don't have to type the dash in the Zip code; the input mask takes care of that for you):

Last Name:	Manger
Street:	111 Eiffel Blvd.
City:	Paris
State:	PA
Zip:	55330-4433

When you entered the Zip code, Access automatically placed the dash in the entry. This is all due to the field mask that you set up when you designed the table.

You also might have noticed that as soon as you moved into the First Name field for Pierre, a customer number (1) was automatically assigned to Pierre. The autonumber field type is doing its job, assigning sequential numbers to your customers as you enter their data. For more information on field types, take a look at Chapter 5, "Turning the Tables: Table Design."

Press Enter again and you will move to the First Name field for your next customer. There is still a little more typing to do. Enter the following customer information (you won't need to type the dash in the Zip code because of the input mask):

Janet	Dugong	12 Coastal Way	Waterford	OH	44240-5567
Bob	Jones	1340 America Dr.	Crystal	PA	65012-6894
Alice	Barney	4443 Maine Ave.	Spokane	PA	65437-1234
Kim	Reech	55 Platinum St.	Los Angeles	OH	44240-9354

The Table window displays your data and provides you with all the tools you need for adding and editing records.

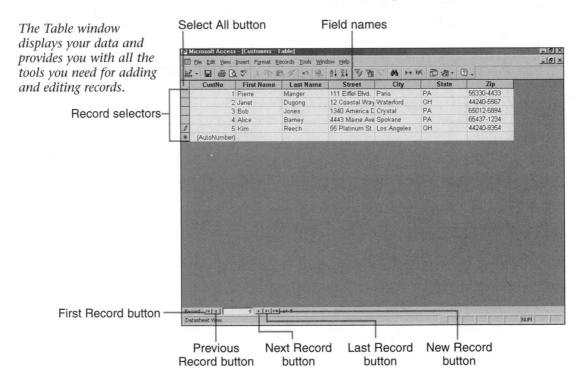

80

Editing Your Data

Editing records is every bit as easy as entering new records. Let's say that Alice Barney dropped by your cheese shop this morning and bought an impressive amount of curd, more than 3 pounds of brie and 7 pounds of cheddar. When she paid for her purchase by check, you noticed that she had a new home address (she purchased the cheese for a house-warming party). As soon as she departed, you rushed to your computer. You're excited, not because she bought so much cheese, but because you get to edit one of the records in your database.

Changing Field Data

Alice is still going to reside in the beautiful garden state of Pennsylvania, but her street, city, and Zip have changed. Place the mouse pointer on the very left edge of Alice's Street field. The mouse pointer will turn into a cell pointer (it looks like a cross or big plus sign). Click once, and all the data in the field will be selected.

Now all you have to do is type the new data. Type 1420 Mineshaft Street. The new data replaces the currently selected old data. Use the mouse pointer (as the cell pointer) to select the data in the City field. Replace Spokane with Big City. We also need to edit Alice's Zip, but only the last four digits have changed. Place the mouse pointer (it becomes an I-beam inside the field) before the first number in the Zip's last four. Hold down the left mouse button and drag the I-beam across the four numbers to select them. Now you can type the new last four; type 8765. The new numbers replace the selected old numbers.

Selection Election

When a single word or number appears in a particular field, you can select the item with a quick double click. In entries that are made up of multiple words or other items separated by spaces or other delimiters such as hyphens (*Kansas City* or a Zip code—44240–5555), a double click will select only the portion of the entry that the I-beam rests on. Those of you who shun the mouse totally when selecting items can use Shift+right arrow key to select items in a field (a character at a time) after you have placed the insertion point in that field.

Navigating the Tossing Sea of Your Table

As you enter data into your table or edit records that are already there, it makes sense to know how to easily navigate around the table. An important area of navigational interest is just to the left of where the horizontal scrollbar normally appears in a maximized Table window (your table is not wide enough to warrant a horizontal scrollbar); this area contains the Datasheet navigation buttons. These buttons enable you to move one record forward or back and to the beginning or end of your records.

Click the First Record button (it's the first button on the left). The record selector moves to Pierre's record. Notice that it selects the text in a particular field. The selected field will be in the same column that you left the insertion point in after your last round of data entry.

Click the Next Record button. The indicator moves to Janet's record. Click the Last Record button, and the indicator moves to Kim's record. Click the Previous Record button, and the indicator moves to Alice's record.

Another phenomenon that you will encounter in Access is that the mouse pointer takes on a variety of shapes, depending on where you've placed it. For example, when you place it at the top of a column, you get a down-pointing column selection tool. When you place the mouse pointer on a particular field in a particular record, you get a cross-like pointer called a cell pointer. You can use it to select one field in a record.

The best way to become familiar with the various mouse shapes is to move the mouse pointer around the table and see what happens. Go on, what are you waiting for?

A Keyboard Sonata (or a Movement in the Key of Board)

The keyboard also offers you several avenues for moving around the fields in your table. Some movements require only one key to get the job done, such as the Tab key (it moves you forward through the fields). In other cases, you must press two keys simultaneously, such as Shift+Tab (this moves you backward through the fields). Take a look at some of the other keyboard movements in the following list:

Key	What It Does
Tab	One field forward
Shift+Tab	One field back
Up arrow	One field up
Down arrow	One field down
Home	The first field in a record
End	The last field in a record

Page Up	Up one screen of records
Page Down	Down one screen of records
Ctrl+Home	The first field in the first record
Ctrl+End	The last field in the last record

Try out some of the keystrokes. After you've tried both the mouse and the keyboard, you can decide which way of moving through the table you prefer.

Sound Practices

When you use the mouse to move around a table, the placement of the insertion point is as easy as one click. However, when you are typing data, it makes sense to keep your hands on the keyboard and use the keys for movement in the table.

Manipulating the Columns

The default column width for the Datasheet view of your tables is 1 inch. This means that you may type data into a field that is not accommodated by the field's column width. You probably have noticed that some of the customers' street addresses placed in the Address field are being cut off because of the narrow column width.

Changing column widths is extremely simple. Place your mouse pointer on the dividing line between the Street column heading and the City column heading. The mouse pointer becomes a column sizing tool.

CustNo	First Name	Last Name	Street	City	State	Zip
1	Pierre	Manger	111 Eiffel Blvd.	Paris	PA	55330-4433
2	Janet	Dugong	12 Coastal Way	Waterford	OH	44240-5567
3	Bob	Jones	1340 America C	Crystal	PA	65012-6894
4	Alice	Barney	1420 Mineshaft	Big City	PA	65437-8765
5	Kim	Reech	55 Platinum St.	Los Angeles	OH	44240-9354
(AutoNumber)						

Column sizing tool

The column sizing tool enables you to change the width of your columns.

83

Click and hold the left mouse button. Using the column sizing tool, drag the column border to the right until the Street column is wide enough to accommodate all your entries.

You can change the default setting for the columns in your new table's Datasheet view. Click the **Tools** menu; then click **Options**. Click the **Datasheet** tab and then put the new column width in the **Default column width** box. Changing this set-ting will not override changes that you make to individual field columns in your tables using the mouse.

Fit to Be Tried

Now you know that you can increase or decrease a column width by dragging the col-umn dividers. There is another way to quickly change a column width: Place the mouse pointer on the column divider between the Street and City fields. When the column width tool appears, double-click. That's right, just double-click. The column widens to accommodate the truncated entry.

This little trick is called *best fit*. Whenever you want a field column to automatically accommodate the longest entry in it, move to the column divider and double-click.

Saving Your Work

When you work in other Microsoft programs (such as Word or Excel), you must save all the information you enter, or you can lose it when you close the application. Saving the data in Access tables is different; the data that you enter is saved to the table as soon as you place it in the field. If you inadvertently exit Access without clicking Save, for example, you will find that all the data you entered is in your table even though you didn't save it. This is one of the (beautiful) enigmas of Access.

Access Warnings

You will find that if you try to exit a table that you have made structural changes to (such as field column–width changes or field deletions), Access will let you know that you need to save the table.

You do, however, have to save your work whenever you make design changes to the table, such as adding a field, deleting a field, or widening or narrowing a column. So, if you change the structure of the table, save it or lose it.

The best advice I can give you is that when you are in doubt about whether you have modified the structure of a table or other Access object, click the Save button on the Table toolbar. This saves any changes that you have made. As for your data, enter it with proud impunity, knowing that it is being saved for you as you place it in the field.

Now that you've entered some data into your table, let's take a look at how you select rows and columns (records and fields) in the table and how you delete unwanted records.

Selecting Rows and Columns

At times it will be advantageous to select an entire record or a field column in your table (such as moving a column or deleting a record). You can click column headings (field names) to select an entire column, and you can click a gray row button (record selectors) to select a record. To select all the records in your datasheet, you can click the Select All button, which is the gray square to the left of your first field.

Select All
button   Field selectors

Access makes it easy for you to select your records and field columns.

Selected record

Record selectors

Moving a Column

Being able to select an entire record or field column makes it very easy to move these items. For example, it might make more sense to have the table fields arranged so that the Last Name field appears before the First Name field.

Place the mouse pointer at the top of the Last Name field heading (the column heading). The mouse pointer turns into a down-pointing arrow, a field selection tool. Click once, and the entire Last Name column will be selected.

Now comes the hard part. Press the left mouse button and drag the entire Last Name column to the left one column. In effect, you are dropping the Last Name column on top of the First Name column.

Moving a field column in Datasheet view is just a click and a drag away.

Don't let go of the mouse button until you have the column in the right place; a dark black line will appear along the border of the column you are moving the column to. Let go of the mouse button, and the column drops into its new position. Click anywhere in the table to deselect the column.

Way to go! You've just become acquainted with drag and drop. You can use this feature to move columns, fields, text, even graphics. Drag and drop is the easiest way to move or copy a selection a short distance.

Broken Record (Deleting a Record)

Life has a way of raising you up one moment and then dashing you down the next. You just finish making all these improvements to your database table when the phone rings. An entrepreneurial colleague who runs a bakery down the street calls to let you know that one of your best customers, Janet Dugong, has moved out of town. After hanging up the phone, you sit down, wondering what you'll do with all that Stilton that you keep on stock for her (what you'll do is fill out your Products table and keep better track of your inventory using Access).

Oh well, you probably should delete Janet's record. Click the selector button for Janet's record (the mouse turns into a right-pointing arrow). Janet's entire record is selected.

 Now all you have to do is delete Janet's record. Courage, I know this is tough. Take the mouse and click the Delete Record button on the Table toolbar.

Janet leaves the table.

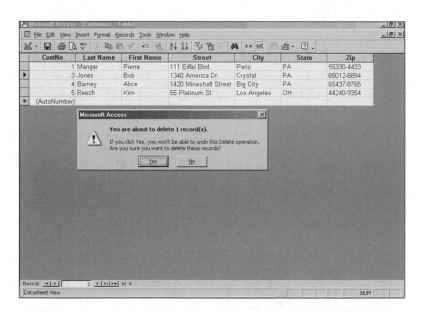

Access is pretty smart. It knows that you are about to delete a record and wants to make sure that you really want to do this. You can delete the record forever (the Yes choice) or let Janet's record live to see another day (the No choice). You really don't need this record any longer, so click Yes. Janet is gone.

When you delete Janet's record, you also delete her customer number from the possibilities. When you use autonumber to number records, the numbers cannot be changed. So when you delete an autonumbered record, it will leave a gap in your sequence. It might make more sense to put a new customer's data in Janet's record if you want to maintain the run of record numbers.

Adding a Field to Your Table

Although you are traumatized by the deletion of Janet's record, you realize that your colleague's phone call has given you a sudden spark of inspiration. Your table does not include your customers' phone numbers. You realize that if you had their phone numbers, you could keep in better touch with them, maybe even become their friend. And then they won't move away like Janet.

Your course is decided: You must add a telephone field to your table. Adding a field to a table is just a matter of adding a new column. Access will add the column to the left of any column you select. In this case, you want the telephone number to go to the left of the Street address. Select the Street field column and then click the **Insert** menu. **Column** is a choice in the **Insert** menu, so click it. A new column is placed in your table to the left of the Street column.

Deleting a field is just as easy as inserting a new field. Select the column (and field) that you want to delete and then click the Cut button. When you delete a field, you are probably deleting some data as well. Access takes this into account and will ask you if you truly want to remove the field from the table. Keep in mind that you can't have it both ways: no field, no data. It's that simple.

Fields can also be added, deleted, and moved in Design view. Any changes that you make to a table's design (such as adding or deleting a field) will be reflected in the table's Datasheet view.

A Name Is Just a Name

Obviously, you will want to name the new field that you've placed in your table. The name that Access automatically sticks in there (Field1) probably isn't going to do the job for you. To replace this field name, double-click the column heading (**Field1**). This selects the text. Now you can type your own field name, Phone. Click anywhere in the table, and your new field name will be centered and you're good to go.

The No Fuss Field

Now that you've added a new field column to the table and named it, all you have to do is switch to Design view, determine the data type, and add an input mask if you like. Because this is going to be a field for telephone numbers, it would be nice to mask the field so that the parentheses around the area code and the dash after the first three digits are automatically placed in your entries.

Click the Design View button on the toolbar. This switches you to Design view. Notice that the new field has already been placed in the table design; it appears just below First Name. Click in the new field's Data Type box.

Because we will be dealing with phone numbers (which aren't really numbers of numerical significance), the field type can remain text. We do, however, want to mask the field to make the data entry easier. Click in the **Input Mask** box in the Field Properties area. Click the Input Mask button to invoke the Input Mask Wizard.

SEE ALSO

> *If you've been working through the chapters in sequence, you've already worked with an input mask. Review the information in Chapter 5, "Turning the Tables: Table Design," under the heading "Masking a Field."*

You Change It, You Save It!

You will be asked to save the table when you manipulate your fields and then switch back to the Table view or call up one of the wizards. Any changes made to the structure of the table must be saved!

The first mask type on the wizard's screen is for phone numbers. Select it with the mouse, and then you can move through each screen as you did for the Zip code mask, if you like. However, because the phone number mask is exactly what we are after, you can click the **Finish** button (again, this button has no relation to any European countries or the body parts of fish) to complete the masking process.

The mask is placed exactly where we want it. Save your table design using the Save button and then use the Datasheet View button to return to Datasheet view. Now you can enter the phone numbers for your customers. Start at the top of the column and press the down arrow key after each entry. You might also want to widen the column to accommodate your entries (remember, you don't have to enter the parentheses or the dash).

Here are the customer phone numbers you should enter:

Customer	Phone Number
Pierre	(216)555-1234
Bob	(216)555-5436
Alice	(216)555-7777
Kim	(512)555-3643

	CustNo	Last Name	First Name	Phone	Street	City	State	Zip
	1	Manger	Pierre	(216) 555-1234	111 Eiffel Blvd	Paris	PA	55330-443
	3	Jones	Bob	(216) 555-5436	1340 America Dr.	Crystal	PA	65012-689
	4	Barney	Alice	(216) 555-7777	1420 Mineshaft Street	Big City	PA	65437-876
▶	5	Reech	Kim	(512) 555-3643	55 Platinum St.	Los Angeles	OH	44240-935
*	(AutoNumber)							

A nice column of phone numbers.

Adding a New Record to a Table

A new customer drops by your shop and is incredibly excited to find such a wide-ranging choice of cheeses. He is so excited, in fact, that he wants to make sure he is in your database so that he can be notified of any special sales or rare acquisitions, such as the Pacific Rim favorite, Hawaiian Coconut Curd. (Okay, so I made it up. Just wanted to see if you were still paying attention.)

Time to enter the new customer's data into the database. You have probably noticed that working in Datasheet view can be distracting. It's hard to concentrate on one record when you can see the entire table. There is a quick and easy way to isolate records for data input and editing—the AutoForm.

Creating a Quick Form for Data Entry

You just want a quick-and-dirty form that shows all the fields in the table and enables you to work on one record at a time. This is basically the definition of an AutoForm. The AutoForm option lets you create a new object, such as a form or report, without going through a long design process.

To use the AutoForm option, click the New Object drop-down arrow button on the table toolbar. A list of possible new objects is displayed. Next, click the **AutoForm** choice on the **New Object** menu.

The New Object menu is a quick-fix solution to creating a data-entry form.

Voilà! Your AutoForm is created. Your form has incorporated all the fields from your table. Your form will appear on the Windows desktop as a new Access Object. Remember that it will have its own button on the Windows taskbar (as does the current database and the table that you were working with).

Working in the Data Entry AutoForm

Pierre's was the first record in your table and appears in the newly created form. You might have to scroll down a little, but this form has a set of navigation buttons just like the datasheet.

The AutoForm uses the fields that were in your table.

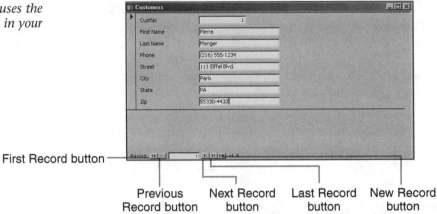

First Record button —

Previous Record button — Next Record button — Last Record button — New Record button

Auto objects such as the AutoForm use all the fields in the table when you create them. Because Auto objects are easy to create, you don't necessarily have to save them after you create and then use them. If you do decide to save an object as a form, you can later delete it in the Database window.

Form Your Own Opinion

Forms can include all or just some of the fields found in a table. Forms can also be designed that include fields from more than one table. You will learn about forms that use fields from multiple tables later in the book.

Click the Next Record button. You have moved to the second record in the table—Bob Jones. It's nice being able to see each record in this isolated manner, but we want to enter data for a brand new customer. Click the New Record button (it's the button with the asterisk).

Now we have a blank record. Press the Enter key and fill in the information that follows (remember to press the Enter key after each field entry):

Field	Information to Enter
First Name	Larry
Last Name	Curly-Moe
Phone Number	(216)555-8444
Street	3 Stooges Lane
City	Hollywood
State	OH
Zip	44240-3210

Way to go! You've added another record to your table. And you probably noticed that the AutoForm also used the field mask that you had created for the Zip field in the table. AutoForms are usually used for quick data entry and then discarded without saving. Click the Close button on the AutoForm. Now let's take a look at the table and see what the record looks like in Datasheet view.

Where's My Record? Viewing Your Table Updates

Mr. Curly-Moe's record does not appear in our table. What gives? Actually, nothing bad has happened. All you have to do is update the data in the table. Make sure that you are in the Table window (not the AutoForm's window). Click anywhere in the table. Hold down the Shift key and press the F9 function key (or select the Records menu and then select Refresh). Ah, there we go. All the records now show in the table.

Now you can continue to enter data, add fields, or even delete fields in Datasheet view. You can also switch to Design view and work on the fields and field types in the table. Just a click back on the AutoForm enables you to continue to enter information into the table. When you are finished with the AutoForm, you can save it or close it without saving it. It's your choice.

Wow, you sure put that table through its paces. As you can see, the table offers the perfect holding tank for your data; its datasheet construction makes it easy for you to see your fields and records in a very simple and easy-to-use format.

The Least You Need to Know

➤ Datasheet view provides a spreadsheet-like view of the information in your table; you can add, delete, or edit records in Datasheet view.

➤ The navigation buttons provide a way to move from record to record in Datasheet view or AutoForm view.

➤ You can select a field column and drag it to a new location using drag and drop.

➤ In Datasheet view, you can add fields to the table.

➤ After you enter data into an AutoForm, click in the table and make sure to press Shift+F9 to update the records in the table.

Chapter 7

Being Manipulative: Different Ways to View Your Records

In This Chapter

➤ Sorting your records like a pro

➤ Freezing fields for easy scrolling

➤ Using the Find feature to search out data

➤ Filtering records by example

➤ Filtering records by form

➤ Hiding fields and then finding them again

Okay, so you got your feet wet with tables and learned how to enter, edit, and delete records. Your first table was a real lightweight, however, nothing more than a quick trip in the wading pool. Now you must take the real plunge into database reality and become comfortable with the fact that most of your database tables can hold a very large number of records. In fact, you can potentially be swimming in records. Everyone into the pool!

In most cases, especially if you use Access to manage business data (a mailing list or a product table), the number of records in a table can be staggering. No reason to panic, however (unless you like to panic; if you do, hyperventilate now). Access provides several clever tools for dealing with massive amounts of data in your tables.

Out of Sorts

You now know (much to your chagrin) that tables can potentially amass hundreds, even thousands, of records. Obviously, you cannot view a table this size in its entirety in the Access window. Not being able to view the records easily increases the chances of data-entry mistakes, even missing field data. You can scroll up and down through the table records, you can even try out an AutoForm to view each record alone, but when you're dealing with many records, you need other strategies to ensure accuracy.

One way to manipulate and reorder your records is with the Sort feature. Access makes sorting very easy; you can sort by any field and sort ascending (*a* to *z*) or descending (*z* to *a*).

Basic Sorts of the Big Kahuna—Northwind

Obviously, if I'm going to convince you of the need to sort your records, I must show you a big database table. Use the Northwind Trader's database mentioned in Chapter 2, "Putting Access Through Its Paces." It's found in the Samples folder inside the Access (or Office) software folder on your hard drive.

When you first start Access, open the Northwind database by making sure the **Open an Existing File** radio button is selected and that **More Files** is highlighted in the file list. When you click **OK**, the Open dialog box appears, and you can use it to locate the database file.

If you want to open the Northwind database and already have Access running, click the Open button on the Access toolbar. In either case, you will be greeted by the Northwind Database window.

The Northwind Database window.

In the Northwind Database window, select the **Tables** icon to the left of the window and then open the **Products** table (double-click its icon). This table has 77 records (take a look at the status bar)—a good number to play around with.

Filters Are Fine, But Queries Really Quake

You will find that sorting, filtering, and finding data work fine when you want to manipulate the records in only one table. For a more advanced way of sorting and filtering data, you can use a query. You can design queries for one table or multiple, related tables. You will work with queries in Chapter 10, "Reforming Your Forms."

Going Down, Please (Descending Sort)

This whole sorting thing is not difficult. All you have to do is select the field and click one of the Sort buttons on the toolbar. For example, you might be in a situation in which you are horribly overstocked; your warehouse is filled to the ceiling with products. Now you can (a) burn down the warehouse and collect the insurance money (and probably go directly to jail) or (b) sell some of your merchandise. Why not start with the products that you have the most of?

The Northwind Products table has a Units in Stock field. You can use this field to sort the records in the table in descending order. This will give a list that places the products with the greatest number in stock at the top of your list.

Click the **Units in Stock** field heading to select the entire column of data. The field column for Units in Stock becomes highlighted. To sort the data from large to small (descending), click the Sort Descending button on the toolbar. As soon as you do, the records are rearranged by units in stock from large to small—or descending—order! If you want to see more fields and records Click the Maximize button on the Table window.

Now you have the data sorted in descending order, which is great. You can see that you have 125 units of something in stock (the item at the top of the sorted Units in Stock field column), and you can probably also see that it is in the Beverages category (in the Category field). What you can't see, however, is the name of the item—the Product Name field column is off to the right of the screen. For you to see the name and the units in stock at the same time, you must scroll back and forth using the horizontal scrollbar. But hold on just a minute, don't scroll yet! There is a way to remedy this little problem so that you can see the name and the units at the same time.

The results of your sort.

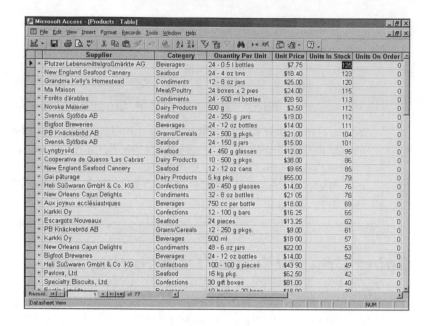

Freezing Columns (Is It Cold in Here, or Is It Me?)

It would be great if you could somehow trick the Product Name field into staying on the screen when you scroll to the Units in Stock column. You know, if you've been reading this book carefully, that there is certainly a way to do this, or I wouldn't bring it up. Freezing columns—that's how you can get the Product Name and Units in Stock columns on the screen at the same time.

So, freeze a column (my teeth are chattering). Click the column heading in the Product Name field column. This selects the entire column of data.

Click the **Format** menu; then click **Freeze Columns** (in this case, it's one column—Product Name). If you did this right, the Product Name column moved over to the first field position in the table. Click anywhere in the table to deselect the field column (you can also select multiple fields to freeze click the first field name (the column heading); then hold down the Shift key and click the last field name that you intend to freeze).

Now see whether this whole freeze action worked. (The last time I tried this kind of thing, I ended up with some Popsicle sticks slumped over in some half-frozen yogurt, but that's another story.) Use the right scroll button on the horizontal scrollbar to scroll toward the Units in Stock column. Notice that as you scroll, the Product Name stays put—that's the frozen column.

Wow! You can scroll horizontally until the Units in Stock column is right next to the Product Name column. The thing that you had 125 units of is Rhönbräu Klosterbier (whatever that is. Some kind of German beer, I guess—oops, this is supposed to be a nonalcoholic-beverage–only book).

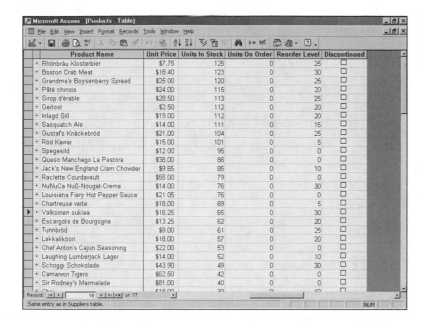

You can freeze columns and then scroll to view columns of data that are many fields apart.

Now you know what items to place on blue-light special in your store to get the inventory down. Notice that the second highest stocked item is crab meat. I guess you need to sell your customers on the idea that crabmeat and German beer really go well together—yum yum.

Spring Thaw: Unfreeze Those Columns

It's easy to unfreeze the columns that you put the freeze on. Just click the **Format** menu and then click **Unfreeze All Columns**. Now when you scroll to the right in your table, the Product Name column does not remain (frozen) in the table datasheet.

You probably noticed that the Product Name column remained in the first position. If you want to put the Product ID back in its original place, select that column and drag it.

Going Up, Please (Ascending Sort)

You've already done a great job with a descending sort, so you probably won't have any problem at all with an ascending sort. Say that you would like to put the records back in their original order, based on their Product ID.

Select the **Product ID** column and then click the Sort Ascending button on the toolbar. Now the records are back in their original order. As you can see, the Sort buttons are somewhat limited; you can sort by one field in either an ascending or a descending direction.

Sorting Adjacent Columns

You can sort by more than one field, using the Sort buttons, if the two fields are adjacent and the fields are in the order by which you want to sort the records. Just drag to select the two adjacent columns and then click either of the Sort buttons on the Table toolbar.

Sorting Out the Details (Advanced Sorts)

As you can see, the Sort command leaves you high and dry if you must sort a table by more than one field, especially if the fields are not adjacent in the table. Not a problem. You just conduct a sort based on multiple fields, which in Access lingo is an *advanced sort*. With an advanced sort, you can sort by as many as 15 fields—if you REALLY want to.

The advanced sort feature is accessed by clicking **Filter** on the **Records** menu. A *filter* is a list of certain criteria (such as customers in Germany) that will give you a subset of the records in your table. Because filtering and sorting are both ways to manipulate your records, they are found in the same menu: Records. We will talk about filters shortly. For now, we'll take a look at an advanced sort using more than one field.

Let's say that you run a company that sells products to other businesses. These businesses would be listed in your Customers table. The catch is that these customers are located all over the world and you would like to see the records in the table sorted by country. Because you have more than one customer in each country, you would like the cities in which these businesses are located to be sorted alphabetically as well.

When you sort by more than one field, you must assign a primary sort field (in this example, Country) and at least a secondary sort field (in this case, the City field) and determine which direction (ascending or descending) you want the sort to follow. When you give Access all these instructions for your advanced sort, you're setting up the *sort parameters*. Setting these parameters is the first step in conducting an advanced sort.

Well, almost the first step. You can't do any kind of sort if you don't have a database table open in Access. The Northwind database provides a Customers table that lists companies. The fields in the table include a field for Country and a field for City. To play out the scenario just described, open the Northwind database and then double-click the **Customers** table to open it. Now you have the raw material that you need (a database table), and you can set your sort parameters.

Setting Your Sort Parameters

The first step in conducting an advanced sort is to enter your sort parameters. You do that in the Filter window. To get there, click the **Records** menu and then point at **Filter**. Click **Advanced Filter/Sort** to enter the Filter window.

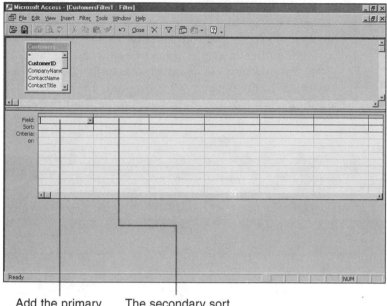

The Filter window is where you set up your sort parameters.

Add the primary sort field here

The secondary sort field goes here

The Filter window has two parts. The upper half of the window shows the current table and the fields that it contains. The lower half of the window is where you get the job done. The area is divided into several rows and columns. The two important rows are Field and the one below it, Sort.

When you sort by more than one field, you should place the field names in the Filter window in the order in which you want the sort to take place. Click in the first field column next to Field; a drop-down arrow appears. Click the drop-down arrow, and wonder of wonders, a list of the fields in the table appears. All you have to do is choose the primary field by which you want to sort the table. In this case, choose the **Country** field. Then click in the **Sort** box and choose **Ascending** from the drop-down list.

Adding Fields to the Filter Window with a Double-Click

You can also add fields to the field columns in the Filter window via the Field Name box that appears in the top half of the Filter window. Click the field column that you want to place the field in. Then double-click the field name in the Field Name box.

Now it's time to add your secondary sort field. Click in the second column across from the Field row heading; Access again supplies a drop-down list of the fields in the table. Choose **City**; then move to the **Sort** box and use the same technique you used before to set the direction of the sort for this field as Ascending.

As I said earlier, in an advanced sort, you can sort by as many as 15 fields and sort some of the fields in an ascending direction and others in a descending direction. It would be a challenge (and people would probably think you're pretty odd) trying to come up with a multidirectional sort that involves more than three or four fields.

You can quickly set up your sort parameters in the Filter window.

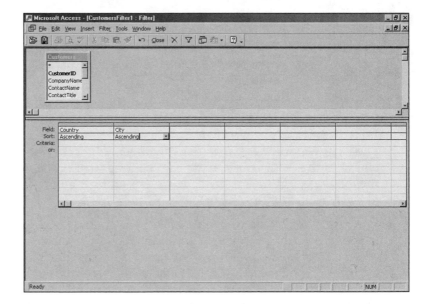

Now Sort!

You've supplied sort parameters to your table; now there must be a button somewhere that will make this a done deal. Aha, there it is, on the toolbar—the Apply Filter button. If you've been playing along, click the **Apply Filter** button. Access looks in the Filter window and sorts your data by each field you selected (moving from left to right in the Filter window).

A Toolbar for Every Occasion!

If you haven't noticed already, each different view (Table, Design, Filter, Form, and many others) that you use to work on your database has its own toolbar. Because you are in the Filter window, the currently displayed toolbar is the Filter/Sort toolbar.

The records in the table are sorted first (ascending alphabetically) by the Country field and then by the City field.

City field   Country field

The table sorted by country and city.

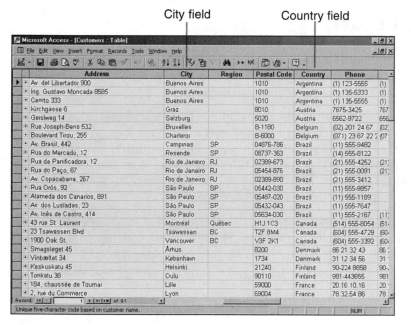

Saving a Sort as a Query!

Although you haven't had the opportunity to work with queries yet, you will find that little difference exists between a query and a complex filter/sort. In fact, queries have both sorting and filtering capabilities. If you design a sort that you would like to use over and over again, you can save it as a query. Click the **Save as Query** button on the Filter window's toolbar. (To return to the Filter window, click the **Records** menu, and point at **Filter**. Click **Advanced Filter/Sort**.)

Using Find (I'm Lost!)

There will be times when you want to quickly find a specific record in a table or take a look at a group of records that have in common the data in a particular field. Well, look no further. Your answer is found, I mean, *find*. The Find feature is a quick way of tracking down records that meet a particular search criteria.

Say you have a table of suppliers (just like the Suppliers table in the Northwind database), and these companies are all over the world, making it hard for you to drop by and check up on their operations. You happen to be taking a vacation to Canada, and you're sure that you have at least one supplier in that country. Even though everyone warns you about mixing business with pleasure, you pull up your Suppliers table in the Access window to search for your Canadian suppliers.

Remember that the Database window for the particular database makes it easy for you to switch between the various tables in the database. After closing a particular table, you can open a new one via the Database window. Just make sure the Table icon is selected in the left pane of the Database window, and the tables in the database will appear in the right pane.

I Need a Replacement!

Notice that the Find dialog box also has a **Replace** tab. Click this tab to search for a particular entry or entries in a table and then replace the item with a new entry that you have entered in the Replace With box in the Replace dialog box. This is a great feature for replacing entries that you know are incorrect or have changed. For example, the area code for customers in a certain geographic area might be changed. You can use Replace to quickly fix them. Remember that the Replace feature works just like the Find feature, only it will change certain entries in the table.

Piece of cake. Scroll to the Country field column. Click in the very first record's Country field (this would be the first field in the Country field column.) Then click the Find button on the Table toolbar (it looks like a little pair of binoculars, I mean, *little* compared to real binoculars). As soon as you click the Find button, a Find dialog box pops up. This is where you tell Access what you want it to search for. As in sorting, these instructions are called *parameters*. The Find dialog box offers all the options you need to set your search parameters.

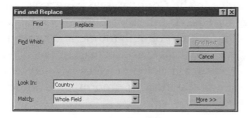

If you're lost, use the Find feature and be found.

Setting Your Search Parameters

Let's take a gander at the various areas of the Find dialog box. In the Find What box, type the item that you want to search for. In this case, type Canada. In the Look In box, specify whether you want to search the current field or the table. First click the **More** button, then use the Search drop-down list that appears to specify whether you want to search all the fields in the current field column (All), or just Up or Down from the selected field. There is also a drop-down box marked Match. This box contains three choices: Any Part of Field, Whole Field (the default), or Start of Field.

If you choose **Any Part of Field**, Access will try to match the entry in the Find What box with any part of the data entered in the selected field. For example, in the case of *Canada*, Access would consider *Canada*, *Canadian*, and *US/Canada* all matches in your search.

Whole Field, on the other hand, would return matches where only *Canada* is found—the whole word only. Finally, **Start of Field** would return matches only where *Canada* is found at the beginning of the field entry. In this case, *Canada* and *Canadian* would both be considered matches because the characters Canada come at the beginning of the field data.

After you type your search string in the Find What box and choose how you want Access to return the matches in the Match box, you can also set additional parameters related to the search. Two check boxes are available in the Find dialog box after you click the **More** button (as already mentioned above): Match Case and Search Fields as Formatted.

The Match Case check box enables you to find text that has the same pattern of uppercase and lowercase characters as the entry you placed in the Find What box. This enables you to search for data that has been entered in a particular way, for example. The Search Fields as Formatted box (when selected) searches for items as they appear in the field. An example of this is a number that is entered as 52000 but appears in the field as $52000.00. You would check the box and do your search for $52000.00. This search parameter is also important for dates; you might have entered a date as a numeric entry (9/12/60), but it appears in a different format (September 12, 1960).

Going Wild with Wildcards

When you set up the search for *Canada* in the Country field, you typed in a complete text string—Canada—in the Find What box. At times, you might want Access to search for parts of words or a particular pattern of alphanumeric characters (letters of the alphabet); you can do this using *wildcard characters* as placeholders. Wildcards can represent one character, several characters, a list of characters, or even a numeric character (you know, a number). Some of the most commonly used wildcard characters and their usage follow:

* The asterisk character can take the place of any number of characters. You can use it at the beginning, middle, or end of a character string. An example would be C*a. A search for this text string in a field column of countries would return countries that begin with a capital *C* and end with *a*, such as *Canada* and *Cambodia*. The number of characters represented by the asterisk can vary.

? The question mark can be used anywhere in your search string to represent a single alphanumeric character. Let's say you use the Find feature to search for the text string f?ll. Some of the possible matches you could get in a search like this would be words that differ by just one character, such as *fill*, *fall*, *full*, and *fell*.

[ ]   The brackets are used to specify a list of possible matches for a single character found in the items you are searching for. For example, you could set up the Find feature to look for the text string Jo[ah]n. Matches to this text string would be limited to *Joan* and *John*.

\#   The number sign is used to represent a single numeric character in a search string. It works very much like the question mark wildcard. Let's say that you have a Product number field that contains data in the form of three-digit codes (such as 142 or 333). Your supplier calls and tells you all the products ending in 22 are going to be discontinued. No problem, you can do a search using #22 to find them.

Wildcards can be a big help when you must use the Find feature and want your matches to consist of items that you just can't find by typing in a whole word (such as *Canada*). Always take a moment to think about what exactly you would like the Find feature to dig up for you. Chances are, you can use a wildcard to produce the right results.

Click and You Shall Find

After you set all the parameters in the Find dialog box, it's just a matter of clicking the **Find First** button to make things happen. You were looking for *Canada*, and that's what Access found; the Find feature takes you to the first record that has the word *Canada* as a field value.

To find the next record that matches the search parameters, click the **Find Next** button. Access finds the next record that contains the *Canada* field value. When you have exhausted all the possible matches, you receive a message that Access has finished searching the records and the search item was not found.

As you can see, Find enables you to move to records in the table that match your search parameters. If you needed to edit or compare many records that share common field values, the Find feature might not be up to the task. It has no capability to group the matching records together or preclude records from your view that don't match the search parameters. But don't despair. Access has you covered. You can use a *filter*.

The World of Filter Feeders

If I called you a *filter feeder*, you might just haul off and bop me in the nose, thinking I was comparing you to an oyster or some other edible sea creature that wears its house on its back. In this case, I'm talking about someone who is in charge of the care and feeding of an important Access tool that can be used to view subsets of the records in a particular table. A filter is a list of criteria that will show only the records in your table that meet the filter criteria. There are two ways to filter tables so that you can view a subset of your records: filter by example and filter by form. You get the same results no matter which of the two filter types you pick.

A word about the Find feature and filters: You already know that the Find feature can be used to move through a table and locate records that meet your search criteria. However, all the records, even those that don't match your criteria, still appear in the table, making the Table window rather busy.

Filters also use criteria to operate. However, filters are superior to the Find feature in that they show you only the records that match the filter criteria. The other records in the table are hidden. This makes working with the records easier. Use Find to quickly locate records that have a field matching certain criteria. Use filters when you really need to take a hard look at a subset of your table—the records matching the filter criteria.

Filtering by Selection

An incredibly straightforward way to filter records is filtering by selection. All you have to do is show Access an example of the field data you want to work with, and it will show you the records that match. For example, in the Northwind Products table, the records in the table each contain a field for suppliers. So if you would like to see the products supplied by just one of your suppliers, you filter the records.

Give this a try. First, select the field data that you want Access to use for the filter. In the Products table, scroll down until you can see the first record that contains *Pavlova, Ltd.* in the Supplier column. Click and drag to select the field text **Pavlova, Ltd.**); now all you must do is have Access perform the actual filtering. Click the Filter By Selection button on the Table toolbar.

Filtering by selection:
Select the field data, and
you are on your way.

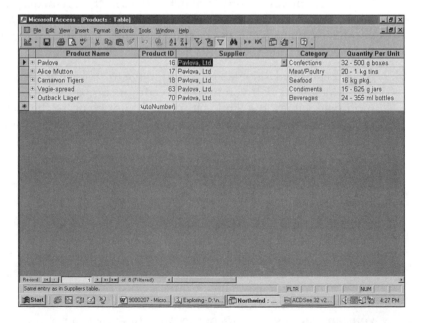

106

Access displays only the records that match the filter criteria, (in this case, Pavlova, Ltd.) in the Supplier field. Now you can edit these records if you want to, and you are not lost in the fog of a huge table with a massive number of records.

Give Me Back My Records

My sister used to say that about her Partridge Family albums. I'd answer, "What records?" Little did she know that the kid next door and I used them as Frisbees (David Cassidy would not be amused).

Anyhow, when you finish using the filtered records, you are certainly going to want to put the table back the way that it was—complete with all the records you had available before. To do this, all you must do is remove the filter.

To remove the current filter, click the **Records** menu and then click **Remove Filter/Sort**. All your records reappear in their original order.

Even though filtering by selection seems like the end-all way to set up a filter, Access does provide you with an alternative: filter by form.

Filtering by Form, Anyone?

When you filter by form, a blank datasheet appears with all the appropriate field columns found in your table. All you have to do is to pick the field or fields you want involved in the filtering. A drop-down arrow appears in each of the field boxes; you click it and select the data that will serve as the filter criteria. Open the Northwind Products table. It provides an excellent venue for trying out the filter by form feature.

The major difference between filtering by form and filtering by example is the number of criteria that you can set. Filtering by form enables you to set criteria in multiple fields. When you filter by example, you can select only one criterion in one field (such as highlighting Canada in the Country field as you did in the Suppliers table). Click the **Filter by Form** button for a bird's-eye view of how this filtering technique operates.

You are looking at a table datasheet with a blank record that contains all the fields used in your table. (If you are in Form view when you click the Filter by Form view, Access provides you with a form view of a blank record instead of the blank.) You can either click in a particular field and select your criteria from a data list or type in the field data that you want the table to be filtered by (enabling you to use wildcards). Say you want to filter the products in the Products table by a certain entry in the Category field. For example, you just want to see the records that are for Beverages.

Click in the empty Category field in the blank filter record. A drop-down arrow appears. Click the drop-down arrow and select the field data from the list—in this case, **Beverages**.

Filtering by form enables you to quickly select your filter parameters.

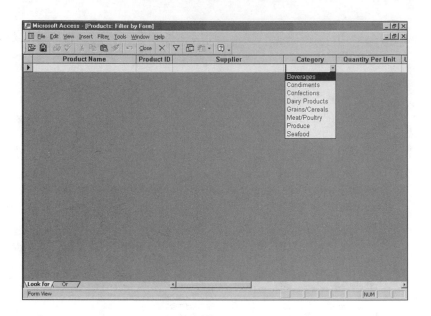

 After you select your filter data in a specific field, click the Apply Filter button on the toolbar to see the results of the filtering.

Alright, Everyone off the Field!

To clear field data already appearing in the filter-by-form record, select the entry and press the Delete key to remove it.

Access shows the records that have an entry in the Category field that matches your filter selection, such as Beverages. Now you can do what you want to these particular records without the distraction of the entire table information. To return the table to normal, use the **Remove Filter/Sort** command under the **Records** menu.

If you wish to filter the table by more than one field (say you want to filter the Products table by a certain category and supplier), select a filter criterion in each of the fields involved. For example, you might want to filter the Products table so that you see only a list of the beverages you buy from a particular supplier, Bigfoot Breweries. To set up this filter in a filter-by-form situation, you would select **Beverages** in the Category field and then select **Bigfoot Breweries** in the Supplier field. The records filtered would then have fields that match both your filter criteria. Pretty cool, huh?

Before we bring down the curtain on our plucky players—find, filter by selection, and filter by form—a few words should be said about when you might want to use these tools. When you want to quickly locate a particular record based on information in one field (in a large table), use Find. When you want to filter a table by just one field, use Filter by Selection. When you want to filter by more than one field you can use

Filter by Form (or better yet, use a query, which you can learn more about in Chapter 11, "Not a Stupid Question—Designing Simple Queries" and Chapter 12, "More Questions—Designing Advanced Queries").

Hiding Out (Hiding Fields in a Table)

You've spent several pages finding (and filtering) records using field information, but what if you want to lose a field—hide it from view? For example, you have an employee table that has salary information in it, and you want to hide that column (it's not a good idea to let employees find out what their coworkers make; it usually leads to a lot of pounding on the boss's door).

Now You See It, Now You Don't

Hiding fields requires only that you specify the field that you want to hide and then let Access know that you are ready to hide it. In the Products table, say that you want to hide the Unit Price field. Click the field heading (**Unit Price**) to select the entire column of data. Then click the **Format** menu and select **Hide Columns**.

The Unit Price field is gone, hidden from view. Now, what if you want that column back?

They're Back

Did they wipe their feet when they came into the house? Although making fields disappear might seem a little scary at first, you'll find that it's no big deal. Restoring the field column to Datasheet view is even simpler than hiding the column in the first place.

To unhide (what is happening to the English language?!) the Unit Price column (or any column), click the **Format** menu. Then click **Unhide Columns**.

The Unhide Columns dialog box appears. The dialog box lists all the fields that appear in the table. A check box precedes each field name. If the check box is empty (not selected), the field

Hiding Multiple Fields

You can hide more than one field at a time. Select each of the fields and follow the steps for hiding the column.

Hiding Multiple Columns Couldn't Be Easier!

You can use the Unhide Columns dialog box to hide or unhide columns. To hide a column listed, simply remove the check mark from the check box by clicking.

is currently hidden. To unhide the field, click in its check box. Select the **Unit Price** check box to unhide the field. To return to the table, click the close (×) button (in cases where you don't want a user sharing a database to view a hidden field, see Chapter 20, "What's the Password?"

You did a great job making those columns disappear and appear! Next you probably expect me (or David Cassidy, since he's gone to Las Vegas) to ask you to pull a rabbit out of a hat. Maybe later. For now, I'll recap some of the important Access features that you worked with in this chapter.

The Least You Need to Know

➤ You can sort your tables by specific field columns in either an ascending or descending order.

➤ In tables that contain a large number of columns, you can freeze fields so that they remain in the Table window as you scroll.

➤ Use the Find command when you want to find records that contain specific information in a specific field.

➤ Use the Filter command when you want to select a subset of the records in your table by a specific entry in a certain field.

➤ You can find most of the commands for Sort, Find, and Filter on the Table toolbar.

➤ The Remove Filter/Sort command on the Record menu puts your table back the way it was before the sort or filter.

➤ You can hide one or a number of field columns in a table by using the Hide Columns command.

Chapter 8

Between You and Me and Access: Table Relationships

In This Chapter

➤ Understanding database relationships

➤ Defining relationships between tables

➤ Sorting out the different types of table relationships

➤ Deleting tables and other objects from your databases

➤ Viewing related records from a table with a relationship

"They're creepy and they're kooky, mysterious and spooky, they're altogether ooky...." Hey, that could be my family! Dealing with database relationships can be every bit as taxing (and as fun) as dealing with personal relations (meaning family members). After all, people are just people and databases are just databases (or is that data?). Having good relationships between your data tables is the key to good database management.

You might remember that early in this book (so early that it might seem like two books ago), I mentioned that one of the strengths of Access (a relational database) is its capability to relate the data in different tables via a common field. For example (looking at the Fromage Boutique database), you could have a Customers table that contains all the information on your customers, including a separate customer number for each record (this customer number would also be the key field for this table).

You could also have a second table, an Orders table, that details every order that you've taken. The Orders table would obviously need to reference which customer made the order. This would be done by entering the customer number in the Orders table. The data in these two sample tables then would be linked (that is, related) by their common field: the customer number.

Tables, Tables, and More Tables

The tables discussed in this chapter can be created from scratch or by using the Table Wizard. The Customers table is the same table you created in Chapter 5, "Turning the Tables: Table Design," and entered data into in Chapter 6, "Going On Record: Adding and Editing Data." To create the Orders table, use the Table Wizard and include the fields in the table that are shown in the figure below. Then enter a few sample orders for your customers. If you need more help in creating these two tables, take a look at the Customers and Orders table in the Northwind database. These two tables have the same type of relationship that you will create between the Customers and Orders table in your own database (such as the Fromage Boutique database). Also keep in mind that you can set up relationships between tables even before any data has been entered. The data appearing in the figures is there to aid you in understanding how table relationships work.

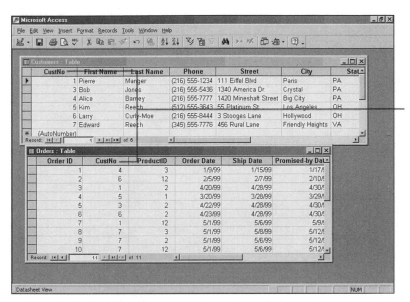

The Customers table and the Orders table share a common field: CustNo.

This link between the tables using the CustNo field is just one possible relationship within this database.

Why Are You Telling Me This?

You are probably wondering what's the point of all this relationship stuff. Well, it's quite straightforward. You design simple self-contained tables that hold subsets of the complete data (all the information) that makes up the database. Then, by linking the various tables by their common fields, you can integrate the information in the different tables in queries, forms, and reports.

As you design your tables, you should keep possible relationships in mind. Well-designed and well-related tables enable you to treat all the data in the separate tables like one big happy family, so you can get the most use (and information) from the data you stored in the database. I feel a group hug coming on.

For example, we have been playing around with a database for a small cheese shop called the Fromage Boutique. Although our treatment of the data has been a bit tongue in cheek (or is that cheese in mouth?), a database for a small business will invariably include tables that track your customers, orders, products, and suppliers, to name a few of the possible tables for this kind of database. As you create these tables, you should always determine which fields can be used to relate two tables together. In a well-designed database, table relationships are the norm rather than the exception.

The Fromage Boutique database in all its glory: Relating tables in the database by using common fields enables you to easily pull the data together from a number of small, self-contained tables.

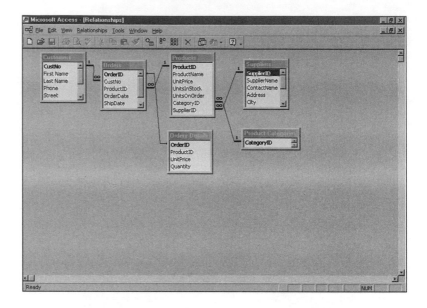

Creating Table Relationships

Let's take a look at how you and Access create these relationships between the various tables in a database. First, you need at least two tables to create a relationship; I happen to have several tables in my database, including Customers, Orders, Order Details, Products, Product Categories, and Suppliers. Two of them you might be familiar with: the Customers and Products tables created when I discussed tables in Chapter 5. (Remember the Fromage Boutique database?) A third table, Orders, is also important to this discussion (you can create it using the fields shown in the first figure of this chapter). The other tables in my database are there to show you how to round out your database in terms of data-holding tanks, meaning the tables themselves and the type of data each holds.

Access makes it easy to initiate the relationship creation process; make sure you have open the database that you want to work with. Then click the Relationships button on the Database toolbar. The Relationships window appears.

Ready-Made Relationships

When you use the Table Wizard, the tables you create with the sample fields often have shared fields. Access knows that you will eventually want to relate the tables, so the sample fields overlap between the different sample table types. The Table Wizard even offers you the option of relating the table that you are making to any of the current tables in the database during the creation process. It asks you whether there is a shared field. What could be easier?

Now Appearing—Your Tables!

In the Relationships window, the Show Table dialog box appears. This provides you with a list of the tables in your database.

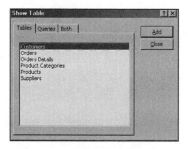

*In the Relationships window, select the table you want and click **Add**.*

Because you want to establish a relationship between the Customers table and the Orders table, you must place both of them in the Relationships window. Click **Customers** and then click the **Add** button. Repeat this procedure to add the Orders table to the window.

It makes sense to get rid of the Show Table dialog box when you are finished with it. Click the close (×) button to shut it down. Now you are resting comfortably in the Relationships window and are ready to establish a relationship between the two tables that you placed there.

If you inadvertently close the Show Table box or have already created some relationships between tables and want to add more, you can open the Show Table dialog box by clicking the Show Table button on the Relationships toolbar.

Database Matchmaker: Using the Relationships Dialog Box

Establishing a relationship between two tables is easier than it sounds. I know I've said this before, but the tables must have a field in common for this to work. This field should be the primary key for one of the tables (this uniquely identifies each record in that table). The field should also appear in the same table. The Customers and Orders tables each contain the field CustNo, so their relationship is based on this common field. Keep in mind that the field does not have to have the same name in both the tables; it only has to hold the same kind of data. In this case, the field contains customer numbers in both the tables. Now comes the fun part.

Drag the **CustNo** field from the Customers table and drop it on the CustNo field in the Orders table. Wow, something's happening. The Relationships dialog box appears.

The Relationships dialog box verifies the relationship that you have created.

Click CustNo here...

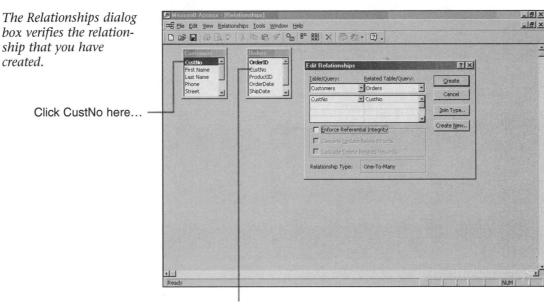

...then drag and drop it here.

The Relationships dialog box shows the two tables that you are attempting to relate—in this example, Customers and Orders. Notice that the field that forms the relationship appears under each table name.

Right in the middle of the Edit Relationships dialog box is a check box labeled Enforce Referential Integrity. It sounds like something you'd never convince a politician to agree to, but it means that you want Access to be certain that any CustNo values found in the Orders table match CustNo values found in the Customers table. From a data entry standpoint, this is a good thing. If you enter a CustNo in the Orders table that does not exist in the Customers table, Access won't let you leave the table until you enter a valid number.

For example, if you enforce referential integrity in the relationship, you could not enter CustNo 100 in the Orders table if a customer in the Customers table did not exist with the CustNo of 100. Pretty neat, huh?

Join Types Often Need No Adjustment

On the right side of the Edit Relationships dialog box, notice the **Join Type** button. Join types enable you to define how the data in the two joined tables relates. This is important when you run a query on a table. The default join type is set so that a query will select equivalent records only, meaning that the values must be the same in the joined field. If you enforce referential integrity, the values must be the same in shared fields. Now this might seem confusing, but 99% of the time, the default join type is the way to go; no adjustments are necessary.

You'll find another important item at the bottom of the dialog box, the Relationship Type information. Relationship types deserve their own discussion, so we'll get to them in just a minute. For now, put this topic aside so that you can complete the steps that form the relationship.

Click the **Enforce Referential Integrity** check box. Click the **Create** button to make this relationship a done deal. Your table relationship shows a line joining the two tables.

Your first relationship!

Notice that a 1 marks the portion of the line attached to the Customers table and that an infinity sign (∞) marks the portion of the line attached to the Orders table. These two little symbols say a lot about this table relationship. Now, before you try to go back to your tables, you have to save the relationships that you created. Click the **Save** button on the Relationship toolbar. To close the Relationship window, click its close (×) button. And speaking of relationships, it's time for that little talk that I've been meaning to have with you…

117

Viewing Related Records

After you create a relationship between two tables, you will notice that when you open one of the tables in the relationship (such as the Customers table in our example), plus (+) symbols appear to the left of each record in the table. These buttons are the Related Records buttons.

When you click the Related Records button next to a particular record (such as Pierre's customer record), a window opens, showing the records from the related table that relate directly to the selected record.

Click the plus (+) symbol next to any record to view related records from the other table for that record.

Related Records buttons

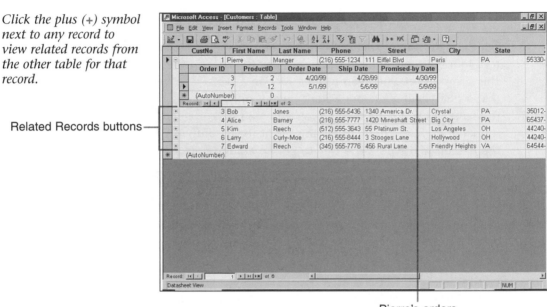

Pierre's orders

For example, in our example we related customers (in the Customers table) to orders (in the Orders table). This means that when you click the Related Records button for a particular customer, you see all the orders that he has placed. This enables you to immediately check the orders for a particular customer right in the Customers table window.

After you click a Related Records button, the plus (+) symbol disappears and is replaced by a minus (–) symbol. To remove the related records window from the current table window, click the minus sign (–), and the related records disappear.

The Types of Relationships

Although you don't want to become bogged down in detail, it wouldn't be a bad idea to take a minute and define the types of relationships you can have between your database tables. You've probably already made up your mind that there are only two kinds of relationships: good and bad. Well, you receive an added bonus in Access; you can have three types of relationships between your tables: one-to-many, many-to-many, and one-to-one.

One-to-Many (Which Is Not the Same as One Too Many)

Let's start with the one-to-many relationship. This is the type of relationship that you have between the Customers table and the Orders table. A unique customer number identifies each customer. This uniquely identified customer can make many orders of your fine cheese products. Access can match each of the records in the Customers table (one) to an infinite number of records (many) in the Orders table. You established this relationship by including the CustNo field in the Orders table.

You now can also see the significance of the little symbols (the 1 and the infinity symbol) that Access stuck on the ends of the relationship line. They define the relationship type for you; the 1 represents the one side, and the infinity sign represents the many side. One-to-many relationships are probably the most common of the three relationship types; however, don't neglect the other two.

...And Then There's One-to-One

Another possibility is a one-to-one relationship. In this case, a record in one table has only one possible matching record in the second table. An example is a publishing company that lets its authors write only one book and one book only (hopefully, there is no such publisher in this fine country of ours). If you had an author table and a book table for the situation described, by sharing the common author number field you would have a one-to-one relationship. Each author record would match one book record.

But Don't Forget Many-To-Many

The third type is the many-to-many relationship. In this type of relationship, each record in the first table of the relationship can have many matches in the second table, and each record in the second table can have many matches in the first table.

Okay, this one is a little fuzzy. An example should help. Say the publishing company publishes huge reference books written by teams of co-authors (it happens, it happens). The company has two tables in its database: one for authors and one for books. Each book is written by a group of authors, so the records in the books table have more than one match in the authors table. At the same time, each author can be involved in writing more than one book, so the records in the authors table have more than one match in the books table, too. Therefore, the relationship between the two tables is many-to-many. Is this starting to sound like a Country Western tune?

The many-to-many relationship is a little more difficult to understand and create in an Access database. This type of relationship is normally created by using a join table as an intermediary between the two tables that have the many-to-many relationship. In the author/book example, a third table (the join table) would include only two fields: the author ID and the book (project) ID. These fields would be the primary keys for their respective tables.

Using the join table creates a one-to-many relationship between the authors table and the join table and a one-to-many relationship between the books table and the join table. The relationship, then, between the authors table and the books table (because of the inclusion of the intermediary join table) would be many-to-many.

Back to Northwind to Test Your Relationship Understanding

A great place to become comfortable with table relationships is the Northwind database, which is no stranger to you. You already know that this database contains quite a few tables, so it should also contain a bunch of relationships.

To view the relationships in the Northwind database, open the database and then click the Relationships button on the Database toolbar. You're ready to become involved in some heavy-duty relationships.

A well-related database.

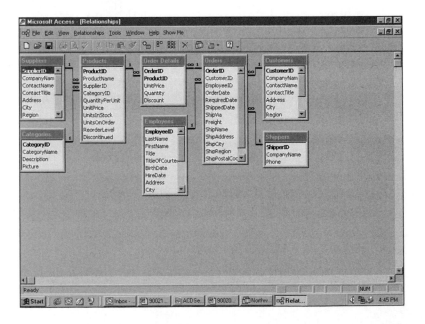

Note that all the relationships defined in the database are one-to-many relationships. It makes sense that, in most cases, one of the tables will have records with many possible matches in the table that it is related to. Remember that Access won't let you establish relationships between two tables using a field that is not a primary key field for one of the tables or a field that has been indexed in one of the tables.

Show Me Tells All

A great addition to the Northwind database is a menu item that says **Show Me** (it's right next to the Help menu when you open the Northwind database). This **Show Me** menu is a feature actually built in to the database using macros. You can use the **Show Me** menu to obtain information on any and all of the objects in the Northwind database. It is a super resource as you work with the Northwind objects such as tables, forms, reports, and queries. Click the **Show Me** menu, and a Help box appears, with great information on all the objects in the database. You will find that the Show Me information works much like the standard Help elements of Access.

Deleting Relationships

You might find it necessary to delete a relationship between two tables; for example, you might want to delete a field from a table that you have related to a field in another table (or you just might be feeling mean). Access will not allow you to delete the field from the table until you delete the relationship that this particular field is involved in (another example would be when you've inadvertently related two fields that should not be related). Open the Relationships window for the particular database; select the relationship and delete away. For example, you might have several related tables and decide that one of the relationships must go.

Say you want to delete the relationship between the Orders table and the Employees table in the Northwind database. Maybe you've decided not to tie Employee information to your order system anymore. Click the line that shows the relationship; this selects the line. Then either click the **Edit** menu and select **Delete** or press the Delete key on the keyboard.

Because you probably won't establish too many relationships that you will later delete, Access wants to make sure that you aim to deep-six the currently selected relationship.

Access and the Office Assistant give you one last chance to save the relationship. If you are using the Office Assistant, it will ask you whether you truly want to delete the relationship (if you have the Assistant turned off, a dialog box appears, related to the deletion). If you want to delete it, click **Yes** in the Assistant balloon. One click, and that relationship is out of your hair forever. Of course, if this is all a big mistake, click **No**.

Relationship deletions are confirmed by Access and the Office Assistant.

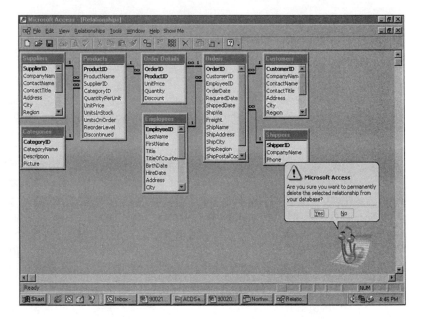

You might also want to remove unneeded tables from the Relationships window after you delete a relationship. Simply click any of the fields in the table and then press the Delete key on the keyboard. Access doesn't give you a second chance; as soon as you press Delete, the table is gone from the window.

Don't worry too much, however; you aren't really deleting the table, just removing it from the Relationships window. You can put it back by clicking the Show Table button on the toolbar. This provides you with a list of all the tables in the database. You can add them to the Relationships window at your leisure.

When you finish in the Relationships window, click its close (×) button to return to the Database window. Access prompts you to save any changes that you've made in the relationships if you've forgotten to save them.

The Importance of Good Relationships

Defining the relationships between the tables in your databases is super important if you ever want to do anything with the data that they contain. Defined relationships enable you to do queries and reports that pull data from more than one table.

Although you might define your table relationships just to manipulate the data, a great side effect is this whole concept of referential integrity. It will help you cut way down on data entry errors.

The Least You Need to Know

➤ Table relationships are possible because the tables involved share a common field. This shared field must be the primary key for one of the tables (or an indexed field in the table).

➤ To establish relationships between tables, click the Relationship button on the Table toolbar. This takes you to the Relationships window.

➤ You can view the related records for a particular record in a table by clicking the plus (+) symbol to the left of the record. Click the minus (–) sign that appears to close the related record for the current record.

➤ Three types of relationships exist: one-to-one, one-to-many, and many-to-many. Most commonly, you will have one-to-many relationships between your tables—the individual records (one) in the table that has the common field as its primary key will potentially have several matches (many) in the related table.

➤ If you don't want two tables to be related, you can delete the relationship.

➤ Relating tables enables you to create database objects, such as queries and reports, using data from more than one table.

➤ Relating smaller tables allows you to avoid ending up with one huge, cumbersome table.

Part 3

So What's the Object?

Our modern society has become obsessed with the notion that everything we do has some sig-nificance; everything has to have a point, an object. We must constantly be growing and learning. The days of couch potatoism and junk TV have gone by the wayside, and we must sit up in our chairs and watch PBS and learn something. Everyone must be growing, and if you're not growing (metaphysically speaking), you must be nurturing someone who is.

Now, you've learned a lot about Access in this book (and have been growing into a real data-base maven). When someone asks you "So what's the object?" you can answer, "Which one?" Access actually offers a number of objects that help you view and manipulate your data. You've already worked with one of the most important Access objects—the table, the place where you keep all your data. In this section, we'll explore some of the other objects available to you, such as forms and reports, items that you can use to improve and streamline the data-base management process. So what's the object? Read on!

It's All in Your Form

In This Chapter

➤ Creating forms for your database tables

➤ Using forms for data input

➤ Working in Form Design view to customize forms

➤ Using the form's toolbox

➤ Creating a new control for your form

I've always been bewildered by high-dive competitions; for the most part, the competitors are judged on their form. Having a problem with dizzying heights (I don't like high places), I've always felt they should all score a perfect 10 just for climbing to the top of that incredibly tall ladder. Your databases can be much like a high dive; people who work online with your database—those entering, editing, and viewing the data—will, in effect, be judging your database by its forms.

Creating a Form

Working with forms is no big deal. Remember, they are just another one of the possible objects in your database bag of tricks. Forms are very useful for inputting, editing, viewing, and even printing data. You already had a quick look at forms in Chapter 2, "Putting Access Through Its Paces." You even created a form when you used the AutoForm feature for data entry in Chapter 6, "Going On Record: Adding and Editing Data." As far as this chapter goes, you are already in good form—so to speak.

The forms you design can use all the fields or just some of the fields that you find in the corresponding table. You can even design forms that use the fields from more than one table, enabling you to enter data in one form that inputs to two tables.

The Wizard Will Know

As with many of the other features that you have already looked at, a wizard is available to help you create a form: the Form Wizard. To create a new form, or any other database object for that matter, you must have a particular database open. In this case, use the Fromage Boutique database (which you created in Chapter 5, "Turning the Tables: Table Design") as an example.

Click Your Mouse Two Times and Say, "There's No Place Like Home"

You can also quickly start the Form Wizard by double-clicking the **Create Form by Using Wizard** icon on the left side of the Database window. Try it. Dorothy and Toto would approve.

With the Database window (for the Fromage Boutique database or any database) open in the Access workspace, click the Forms icon on the left panel of the Database window. This lets Access know that you want to either work with an existing form or create a new one. Click the **New** button.

The New Form dialog box appears. This dialog box enables you to choose the kind of form you want to create and how to create it. You can start from scratch in Design view (just as you did when you created a new table) or use the Form Wizard (I vote for this choice). You can also use the AutoForm feature (remember, this uses all the fields in the table) to create three kinds of forms: columnar, tabular, and datasheet. There are also two other choices: Chart Wizard and Pivot Table Wizard, advanced features that you can ignore for the moment. The Chart Wizard enables you to create various types of graphs to accompany the data in a particular table when displayed in Form view. The chart (or graph) appears on a special form. The Pivot Table Wizard is a special cross-tab feature that enables you to compare data in a variety of views.

Select the form creation method and the table you want to base the form on.

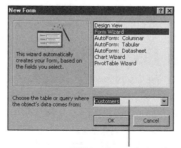

Table drop-down box

Click **Form Wizard** to make it your choice in the New Form dialog box. Now all you have to do is tell Access what table you want to create the form from. This means that the form will use the data and fields currently in the selected table. Click the drop-down box to choose the table. All the tables (and queries) in your database appear.

Keep this first form simple; base it on a simple table, Customers. Select **Customers** from the table list. Now all you must do is click **OK**, and the wizard will walk you through the form creation process.

Picking Your Fields

The Form Wizard moves you to the next step in the form creation process; you pick which of the table's fields you want to use in your form. Use the series of command buttons to include fields in the new form or remove fields from the new form. This screen also provides you with a Tables/Queries drop-down list if you select the wrong table in the preceding step. See, the wizard is a nice person!

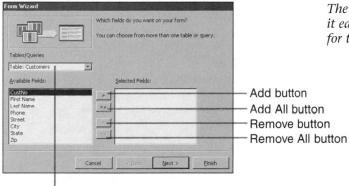

The Form Wizard makes it easy to select the fields for the form.

— Add button
— Add All button
— Remove button
— Remove All button

Tables/Queries drop-down box

Such Similarities

The Form Wizard dialog box is very similar to the Table Wizard dialog box that you use to create a new table. Access supplies a list of possible fields and a series of buttons that enable you to select or remove fields from your new database object. Hopefully, you're getting the feeling that the Access wizards you use to create new objects will operate in pretty much the same general way.

If you want to include a particular field, for example, the CustNo field, you must select the field in the Available Fields list and then click the Add button. Because you are going to use all the fields for your form, click Add All rather than move each field individually (it saves your clicking finger for playing games). After you select the fields, click Next to move to the next step.

Don't Be a Lay-About, Choose a Layout

Although the wizard does a lot of hand holding during the form creation process, it won't make the choices for you. You must decide how you want this new form to look. You have four layout choices: columnar, tabular, datasheet, or justified.

A *columnar* layout places each of the fields on its own line in a vertically oriented form; this type of form shows only one record at a time. A *tabular* layout places the field names at the top of the form in separate columns and then lists the data records, one per line, below the column headings. The *datasheet* layout sets up the form to look like a table, using rows and columns. The *justified* layout places the fields in equal rows across the form. These field rows line up or are justified on the right and the left.

To see a preview of a particular layout, click its radio button; the preview appears in the left half of the Form Wizard dialog box. When you've decided on a particular layout, make sure its radio button is activated. Then, to select the type of form layout you want, click the appropriate radio button.

The Form Wizard makes it easy for you to choose the layout of your new form.

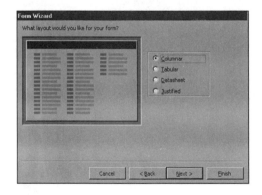

Putting Your Layout on the Line

The type of layout you choose for your form will affect the onscreen arrangement of the fields. It's important to create a form that is easy on the eyes and makes data entry a snap. The columnar layout is great for creating a form based on a table with only a few fields. This layout type also enables you to view records separately. The tabular layout works well when you have many fields and want to view several records at once. The datasheet layout can be used to hide certain fields from whoever is doing your data entry (things such as a salary field), while still providing them with a datasheet-type environment in which to do data entry. The justified layout is similar to the columnar layout, but places the fields in equal rows. Make sure you choose a layout that suits your data entry style!

The columnar layout (already selected) will work fine for the particular form that you are creating, so click **Next** to move ahead in the process.

You've Got to Have Style

In the next dialog box offered by the wizard, Access tests your personal taste as you choose the style for the new form. The style is nothing more than the backdrop for your forms. For example, you can decide to have your data overlay a graphic of the world (International) or rest on a textured design (Ricepaper). A style type can be chosen by clicking its name in the dialog box.

Because this form is for your Fromage Boutique database, use the Sandstone style because it looks sort of like an extreme close-up of a block of Havarti cheese. Obviously, you could use a less arcane (or strange) process to decide on a style for your forms, but, hey, I'm writing this book. Click **Sandstone**. Click **Next** to move to the next step.

It Was Fun While It Lasted

All good things must come to an end, and form creation is no exception. The last dialog box of the Form Wizard asks you to do two things: Name the form and then decide what to do next.

Every object that you create for a database needs a name, and Access is pretty good about coming up with names for you. In this case, you are basing this form on the Customers table in the Fromage Boutique database. Access figures that the form should have the same name as the associated table. You can, of course, change the form's name by typing in a new name. In this example, however, you can leave the name as is, Customers.

You must also decide whether you want to open the form that you created, to enter or view data, or whether you prefer to enter Form Design view and immediately alter the appearance or structure of the form. It makes sense to take a quick look at the form with the table's current data in it to see how much reworking it might need.

Make sure to select the **Open the Form to View or Enter Information** option button. Then click **Finish**. Congrats, you've designed a form!

Help You Can Count On

You already know that the Office Assistant and the Access Help system offer you a lot of help as you work with the different database objects. The final dialog box of the Form Wizard has a check box named **Do You Want Help to Display When Working on the Form?** If you do, select the check box.

Truly an Art Form

So you have a form, a very nice-looking form, in fact, and you're probably wondering what to do next. Well, you can enter new data, edit old data, or just sit there and stare at the form. But hey, I know that you're too motivated to just sit there and stare (I'm giving you the benefit of the doubt).

Your new form appears! This one shows the first record in the Fromage Boutique database.

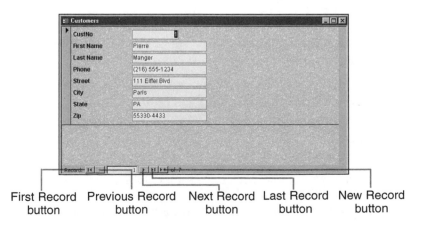

First Record button   Previous Record button   Next Record button   Last Record button   New Record button

Notice that the form has the same kind of navigation buttons that your tables have. You can move forward and backward through the records, using these buttons. If the table you based the form on already contains data, the form will display the first record. You can also easily move through all the records in the table. The New Record button (a right-pointing arrow followed by an asterisk) moves you to a blank record that's ready for data input.

Say that you're looking at the form and you don't like it. You want the fields to be ordered differently on the form. Believe it or not, you have complete control over the form's layout.

Customizing Forms

Customizing forms is one of those things that might seem very simple on the surface but can become quite complex, depending on what you want the form to do. Of course, you're saying, "I want the form to be a data input platform." (That *is* what you're saying, isn't it? You're so Access savvy!). And, of course, this is one of a form's primary purposes. But you can set up your forms to do all sorts of things, such as automatically fax a product order to a supplier or print an invoice for a customer.

Start with several of the basic form customization options, and then in the next chapter, you will take a look at some of the more elegant things that you can do to a form.

 To enter Design view for the form, click the Form View button on the Form toolbar.

Form Design Geography

It's always a good idea to get a feel for a new area such as the one you're about to work with, the Form Design window. An understanding of the basic geography can save you many headaches later. For example, I don't know how many times I've stood in front of those maps at the mall and realized that knowing "you are here" only reaffirms the fact that I am lost.

You might want to work with the Form Design window maximized, so click its Maximize button. When you work in Form Design view, you have the option of viewing a ruler and grid to help you place items on the form. To see either of these items (if they are not shown by default) click their respective menu choice on the View menu.

 You should also see the Form toolbox in the Design windows by default. If you do not, click the Toolbox button on the toolbar.

The Form Design window is where you do all sorts of cool things to your forms.

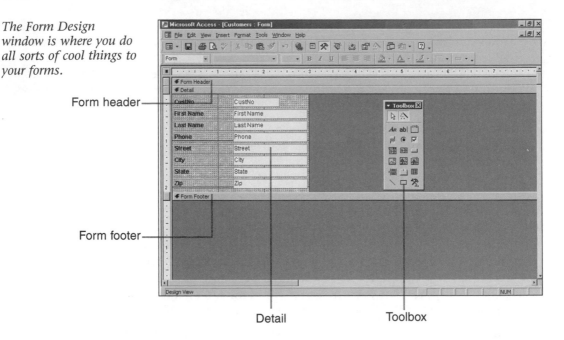

Form header

Form footer

Detail

Toolbox

The Form Design window has three parts: header, detail, and footer. The *header* area is where you display the name of the form and any other information or items that you want repeated when you view the records in Form view, such as any special command buttons that you create to open related forms or do special things such as print the form. The *detail* area contains all the fields and actually appears on the form when you are in Form view or print the form. The *footer* area is at the bottom of the form window, and you can use it for items such as the date or other information that you want to appear on each of the records as they are viewed, including short directions on how to use the form.

Headers and Footers from Top to Bottom

There are two different types of headers and footers related to forms. *Form* headers and footers appear on your form when you are in Form view; each record or form screen shows the header and footer information. *Page* headers and footers appear on each printed page of a form.

You can enlarge or squish any of these three areas to accommodate a change in its size or another area's size. If you place the mouse pointer on any of the lines that divide the areas, the mouse pointer becomes a sizing tool (go ahead and try it). Click and drag the sizing tool to increase or decrease the size of one of the form's areas.

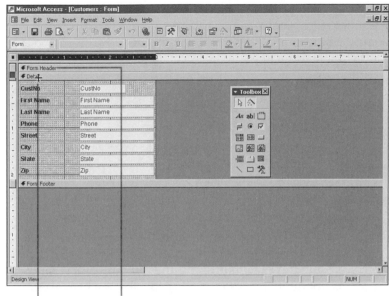

The sizing tool makes it easier to change the size of any of your form's areas.

Sizing tool   Form header

Taking Control of the Form Controls

Pay special attention to the detail area of the Form Design window. This area is where you decide how the data will be entered and represented in the form. For example, you will usually want your data to appear as you type it. Text will be text, and numbers will appear as numbers. However, you can set up a numeric control that charts the data rather than display it numerically, for example. We'll talk about some of this advanced control stuff later.

Two kinds of boxes appear: labels and controls. The *labels* are the field names that you create when you design the table the form is based on. The *controls* dictate how the data is input into the form. (You will work more with the various control possibilities in the next chapter.)

You can rearrange the labels and controls on your form to make the data entry process easier. You can also add or delete labels and controls. If you delete a particular field control in the form, however, you no longer have a place to enter data that is normally contained in the table that the form is based on.

135

Your (Form's) Name up in Lights

The first thing you should do is give this form a title. Yeah, I realize you named it when you created it using the wizard. But this title will be big and beautiful and will appear in the header area of the form.

First, you must make some space for your title in the header area. Place the mouse pointer on the line that divides the header area from the detail area. A sizing tool appears. Hold down the mouse button and drag the header border downward about a half inch (use the ruler to help you estimate).

Now you add text to the header area.

Missing Toolbox?

If you can't find the toolbox, don't worry. Simply click the **View** menu and then click **Toolbox** or click the Toolbox icon to display it.

The Toolbox

In Form Design view, a set of tools is available to help you customize your forms. This set of tools appears on a Toolbox toolbar. You can drag the toolbox around in the window until you find a spot that you like.

In this particular situation, you want to put new text in the header area. Do this by clicking the Label button on the toolbox. A new mouse pointer appears (a cross shape above a capital *A*). This pointer is a drawing tool.

Place the mouse pointer where you want to create the new label (in this case, in your form's header area). Hold down the mouse button and drag the mouse pointer to draw a rectangle in the header area. When you let go of the mouse, the rectangle becomes opaque, and an insertion point appears in the upper-left corner.

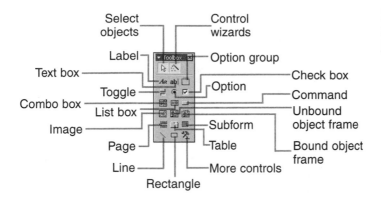

Select objects
Control wizards
Label
Option group
Text box
Check box
Toggle
Option
Combo box
Command
List box
Unbound object frame
Image
Subform
Page
Table
Bound object frame
Line
More controls
Rectangle

The Toolbox gives you all the tools you need for form design.

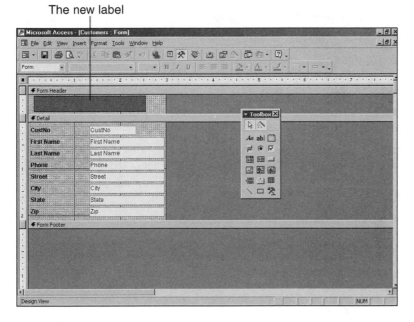

The new label

The label tool makes it easy to add a title or text to your form.

Now all you have to do is type the text that you want to put in the box. In this case, type Customer Information. You're halfway toward creating a great title for your form.

137

A Text Box of a Different Color

You will find that the background color for a new text box or control in your form is based on the default color for the style that you chose for your form during the creation process. If you want to change a text box's background color, click the edge of the text box to select it. Then click the Fill/back color button on the Form Formatting toolbar and select a new color.

Appearance Is Everything

Things are looking good. You have your label in the header area, and you typed text into it. Now it makes sense to format the text so that it looks good. Move the mouse pointer to the edge of the title rectangle. When the mouse pointer becomes an arrow, click. The insertion point disappears, and the text rectangle is selected.

With the text area selected, you can take advantage of all the great font attributes available on the Form Formatting toolbar. You can change the font style, change the font size, or make the text bold, italic, or underlined. (Remember that if you forget what a particular button does, you can always point at it with the mouse, and you will see a ScreenTip that displays the button's name.)

The Form Formatting toolbar puts you one click away from several features and commands related to forms.

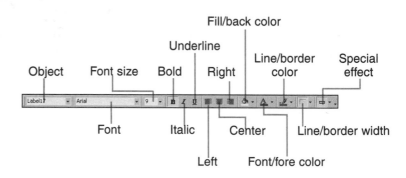

By using the appropriate buttons on the toolbar, you can increase the size of the font and also make the text bold and italic. First, make sure to select the label box you created (click any border on the box). Then click the drop-down box for font size; select the new size, **18**. Click the Bold and Italic buttons to add these attributes to your text (If your text does not fit in the label rectangle you created, place the mouse on any of the square sizing handles, and drag to increase the size of the rectangle until it accommodates the size of your text.)

Give Yourself a Hand Moving Controls

You can also reposition a label box on the screen. Lay the mouse pointer anywhere on the rectangle border (not on the sizing handles), and a hand appears. Don't worry, it's a friendly hand. When you see the hand, click and drag to change the position of the rectangle. This ability to reposition a label box enables you to tweak your form's design. You will find that any and all labels and controls can be moved using this method, which gives you complete control over your form's appearance.

You Have Complete Control!

You can move and size every control and label in the detail area exactly the same way that you did for the title text. You can even offset the label from the control by using the alignment handles (large black handles at the top of the boxes) that appear when you select the label and control for a particular field.

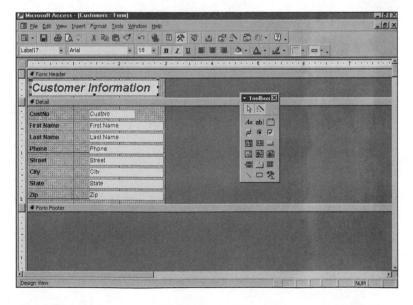

Repositioning the title text in the header area.

You've done a fair amount of work on this form, so it would be a shame to lose it. Whenever you want to save the design changes that you make to a form, click the Save button on the toolbar.

It's Always the Details

Now that you have a great-looking title for your form, you can move on to the detail area. You have probably noticed that the controls in the detail area are vertically oriented, one on top of another (that's because you created this as a columnar form). This form would probably be more appealing and easier to use if you reoriented the controls to a horizontal positioning. To do this, you must widen the form.

Widening the form is no more difficult than sizing any of the label or control boxes you find in it. Lay the mouse pointer on the form's right edge (you can't miss it—everything to the right of the line is gray). The mouse pointer becomes a sizing tool; then drag it to a new position. This is where the ruler comes in handy. Drag the form border to the 7-inch mark on the ruler.

You can widen your form by dragging the right border to a new position.

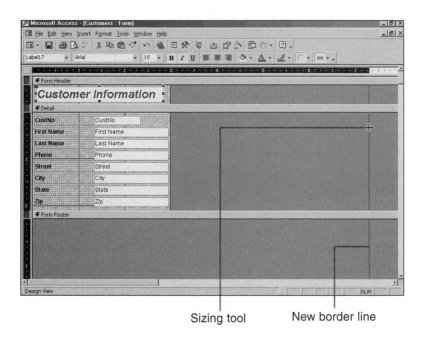

Sizing tool   New border line

In Complete Control

The controls and their accompanying labels are basically what you used to call *fields* back when you were working on tables. When you drag a control to a new position, its label accompanies it (the opposite is also true). Notice, however, that the labels and the controls reside in separate, but connected, boxes. You can size each of these boxes separately and exactly the same way you sized the title label box in the header area—using the sizing handles that appear when you select the box.

140

Start rearranging some of the controls. The CustNo label box and control box (the CustNo label box is on the left; the control box, on the right) are already in a good position—the upper-left corner of the detail area. The First Name label and control box are lined up right under the CustNo label and control. It would be nice to drag the Last Name label and control to the right of the First Name label and control. Position the mouse pointer on the Last Name box's border. You see a hand pointer, which enables you to drag the control and its label to a new position (if you place the mouse pointer on a sizing handle, you get a sizing tool). Drag the Last Name control just to the right of the First Name control. This leaves a big gap in the form, so you might as well move the Phone control under the First Name control.

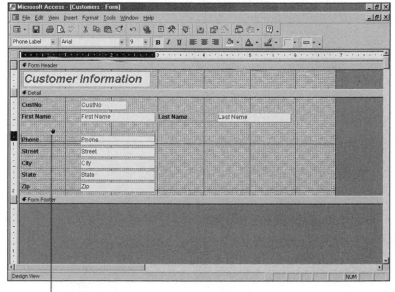

Select a control label and then drag it to a new position on the form.

Mouse pointer

This rearranging of the controls should make data entry in the form a little easier. You expect someone's last name to follow his first name. It's also a good idea to arrange the Street, City, State, and Zip controls on the same horizontal line. To do this, however, you must resize the label and control boxes associated with each field.

Sizing the Labels and Controls

Changing the size of the labels and controls is easy. Click the label or control to select its box and then use the mouse sizing tool to increase or decrease the height or width of the selection.

141

In this form, you must change the width of the address controls and their labels to make them all fit on one line. Move the Street control under the Phone control. Now comes the tricky part. Select the label for the Street control. Place the mouse pointer on the sizing handle on the box's right side. Drag the sizing handle to the left to decrease the width of the label.

You can easily size the form's label and controls.

Alignment handle

Street control

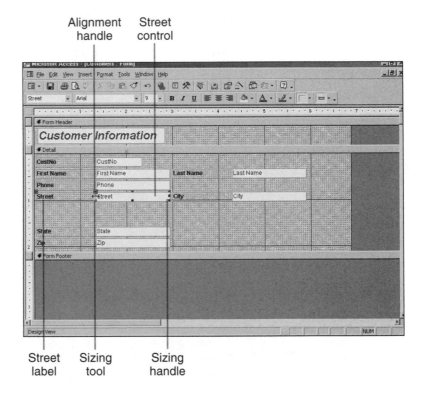

Street label   Sizing tool   Sizing handle

Notice that the Street control box remains in its original position; it does not move to the left to take up the space that you opened up when you decreased the width of the Street label. Click the **Street** control box to select it (it's the rectangle hooked to the Street label). Use the sizing handle on the control box's left side to drag it toward the Street label. This closes up the space between the label and the control. Then all you have to do is use the sizing handle on the control box's right side to decrease its width slightly so that it's nearly the same size as when you started.

Out of Control

Now comes the real test. The plan here is to fit all the address information on one line. This means that you must size and move the labels and controls for the City, State, and Zip fields. (Remember that the controls must remain wide enough to display the data that you will eventually input into the fields using this form.)

142

Techno Talk

Don't Lose Control with a Double-Click

If you inadvertently double-click one of the controls, you will open the control's Properties dialog box. This box enables you to set several parameters related to the control, such as the control source (where the data for the field is coming from) and additional field validation rules. To close this dialog box, click its close (×) button in the right corner.

When you line up all the address controls on one line, you will have a lot of open space on the form. You can close up some of this space by dragging the detail area's bottom border until it is just below the address line. The form looks great.

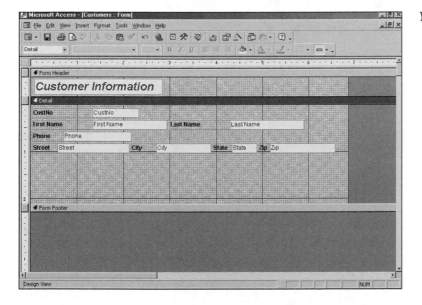

Your form is the best!

Wow! You did a good job creating this form. It is definitely ready for some heavy-duty data entry. In the next chapter, you will raise the stakes of form construction and look at some elegant form design possibilities that will amaze coworkers, friends, and family.

The Least You Need to Know

➤ The easiest way to create a form is with the Form Wizard.

➤ If you don't like the way the form turns out using the Form Wizard, customize it in Form Design view.

➤ In Form Design view, your form has three areas: header, detail, and footer.

➤ The detail area is where you build and arrange the controls used for data entry on the form.

➤ Use the header and footer areas for information that you want to see on each record when you use the form to enter, edit, or view your data.

➤ You can move, size, and delete controls and labels in your forms.

YOU ARE GONNA TURN OVER A NEW LEAF, MISTER!

Chapter 10

Reforming Your Forms

In This Chapter

➤ Adding a text box to a Form Footer

➤ Working with the Expression Builder to place a date in a control

➤ Creating list boxes and combo boxes for easy data entry

➤ Adding a command button to a form

➤ Adding a subform to a form

➤ Using color, borders, and shading to make your forms look great

In the last chapter, you explored some design aspects of the database form. Now you are going to take one more giant step and take a look at several things you can add to your forms that will bring you a standing ovation at the office water cooler. Plus, you will put together a form that makes the data entry process extremely easy. Go for it!

Putting Your Foot(er) in Your Form

You can add new labels and controls to your forms when you are in Form Design view (but you already knew that from the last chapter). It's a matter of using the right tool from the toolbox. So that you're not accused of dragging your feet in regards to your footer, you will find that the footer makes a great place for placing new controls, such as a page number or date.

Techno Talk

Taking Control of Your Form Controls

The controls in your form are made up of two parts: a label that denotes what kind of data can be found in the control (a label for the date control might be Date) and the control itself, which holds the data. Some controls are tied to specific fields in the table that the form is associated with (such as First Name and Phone). A control tied to a particular field in the associated table is called a *bound control.* You can also place math formulas in your controls, using the Expression Builder. Expression types can range from a formula that adds your data, to an expression that places the current date in the control.

For an example, use the same form as in the last chapter, the Customers form from the Fromage Boutique database (or create a new form based on any table you have available; you can quickly create a form by using the AutoForm feature). When you are in Form Design view, drag the footer border down so that you have a little room to work in. Now you can create the control.

You can expand the form footer with a quick drag of the mouse.

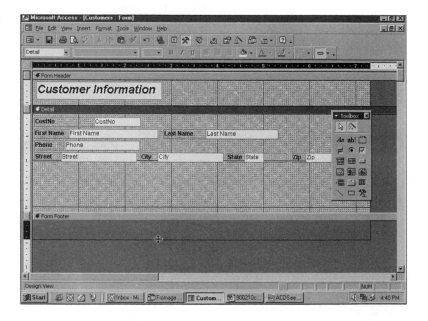

Click the Text Box tool in the toolbox. Drag a small rectangle on the left side of the footer area. A new control is created. Notice that Access created an empty label (it does have a label box number in it). Place the mouse pointer in the label box until the pointer turns to an I-beam. Click and drag the current text in the label box to select it and then type Date. You can widen the label box using the sizing handles, if necessary, to accommodate the text entry.

Controls Unbound

Notice that the new control you added to the form is currently *unbound*, meaning that it isn't associated with any particular data. The other controls in your form are *bound*. Controls such as First Name, Last Name, and Phone are all bound to their field namesakes in the Customers table. Whenever you use a wizard to create a form, all the controls created are bound to their respective fields in the table or tables you told the wizard to use in the form creation process.

Controls can also contain data that is not associated with a particular field in the table that the form is based on. These controls are called *calculated controls*. You use the Expression Builder to create the expression that goes in the control; this can range from a complex math formula to a simple expression that returns the current date.

So you can take an unbound control and either associate it with a particular field in a table, making it a bound control, or place an expression in it, making it a calculated control.

If you add a new control to a form that is going to be used to enter data in the associated table, it must be a bound control. If you want to add a control to a form that will be bound to a field that already exists in the associated table, click the Field List button on the Form toolbar. A list of all the fields in the table appears. To add a control for a particular field, drag the field onto the form. It's as simple as that.

In our current situation, we want a control in the form footer that gives the current date. We're dealing with a situation in which we need (yes, you guessed it) a calculated control.

Double-click the edge of your new control box. The Properties dialog box for that control appears. This box enables you to choose the format and the source of the information that will appear in the control. Click the **Data** tab in the dialog box. You want to attach to this control an expression that provides the current date. Click the **Control Source** box.

The new label and control box in the footer.

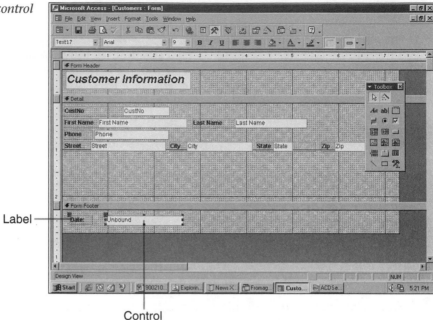

Label ———

Control

The Right-Click Is the Right Click

To get to shortcut menus that give you quick access to the features and commands you want quickly, right-click any database object or control. For example, right-click a form control and then click **Properties** to set up the control for data input. The shortcut menu that appears also enables you to manipulate the various background and foreground colors associated with the label or control that you are working on.

Control
Source box

*The Properties dialog box
for the control text box
gives you the ability to
attach an expression to
your form.*

Notice that the Control Source box contains a drop-down arrow and a button marked with an ellipsis. The drop-down arrow (when you click it) displays a list of the fields contained in the table associated with this form. This form is associated with the Customers table (or the table that you based your form on); that table's fields appear in the Control Source box.

The button marked with an ellipsis takes you to the Expression Builder feature. Click the **Expression Builder** button to take a look at this great feature.

Express Yourself with the Expression Builder

The Expression Builder enables you to build calculated controls. These can be as simple as a control that takes the First Name and Last Name fields and places them side by side in the new control (although not truly calculated because these are text fields, it still allows manipulation of field data). Or you might want to build a control that returns the answer to a mathematical calculation. For example, you might have a form in which you want to take the units in stock and multiply that by the unit price of the items in stock. This would be an excellent calculation for using the multiplication operator (*) on a form that tracks the products in your warehouse. Obviously, calculated controls can be complex and involve a lot of math, or they can be straightforward, such as creating a calculated control that displays the current date.

In the first column of the Expression Builder is a list of possible items that you can use to build an expression for your control. These items include such things as tables, queries, forms, and reports that currently exist in the database and other items such as functions, constants, operators, and common expressions. You can see that building an expression for a control can be complicated. Keep it easy by using one of the common expressions (no, not a smiley face).

Click the **Common Expressions** folder in the first column of the Expression Builder lists. In the second column, you now have a list of ready-made expressions—items that will put the page number or the current date in your control. At this point, I know it might be hard to remember what you were doing with the Expression Builder in the first place, but all you wanted to do was to create a control that would return the current date in the footer area of the form.

The Expression Builder enables you to attach several expressions to a control.

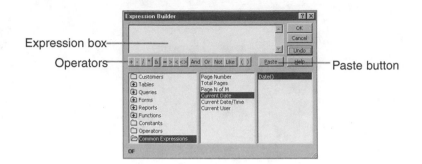

Expression box

Operators

Paste button

Click **Current Date** in the second column of the Expression Builder. The element that will end up in the expression you are creating appears in the third column of the Expression Builder—Date( ). Notice that it is selected. Now you must paste the expression element into the Expression box (at the top of the Expression Builder), so click the **Paste** button. Now that you have the expression in the Expression box, all you have to do is click **OK** (which you should do now).

You still have to close the control's Properties dialog box, so click its close (×) button. The date expression appears in your Control Source box. Now you can return to the form.

Techno Talk

Some Smooth Operators

The operators that appear in the Expression Builder window are used to create the various expressions that you place in your calculated controls. You will notice that many of these operators are typical math symbols, such as +, −, and *, characters that serve as the addition, subtraction, and multiplication symbols. You would typically employ these symbols to build expressions that do some mathematical calculation on a field or group of fields. For example, you could build an expression that multiplies a field containing the number of items sold by the price of each item, which appears in another field. Other operators are also available, such as And, Or, Not, and Like. These operators can be used to build conditional statements that return only data that meets certain criteria.

Is It a Date?

Dealing with the creation of a new control and the complexities of the Expression Builder might have tired you out, but you have still one more step to perform. You want to see whether the expression you placed in the footer actually works. The easiest way to do this is to leave Design view and return to Form view. Your moment of truth is just a click away.

Click the Form View button on the toolbar. Access displays the first record in the Customers table in your revised form. And hey, look at the bottom of the form. There's the current date!

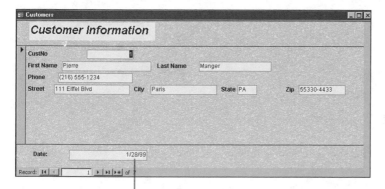

It is indeed a date!

A date in a form footer

That was some slick work you did there. You will find that it can be very useful to include certain types of information in a form's footer. The Common Expressions folder in the Expression Builder provides you with ready-made expressions that make it easy for you to place the date, page numbers, and even your name (current user) in a form's header or footer area. Other expressions that you might want to create and place in the form's detail area (such as the addition or multiplication of two or more fields) require that you specify particular fields in the table (using the appropriate folder to the left of the Expression Builder) and then use the operator—such as the addition (+) or multiplication (*) symbol—from the operator's toolbar that provides you with the correct calculation. Continue your exploration of form design and look at some great ways to make data entry a piece of cake.

Adding a List Box or Combo Box to a Form

You're probably getting a feel for the fact that a well-designed form can make your data entry chores much easier. Each record can be viewed separately, different form layouts give you a choice of how the controls are arranged on the form, and new controls can be created that can place a date or the result of a math expression into your form. Well, hang on, because you're going to be introduced to two more types of form controls that really make data entry a breeze: the list box and the combo box.

151

Both these control types take advantage of the fact that certain tables in your database will be related. Let's put our thinking caps on for a second and discuss the nuts and bolts of table relationships that make list boxes and combo boxes possible. When two tables are related by a common field, the field must be the key field for one of the tables. An example would be a Products table that is related to a Suppliers table by a common field, SupplierID; this field will be the key field for the Suppliers table. (You might want to build a Products table and a Suppliers table based on the fields shown in the Relationship window. You can create either easily using the Table Wizard, and then fill in some sample data.)

The SupplierID field is shared by the Products and Suppliers tables, making it easy for you to create a form that uses a list box or combo box for data entry.

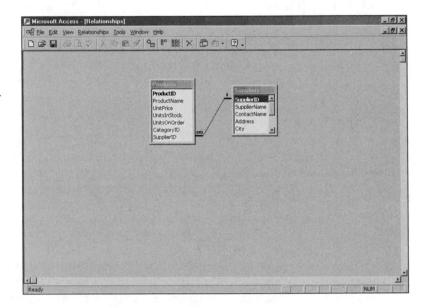

Every time you add a new supplier to your Suppliers table, you assign a SupplierID to it (or let Access autonumber the suppliers via an autonumber field). You also must have the SupplierID information appear in your Products table. Why not set up a situation in which you can view a list of the SupplierIDs from the Suppliers table when you must enter this information into the Products tables? Taking it even one step further, wouldn't it be nice if you could use the mouse to select from a list of the suppliers and their IDs when you must enter them in the Products table during the data entry associated with a new product?

That is exactly the purpose of the list box and combo box controls; these controls supply you with a list of the correct field data. All you must do is to click one of the choices, and it appears in your form. You enter data into the form, and it ends up in the associated table or tables, without any typing. It's all mouse work. Using combo boxes and list boxes greatly improves the accuracy of the data entry into your database because the data entered is pulled from a related table. What could be easier?

List boxes and combo boxes can be created for any form. For example, say that you create a Products table (as you did in Chapter 5, "Turning the Tables: Table Design") for the Fromage Boutique database (or any database you are working with) by using the Form Wizard. When you have the form, switch to Design view. This is where you create the list box or combo box control that will supply you with a list of suppliers.

Access 2000 Automatically Creates Subforms on AutoForms When Tables Are Related

You will find that when you create an AutoForm for a table already involved in a relationship (the table contains the field involved in the relationship as the primary key field), a subform (it looks like a datasheet) for the other table in the relationship is automatically placed at the bottom of the new form. This enables you to view related records in the two tables on one form. For more discussion related to subforms, see the section "Adding a Subform to a Form" later in this chapter.

You're on My List (Box)

When adding a bound control to a form, you will probably want to make space for it in the detail area (calculated controls such as date or page number can go in the header or footer area). This means you might have to move controls currently in the detail area or increase the size of the detail area. Remember that you want this new control bound to the SupplierID field in the Products table. Because you are creating the control from scratch, you must designate which field in the Products table the control is associated with.

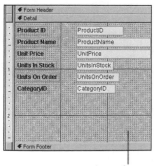

The detail area is expanded to accommodate the new control.

Area for a new
SupplierID control

I'll Take Box Number One, Monty

Adding the new box to the form is easy, just a matter of making a choice from the toolbox. Access provides two types of controls for list boxes: list box (surprise, surprise) and combo box.

The *list box* enables you to create a control that will pull its choices from a table, a query, or a list that you type in. A *combo box* is even cooler. It sets up a control that does all the things the list box control does, but it also lets you manually type in the data that you want, totally ignoring the offered list. You will find that a combo box is very useful when the data that appears in the drop-down list is not the correct data. For example, you could have a new supplier that you haven't entered into the Suppliers table yet. Because the supplier's name won't appear on the list, you can type it into the form control.

Go ahead and set up this new combo box control.

Creating the Combo Box

Creating the combo box control and its accompanying label takes a tiny bit of artistic ability on your part. Well, not really. Simply drag the mouse to draw the combo box on the form.

One other important thing that you should know about is the Control Wizards button on the toolbox. When this button is selected (it will be a lighter gray than the other buttons), you get assistance from a wizard when you use tools on the toolbox, such as the combo box and the list box. For example, if you have the Control Wizards button selected, when you create your combo box, the Combo Box Wizard appears and walks you through the necessary steps. It makes sense to take advantage of this wizard whenever you can; make sure to select the Control Wizards button.

Now create the box. Click the Combo Box button on the toolbox. Place the mouse pointer in the detail area of the form (or where you plan to place the new control). Then drag to create a rectangle below the other controls in your form that will represent the combo box. As soon as you do this (it takes a second or two), the Combo Box Wizard appears.

The Combo Box Wizard helps you create your combo boxes. It starts off the creation process by asking you to select one of three methods that the wizard can use to get its value. You can have the combo box look up the list values from a table or query, you can type in the values for the list, or you can have the wizard find a record in the current form, based on the value in the combo box.

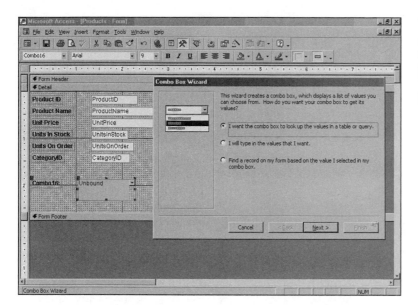

When you draw the combo box rectangle in the detail area of the form, the Combo Box Wizard knows you mean business.

The first choice, a combo box that lists values found in a table or query, is the best choice because when new data is added to the field that the combo box is bound to, your list of choices will reflect the new data—it is updated on the fly. For example, if six new suppliers are added to the Suppliers field in the table, these new choices will immediately be available in the combo box. The second choice, typing in the values, will give you a usable list of possibilities, but you must manually update the list if the available choices change. You can completely ignore the third possibility, using the control to find records in the current form, because it will not give you a bound control (remember, a bound control is tied to a specific field in the table that the form relates to). This type of combo box is used to find records that contain data matching the combo box list.

Make sure to select the **I Want the Combo Box to Look Up the Values in a Table or Query** radio button. Click **Next** to go to the next step.

I'd Like the Table by the Window, Please

Now the wizard wants to know which table in the database you want to derive the list of values from (in this example, the Fromage Boutique database that you played with earlier). You want to be able to choose supplier information from the list, so it makes sense to get the list of values from the Suppliers table.

155

*The Combo Box Wizard
wants to know what
table to use for the
combo box.*

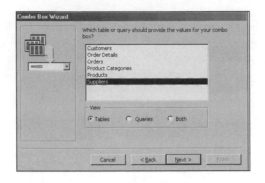

**Using the Northwind
Database to Explore Combo
and List Boxes**

If you didn't create the Products or
Suppliers databases that have been
discussed in this chapter (as part of
your Fromage Boutique database),
you can also explore combo and
list boxes using the Products and
Suppliers tables in the Northwind
database supplies with Access.

The wizard wants you to select the table that will supply the combo box values. Select the table that you
want—in this case, **Suppliers**—and then click the
Next button.

Now the wizard displays the fields that are in the
Suppliers table. This is where things get tricky.

Choosing the Field for the Combo Box List

Let's recap what you are trying to accomplish by creating this combo box. You want to create a control that
provides a list of data. In this particular case, you have
a Products form that requires you to enter the supplier
ID for each product. The combo box list will be derived
from the supplier IDs already entered in the Suppliers
table.

On the surface, this all seems fine and dandy. However,
there is a small, yet annoying, flaw in this plan. The combo box will give you a list of
numbers (1, 2, 3, and so on). You will have to memorize the supplier name associated
with each ID number. Otherwise, you won't be able to enter the supplier ID for a particular product into the form.

Don't despair, there is a way to set up the combo box so that it gives you a list of the
supplier names but actually enters the supplier ID into the SupplierID field in the
associated table. It might sound like magic, but it's not all that hard to do.

The wizard wants you to choose which field in the table will supply the values for
your form's combo box. Well, you want the list to display the suppliers' names. So, in
the Available Fields box, click **SupplierName**; then click the **Add** button. Now you
want this combo box in your form to enter the supplier ID in your table, so click the
SupplierID field and then click the **Add** button to add it to the Selected Fields box.
Click **Next** and move to the next step.

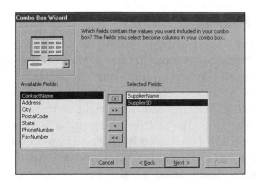

Add the field you want to view in the form's combo box, and add the field that will supply information to the table.

Sizing Your Combo Box

Now you must determine the width of your combo box. You can size it just as you would a column in a table or any other control on a form. Place your mouse on the box's right border and drag to the right or left.

A more important aspect of this particular screen is the Hide Key Column check box. This box is selected by default and makes sure that only the SupplierName field information (or other fields that you choose) appears in your combo box. SupplierID, which is the key field for the Suppliers table, will be invisible.

The reason that this box is selected by default is that it sets you up with a combo box that shows only the information that you want to appear in the form (in this case, the supplier name). Because SupplierID is the unique identifier for the table, it must be associated with the list (any list box or combo box you create will have this same option) supplied by the combo box. Access figures that you won't want to view a two-column list in your combo box, so by default, it hides this information.

The Hide
Key Column
check box

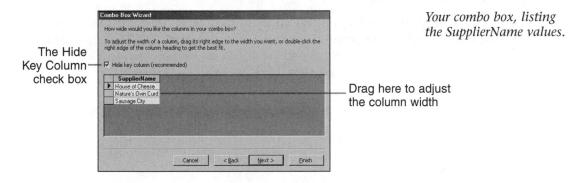

Your combo box, listing the SupplierName values.

Drag here to adjust
the column width

You won't always have to adjust the width of your combo box columns; you can double-click the right edge of the box to get the best fit. When you finish, click **Next** to continue the process.

157

Telling Access Where to Put the Data

The next step in the process gives you the choice of having Access remember the values that you have in your combo box, for later use, or having it store the values in a particular field. You might ask yourself, "When would I have Access remember the values in the combo box for later use?" You could have a situation in which the value in the control is used in a mathematical calculation. The result of the calculation is much more important than the value you choose from the combo box, and you don't want the value in the combo box field to be entered in the associated table. Access will remember the value so that the calculation takes place and returns the result in the appropriate field elsewhere on the form. Selecting this radio button creates an unbound control. Access will not store the data in a field in an associated table. However, it will list the data that appears in that field.

In most cases, you will want the second choice, **Store That Value in This Field**. Remember, the purpose of the combo box that you are creating is for data entry (in cases where the information in the field will be involved in some sort of calculation where the result will appear in the field, you can choose to have Access remember the data rather than store the data in the field). The data that you select from the combo box list will be entered on the form. This means that the data will also be entered into the appropriate field in the associated table. It certainly makes sense to have Access store the data in the field.

Click the **Store That Value in This Field** radio button. Click the field drop-down list and select **SupplierID**. This is the step that you don't want to miss. It creates the combo box so that it shows you a list of supplier names that you can pick from (that's the field you chose in the first step of the wizard). The supplier name will also appear in the form. However, if you check the associated table (Products), you will find that although the form shows the supplier name, the actual data that is being placed in the table is the supplier ID. Pretty cool, huh?

Now you can cut to the chase and finish off the combo box. The wizard would like you to enter a name for the control. Type Suppliers and then click **Finish** to end the process. You might have to decrease the width of the combo box control to see the combo box label in Form Design view.

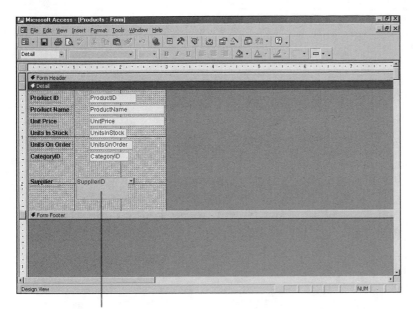

*Your new control is ready
and waiting for some
heavy-duty data input.*

The new control

Using Your New Combo Box

To see the combo box in action, you must return to Form view. Click the Form View
button on the toolbar. Go ahead and try the combo box; click its drop-down arrow.
The possible supplier names appear in the drop-down box. If you use the new form to
enter data for a new product, all you have to do is enter the product's information
and choose the supplier of the product from the combo box list. The great thing
about all this is that the information entered in the form goes directly to your
Products table. Now wasn't that a great "combo" of working with a new feature and
having fun?

Techno Talk

Creating Combo Boxes and List Boxes for Your Tables

You can also add combo boxes and list boxes to fields in tables. When you are in
Table Design view, click the field you want to assign a combo or list box to. In the
Field Properties window, select the **Lookup** tab. Designate the type of box in
Display Control and the value source (the field in another table that the data
will come from) in **Row Source**.

159

Your form with the new combo box in action.

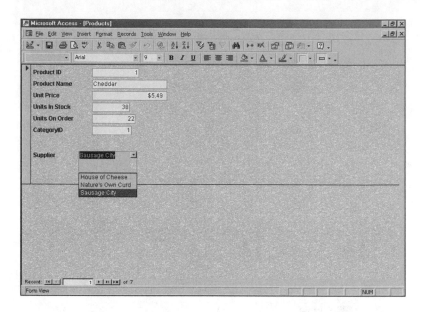

List boxes perform exactly the same way as combo boxes. You can either derive the values from a table or create your own list. A list box, however, will not allow you to enter a value that's not on the list.

Adding Command Buttons to Forms

Now that you have added a couple of controls to some forms (in this and the last chapter), you're probably starting to feel confident, in command. We'll take this form fun one step further and see how easy it is to add commands to your forms.

Commands are all around you in Access; you find them on the various toolbars as buttons and on the menu system as choices. Commands can start a quick and easy process, such as print or save, or embroil you in all sorts of choices, such as build, which invokes the Expression Builder.

You're in Command

Adding a command button to a form is very straightforward. Access already has scads of built-in commands that you can use to create buttons, or you can make a button that fires off a list of instructions that you've compiled as a macro or written in Visual Basic language (you'll deal with macros later).

As a guinea pig for command button creation, let's use the Products form on which you stuck the combo box. To create a command button, you must be in Form Design view.

Create the command button, using the toolbox (just as you did for your combo box). Make sure to select the Control Wizards button if you need help creating the button. Command buttons go very well in the header area of a form, so expand the header area for this particular button.

Next, click the Command Button tool on the toolbox and use the mouse to drag a button out on the form (in this example, in the header area). As soon as you do this, the Command Button Wizard appears.

What's a Button to Do?

The Command Button Wizard lays it right on the line, asking you what you want to happen when the button is pressed. It also gives you a box of command categories to choose from. Because the person doing your data entry with this form might not know Access that well, it would be a good idea to put a button on the form that will close it.

To tell Access what you want the button to do, click a category of commands. For example, click **Form Operations**. The wizard gives you a list of commands in the **Actions** box related to form operations. The button you're creating is supposed to close the form, so select **Close Form** in the **Actions** box.

Buttons That Print

Placing a Print button on forms is a good use of the Control Button feature. That way you are just one click away from a printed copy of the current record.

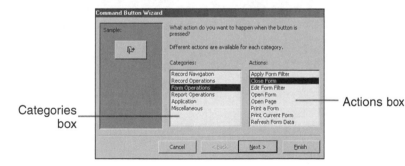

Categories box

Actions box

The Command Button Wizard gives you a list of commands that are perfect for your form.

The wizard gives you a preview of what the command button will look like for the selected action. Click **Next** to continue the process.

Sew On Your Own Button

The wizard gives you one last chance to edit the appearance of the button that will appear on your form. You can use the Exit button or a Stop button (my personal choice), or you can choose to mark the button with text of your choice rather than use a picture. So you select the picture (the Stop button), or you type in the text you would like. Then you click **Next** to continue.

All you must do is name the button and decide whether you want the wizard to display help that will assist you in the customization of the button. Say you name the button Exit button and then reject the offer of help by clicking **Finish**.

The completed command button, in Form Design view.

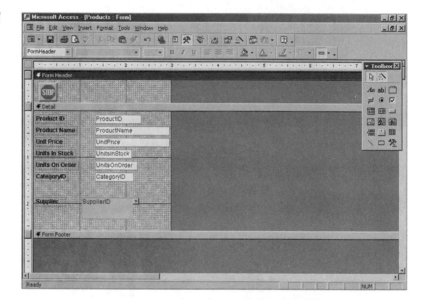

A Command Performance

Your finished button appears on your form. To test the button, return to Form view. When you finish entering data in the form, click the button. It closes the form (or performs whatever action you selected back in the Command Button Wizard).

Adding a Subform to a Form

Because we're on the subject of adding things to forms, you might as well push the envelope a little bit and look at some of the other stuff you can stick on them. *Subforms* provide you with a way to view and edit data from two completely different tables. A subform is like any other form and is associated with a particular table. All you have to do is to take a form that you've created (such as your Products form) and

162

make a place on it for the subform. The original form is now referred to as the *main* form. The subform is often referred to as the *child* form. One thing you must keep in mind is that for this to work, the two tables must have a relationship. This means that they share a common field.

When you use the AutoForm command (it's on the New Object list when you click the New Object button) to create a quick form for an open table, Access 2000 automatically creates a subform on the main form created for the current table. This happens only when you have already related the current table to another table. The subform also appears for related tables only when the field used to create the relationship is the primary key in the currently open table. For example, if you relate a Customers table to an Orders tables, you would probably use the CustNo field to relate the two tables. The CustNo field would be the primary key in the Customers table and the foreign key in the Orders table.

SEE ALSO

> *If you're still confused about table relationships, take a look at Chapter 8, "Between You and Me and Access: Table Relationships." Also, play around with the Northwind database that comes with Access; it contains many examples of related tables, forms, and subforms.*

Main form

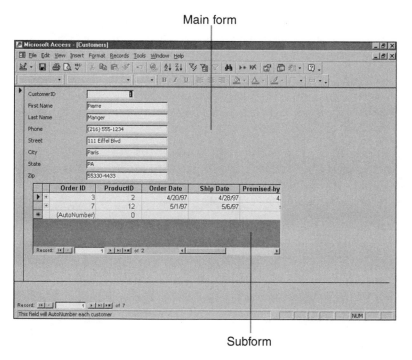

Using AutoForm to create a form for an open table also creates a subform if the open table is involved in a relationship.

Subform

You can also create subforms for previously created forms (before the table the form was based on became involved in a relationship) or when you create forms using the Form Wizard (creating forms using the Form Wizard will not automatically create subforms for appropriately related tables). Again, remember that to create a subform on a main form, a relationship must exist between the tables. For example, say you would like to place a subform on a Products form that gives you access to associated records found in the Orders table. Because the Products table and the Orders table are related (by the ProductID field), you can create the subform. When the main form and subform are viewed in the Form view, you will be able to see related records. For example, if you go to a record for a particular product on the main form, the subform will show related orders for that product.

You're the Sub(form), Commander

So you have a Products form. It tells you the ID of a particular product, as well as the product's name, the unit price, the amount in stock, the amount on order, and the supplier—information that would be very useful for you to see as you add new customer orders to your database. Attaching an Orders subform to the Products main form enables you to enter your new orders and also keep an eye on how much of a particular item you have in stock as the orders are filled. By combining these two forms, you are able to watch two tables of data at once. You end up with one great form (consisting of a main form and subform) that can be used to enter or edit data in the two tables.

Because the Products table and the Orders table are related by the product ID (its a one-to-many relationship: product to orders), it's a snap to set up a form (containing a main form and a subform) that uses the fields from both tables.

You already know how to build a form: With the **Forms** tab selected in the Database window, click **New**. Select Design view or the Form Wizard and then designate the table that the form will be based on. In this particular case, you will build your new form based on the Orders table. This supplies you with the subform.

You already have a form that can be used as the main form in this process, the Products form. Make sure you have the form open and that you are in Form Design view. Just as when you added controls and command buttons to this form, the first step is to make room on the form for whatever you plan to add.

Most likely, you will place a subform at the bottom of the current form, below all the already existing controls. Expand the detail area of the current form to make a space for the subform.

As you get ready to add the subform, keep in mind that this is another situation in which you will want the Control Wizards button in the toolbox selected. That way, when you select the new object to go onto the form, Access will invoke the appropriate wizard.

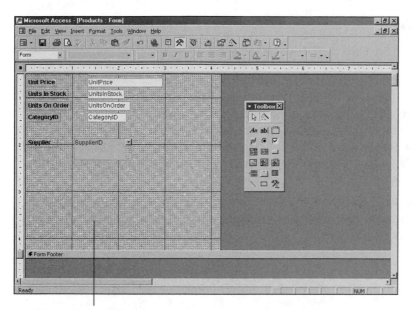

The expanded detail area makes a perfect spot for you to place the subform.

Expanded detail area

Click the Subform/Subreport button on the toolbox. A subform pointer replaces your mouse pointer, and all you have to do is to drag out a rectangle on the current form. As soon as you draw the subform rectangle, the Subform/Subreport Wizard jumps into the process.

Help, Mr. Wizard!

The Subform/Subreport Wizard walks you through the subform creation process. First, you must decide whether to build the subform from a table, meaning that you build a new form from scratch (my choice) or use an already existing form. You would choose the latter if you had already created a form based on the Orders table using the Form Wizard.

Both these procedures for creating the subform work equally well. Obviously, the process will move along a litter faster, though, if you have already created the form you will use as the subform. For a better understanding of the overall process, let's build the subform from scratch. Click **Next** to move along.

Now the wizard wants you to select the fields that will go into the subform. This is easy. Select the table from which you want to get the fields; then add the fields that you want to use. In your example, select the **Orders** table and add all the fields. Once again, click **Next** to advance to the next step in the process.

165

The Missing Link

The wizard would now like to know how you want to link the subform to the main form, meaning that you must select a field that the forms have in common. Your example has two possibilities: ProductID and SupplierID. Use ProductID because this is the field that defines the relationship between the two tables. It is the primary key for the Products table and is also contained in the Orders table. This is a necessity if two tables are to be related (SupplierID is not the primary key for either table, making it unusable as a field that relates two tables). The type of relationship that is common between the Products table and the Orders table is one-to-many. Each product (one) can appear in the Orders table a number of times (many).

It is the relationship between the two tables (Products and Orders) that gives you the ability to combine the two forms based on these tables. The linking field provides the connection between the forms.

Choosing the field that will link the forms together.

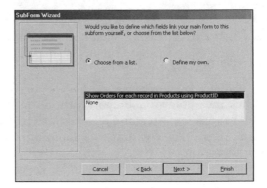

After you select the linking field, you can move to the next step by clicking **Next**. The last step in the subform creation process requires only that you name the subform (you can always go with the name that Access gives it) and decide whether you want help displayed as you work with the subform. Then click **Finish**.

Your Finished Subform

The best way to view the finished subform and get a feel for how it will work with the main form is to switch from Form Design view to Form view. The forms are linked by the ProductID field. It is the primary key in the Products table and also appears as a foreign key in the Orders table. Now that you have a form and subform that tie the data together in these two tables (because of the shared ProductID field), when you view a record in the Products portion of the form, all the associated records in the Orders table appear on the subform. Holy subform, Batman—sorry, Batperson—is this database business great or what?

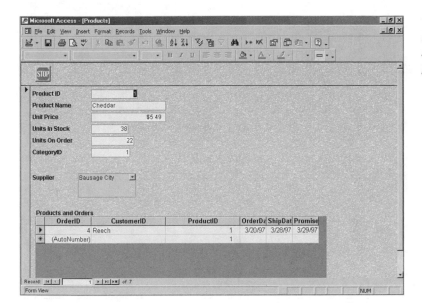

The finished multiform links the main form and subform together by one field, ProductID.

Drag and Drop to Create a Subform

For those of you who like to do things fast, there is another way to quickly create a subform on a main form. You can drag and drop an existing form onto an open form to create a subform. Again, the tables on which the two forms are based must be related, and you drag the form that will be the subform and drop it on the main form.

For example, say that you already have a Products form and a Suppliers form and that you would like to place the Suppliers form on the Products form as a subform.

Open the Products form in Design view and expand the detail area to make room for the subform. Click the Restore button on the Form Design window if you have the window maximized. Size the Form Design window by holding the Products form so that you can see the expanded detail area. Also, make sure that you can see the Database window, which lists the available forms in the database.

After you have the Database window and the Form window located so that you can see both of them in the Access application window, grab the form that will serve as the subform from the Database window and drop it on the detail area of the main form in the Form window.

A new subform will be created from the form that you dropped on the detail area of the main form. You can now save the new compound form and manipulate its look just as you did the other main forms or subforms you have created.

You can drag a subform from the Database window and drop it on a main form in the Form Design window.

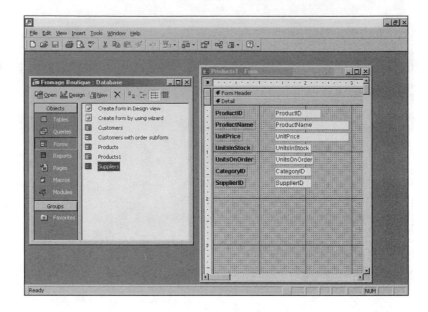

Dressing Up Your Forms with Color and Borders

Because you're on a roll with forms, take a look at a couple of ways to make them look better (think of it as a kind of form makeover). You can change the borders and colors of the controls and labels on your forms. All you have to do is to be in Form Design view.

On the far right of the Form toolbar is a group of buttons that will assist you in changing the appearance of the form:

Fill/Back Color button

Font/Fore Color button

Line/Border Color button

Line/Border Width button

Special Effects button

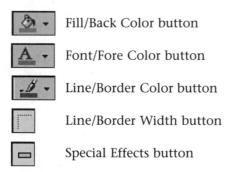

To change a label or control's appearance, select the item and then use the appropriate button to change a specific attribute. The only button that might seem a little mysterious is the Special Effects button. It can do things such as add a shadow effect to a control or make the control look raised, sunken, or etched.

The Least You Need to Know

As you can see from the last two chapters, you can do many things with forms and to forms. Forms are definitely a formidable tool in your bag of database tricks. Here are the critical points to remember from this chapter:

➤ You can add controls to your forms that are bound to specific fields in your database tables, or you can link a control to an expression that will insert an item such as the current date.

➤ Expressions are the domain of the Expression Builder; use the Expression Builder to build expressions involving fields or expressions that return a specific result.

➤ You can create controls (list boxes and combo boxes) in your forms that take their values from a list based on a specific table's field or from a list that you create.

➤ You can place command buttons on forms to close, print, or complete other actions.

➤ You can link subforms to a main form, enabling you to see the data from more than one table on one form.

➤ AutoForms created for an open table automatically create a subform on the form if the table is related to another table, when the open table has the linking field as the primary key.

➤ You can create subforms by using the Subform Wizard or by dragging and dropping an existing form from the Database window onto a form in Design view.

➤ You can do almost all the special things to a form, using the Form toolbox.

Chapter 11

Not a Stupid Question— Designing Simple Queries

Questions—sweet mysteries of life. Answer a mind-boggling question, and you might win the Nobel prize. Fail to answer a simple question on your driving test, and you might spend your mornings waiting at the bus stop. You can find questions everywhere; unfortunately, answers aren't as easy to come by. Not so in Access, my plucky database maven. In this chapter, you will find out how easy it is to ask your Access database tables queries—and always get the correct answers.

Understanding Queries

A *query* is a question that you pose to your database table or tables (yes, you can query more than one table at a time). You might want to know which of your sales-people have reached their sales goal for the year, or you might want to see a list of customers who live in a certain state. You can handle both these situations with a query. In Access, you use different types of queries, depending on the type of response you need.

As you work with databases, the most common type of query that you will run into is the *select query*. A select query finds and lists the records that satisfy the question you ask.

You can also design queries that do something to a table; these are *action queries.* Action queries can be used to delete duplicate records in a table or move records to another table. Action queries always result in some kind of change to the table or tables involved in the query. You can even create queries that display their results in a crosstab format that looks much like a spreadsheet. These tables are called *crosstab queries* and provide you with a very unique way to look at the information that results from the query.

Access makes it easy for you to design queries. As with tables and forms, you can create queries from scratch or use a wizard. For your first foray into the wonderful world of queries, you will start by creating a simple query that lists a subset of the customer records you have in a Customers table (we'll use the Fromage Boutique Customers table as an example).

Creating a Select Query

Say that the Pennsylvania Legislature is debating a new bill that would place a surtax on cheese products. You decide that you had better get a letter out to your Pennsylvania customers, asking them to write their legislators and condemn the proposed tax. Your Customers table contains customer records from two states: Pennsylvania and Ohio. You must come up with a simple query that will list just the Pennsylvania folks.

Creating Database Objects from Query Results

After you query a database table, you can use the query results to create a new table or a database report. Because Access makes it easy to create a report type that produces mailing labels, the logical outcome of this simple select query would be to eventually create mailing labels (maybe even form letters, using Microsoft Word) for the Pennsylvania customers.

Before you start the query, make sure the Database window for the database that you're going to use in your query is open (in this case, the Fromage Boutique Database window). Then it's just a matter of clicking the **Queries** tab and then clicking the **New** button. The New Query dialog box opens. If you want to bypass the New Query dialog box and jump right into the creation of a query in Design view or by using the Query Wizard, double-click the Create Query in Design View icon or the Create Query Using Wizard icon, respectively, in the Database window.

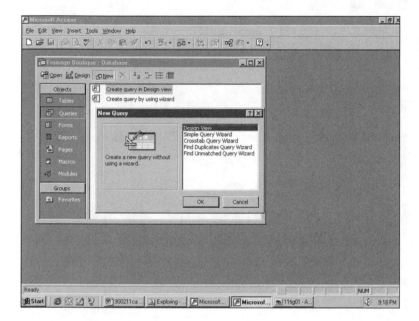

The New Query dialog box offers you several ways to create your new query.

Keep It Simple

Access gives you several choices for creating your new query. You can create a new query from scratch, use a wizard to create a simple query, use a wizard to create a crosstab query, use a wizard to find duplicate records, or use a wizard to find records in one table that have no related records in another table (these two tables would obviously have a relationship defined between them).

After you have used the different query wizards a couple times, you might find that the fastest way to create a simple query is by creating it from scratch. However, the wizards make the whole process extremely straightforward. Because this is your very first query, select **Simple Query Wizard**. To move to the next step, click **OK**.

You Need Fields

You are probably getting the feeling that almost all this database stuff revolves around the data fields that you find in the records. Well, pass Go and collect 200 dollars because the next step in the query creation process is to pick the fields that you want to use in the query.

The first screen of the Simple Query Wizard is where you select the table and the fields that you want to include in your query.

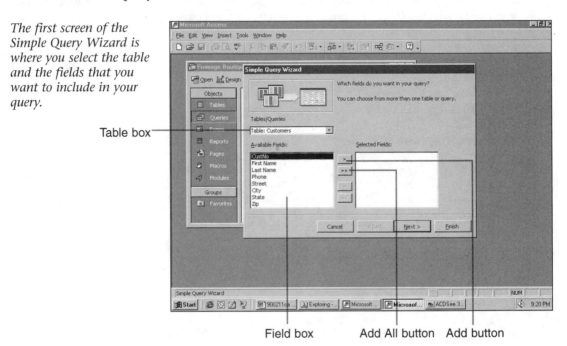

Table box

Field box   Add All button   Add button

First, in the Tables/Queries drop-down box, select the table or query you want to use for this particular query (in this case, choose the **Customers** table). After you select the table, you can include all the fields available or use only some of them. Because you are designing this query to find a subset of your customers (the people in Pennsylvania, remember?), including all the fields wouldn't hurt. To include all the fields, click the Add All button. Then advance to the next screen in the Query Wizard by clicking the **Next** button.

Pulling Up to the Query Wizard Finish Line

The Simple Query Wizard doesn't waste your time. You reach the last step in the process quickly. You are given two choices on the final screen of the Simple Query Wizard: You can open the query to see the results, or you can immediately modify the query in Query Design view.

If you've been paying attention to the Simple Query Wizard screens, you might have noted that you haven't done a whole heck of a lot to create this particular query. All you did was choose a table and some fields from the table. You haven't defined the question that the query will ask.

Obviously, you are going to have to modify this query's design to get the results that you want—a list of your customers in Pennsylvania. So click the **Modify the Query Design** option button. Now all you have to do is name the query (or go with the name the wizard picks) and click the **Finish** button. (For those of you who want additional help as you work with the query, click the Help check box on the final wizard screen.)

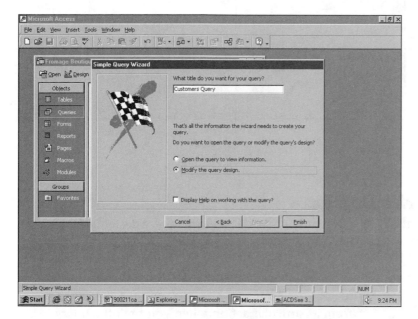

The final screen of the Simple Query Wizard asks you to name your query.

When you exit the Query Wizard, you are taken directly to Query Design view, and your query (actually, your query to be) is ready and waiting to be modified.

The Query Design Window

When you enter Query Design view to either create a new query or edit an existing query (which is what you're doing now), you will find that the Query Design window is divided into two panes. The top pane shows the table or tables that have been selected for the query. You can add tables to the query by clicking the Show Table button on the toolbar. To remove a table, click anywhere on the table and then press Delete on the keyboard.

175

The Query Design window lets you specify the tables and fields to be used in your query.

Tables selected for the query

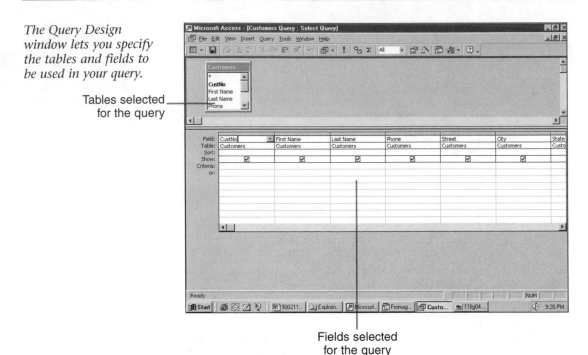

Fields selected for the query

A Real Pane in the Bottom

The bottom pane of the Query Design window displays the query design grid, which lists the fields that you designated in the Query Wizard. These fields appear in a series of boxes (from left to right). Each field lists the name and the table that the field is from.

Cleaning Up the Window Pane

If you do not want the Table row to appear in the lower pane of the Query Design window, you can use the Table Names command on the View menu to hide it. (If you are using the personalized menus, hold the View menu open until all the commands available appear.)

Access associates other criteria with the field that perform a particular action when you fire off a query. Some examples are a sort parameter associated with the field, whether the field should be shown in the query, and any selection criteria associated with the query. Remember that you only want to list the customers in Pennsylvania. Do this by putting a match criteria (the abbreviation PA) under the State field.

You can change all the query parameters associated with each field. The field selected, the table selected, sorting parameters selected—you control these three items using drop-down boxes.

For example, if you want to sort the records that appear in the query by the Last Name field, click in the **Sort** area under this particular field and either select an **Ascending** (my choice for an alphabetical listing of the customers) or a **Descending** sort. You will make your sort selection (Ascending, Descending, or not sorted) via a drop-down box that appears when you click in the field's sort area.

You should also keep in mind that some customers might have the same last name. You might also want to set up your sort so that it sorts in ascending order by the First Name field as well. Click in the **First Name** field sort area and then select **Ascending** from the drop-down box.

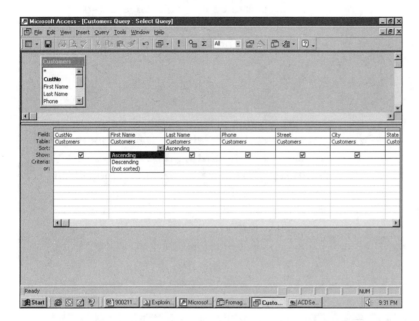

Clicking in the Sort row enables you to select the type of sort you want to accomplish when you run the query.

For this sort to work correctly, the Last Name field must appear in the query box before the First Name field. This is because the sort proceeds from left to right. The field you want to sort by first must be the first field designated in the query box. The other fields involved in the sort then follow, in the order that you want to sort them by.

It is very easy to change the order of the fields shown in the query box. Click in the **Field Name** row for a particular field. A drop-down arrow appears. Click the drop-down arrow, and Access supplies you with a list of all the fields that you included in the query (yes, fields from all the tables that you select for the query will appear). Select the fields so that they are ordered appropriately for a sort that uses more than one field. In this particular situation, you would click the **First Name** field name in the Field row. To change to a different field, select **Last Name** from the list. Now all you have to do is change the second Last Name field to First Name by repeating this action and selecting **First Name** from the field list box. In effect, you've flip-flopped the order of the fields to be sorted.

177

Techno Talk

Index Your Tables

There is a way to speed up queries when you are dealing with large database tables—indexes. Access uses indexes to look up data, which means it can find an indexed field or sort a table more quickly. The primary key field in your database table is already indexed. However, you can also index other fields, especially those that you use frequently in queries where the field is *related* (joined to a field in another table).

To index fields and view the indexes already in a particular table, make sure you have the table open in Design view; then click the field you want to index. In the **Field Properties** box for the record, click in the **Indexed** box; then select **Yes (Duplicates OK)** or **Yes (No Duplicates)**. Duplicates OK allows more than one record to have the same data in the index field (such as a last name field). No Duplicates assures you that no two records will have exactly the same data in the field. Indexing a field also enables you to create a relationship between the indexed field and that field stored in another table. It is not unlike creating relationships between primary keys and foreign keys in two tables.

Clicking in the Field row enables you to control the order that the fields are sorted in.

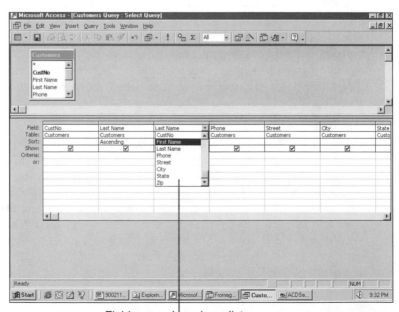

Field name drop-down list

Fields: To Show or Not to Show

You can also decide not to show some of the fields currently listed in the lower pane of the Query Design window. For example, you might not want the CustNo field and the Phone fields to show up in your final query (especially because you might want to use the query to generate mailing labels later).

A check box for each field appears in the Show row of the Query design grid (just below the Sort row). Select the Show check box below **CustNo** to hide that field in the query; Access removes the check mark, and the field will not appear. Do the same thing to the Phone field, and it will also not show up in the query results.

What's My Criterion?

Queries get their power from the *conditional statements* that you place in the Criteria row of the Query Design grid. "What is a conditional statement?" you ask. It is a limiting parameter that makes the query produce a subset of your original table or tables. These statements can be as simple as =PA, in which you are saying that you want only the records that have PA in their State field, or as simple as >500, in which you want only the records where a particular numeric field has a number of more than 500 in it.

The Or box enables you to expand the conditional statement so that the query will satisfy either the condition you place in the Criteria box or the condition you place in the Or box. An example would be a query that displays fields for customers from more than one state (you would type PA or OH in the Criteria box).

In your sample query, you want to see only the records that have PA in the State field. To accomplish this, scroll to the State field in the lower pane of the Query Design window and type PA in the Criteria box.

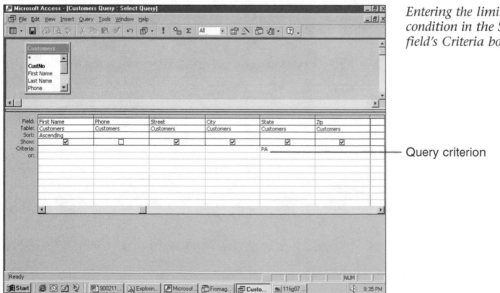

Entering the limiting condition in the State field's Criteria box.

Query criterion

179

Every Query Has a Toolbar

One incredibly helpful bag of tricks that we should not neglect to discuss is the Query toolbar. Buttons on this toolbar enable you to run the current query, change the query type, and display a Totals row in the grid box that you can use to put formulas in the query. There is even a button that enables you to add more tables to the Query window.

A Query with a View

You can also use the Query view button to switch back and forth between the results of your query and the Query Design window. This enables you to fine-tune your query on-the-fly.

The Query toolbar provides quick access to a bunch of useful features.

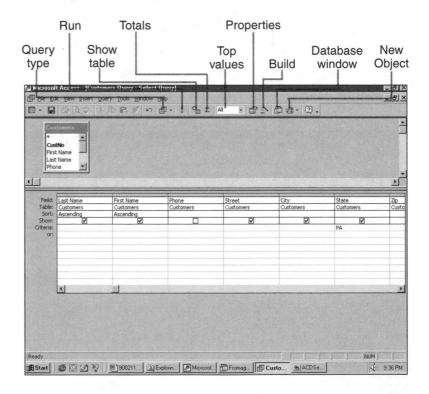

The buttons that you use on the Query toolbar will obviously depend on a particular need as you build your queries. The following is a quick summary of what some of the more important buttons on this very useful toolbar do:

The Query Type button (click the small arrow on the right of the button itself) enables you to change the type of query that you are designing on-the-fly. You can choose from a number of query types, including select, crosstab, and make-table.

This one is easy; click this button when you are ready to run your query.

The Show Table button opens the Show Table box, enabling you to add tables to your query.

The Totals button adds a Totals row to the query grid box. You can use this row to perform calculations such as totals, averages, or counts.

The Top Values box can be used to find the highest or lowest values resulting from the query. For example, you might want to see the top 25% of your sales, using a query. You would set up a query that would sort sales in descending order, and then you would place 25% in the Top Values box. Only the top 25% of your sales figures would appear when you run the query.

Running the Query

After you establish the criteria for your query, you are ready to run it. The Customers query that you have been working on will (we hope) select the records for the customers who live in Pennsylvania and sort the records ascending by last name.

To run the query, click the Run button on the toolbar. Way to go! You set up (with Mr. Wizard's help) and ran a select query. Your sample query produced a sorted subset of the original Customers table, the customers who live in Pennsylvania.

*The query results—
a sorted subset of the
original table.*

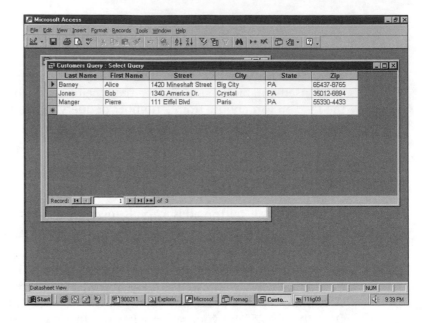

Doing the Math—Formulas in Queries

Setting up the select query was really straightforward, so cook some of that gray matter of yours and work with a query that incorporates a formula. Getting your queries to do math is easier than you think. Say that you have a Products table that tells you how many units of each product you have in stock and also tells you the unit cost of each item. You can run a query that will give you the total dollar amount that you have invested in each item in your inventory.

It takes only a second to set up, from scratch, a simple query that includes a math formula. You select the Queries icon on the left side of the Database window and then double-click the **Create Query in the Design View** icon on the right of the Database window. Access opens the Show Table dialog box, letting you know that this query isn't going to get very far if you don't choose a table.

*Select your table or tables
for the query in the Show
Table dialog box.*

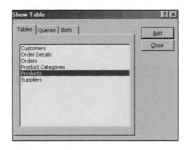

182

In this case, select the **Products** table and click **Add**. After you add all the tables you plan to use in the query, click **Close**. As soon as you click Close, you are taken to the query grid box area, where you can refine or edit the query.

Selecting the Fields for the Query

The query grid box is familiar territory; this is where you place the fields that you want to use in the query. To add a field to the grid box, click in the appropriate field box and then on the drop-down arrow. All the fields in the table that you select will appear in the drop-down list. To select a field, click the field you want. If you ever have to clear the query grid, click the Edit menu and then select Clear Grid. Then place the fields in the query grid box as needed.

In your sample query, place ProductName, UnitsInStock, and UnitPrice in the grid box. Remember, you can keep this query simple because all you want is the total investment you have in each product in stock.

Adding Fields from the Selected Table

You can also add fields directly from the table or tables in the top pane of the query window. Double-click a field contained in the table's box, and it will be placed in the next available column on the query grid.

Expressing Yourself: Creating the Expression

Think about what you want to accomplish here; it doesn't require brain surgery. You want to set up a formula that multiplies the units you have in stock by the unit price of the products that you have in inventory. You create this simple formula using the Expression Builder.

Make sure that you click in the field box just to the right of the two fields that you want to multiply (UnitsInStock and UnitPrice). This will put the answer in the last column of the query. This column, in effect, becomes your summary field in the query.

You can place a new query column in your query to help summarize your data.

Fields in query

Expression Builder button

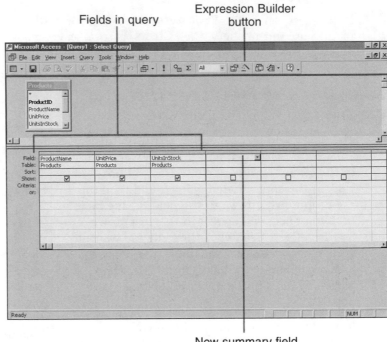

New summary field

After you place the insertion point in the field box that you will use for your total investment formula, click the Build button on the Query toolbar. Then you meet an old friend.

The Expression Builder

You can't say that you've never seen this thing before; you are now in the Expression Builder. You used the Expression Builder to put the date in one of your forms in Chapter 10, "Reforming Your Forms."

The Expression Builder is divided into two areas: The upper part is the Expression box, where you paste your formula, and the lower part is the identifier area, where you select the things that you construct the formula from.

Now it's time to use the Expression Builder to create your formulas. In this case, you want to multiply two fields together. Because you find fields in a table, it makes sense to click the **Tables** folder in the identifier area.

All the tables in your database are listed. You just have to double-click the table that you want to get the fields from. In this case, you should double-click the **Products** table. As soon as you select the table, the fields in the table are listed in the second box in the identifier area. Now you are ready to build the expression. (Remember that the Expression Builder has its own Help button, so don't hesitate to press it if you need some direction.)

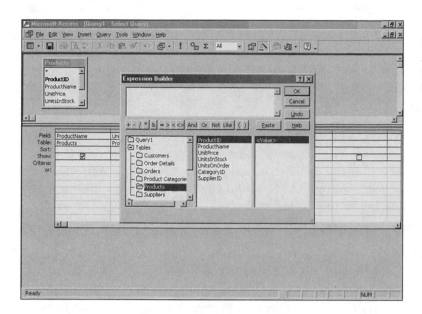

Working your way through the Expression Builder decision tree is a matter of a few double-clicks.

Click the first field that you want to include in the formula, **UnitPrice**; then click the **Paste** button. Access pastes the field name into the Expression box.

Now you have to place a multiplication sign in the formula. The Expression Builder supplies a whole set of math symbols below the Expression box. Click the Multiply button (it has the asterisk on it) to place this symbol into the formula. Now all you have to do is paste the second field into the expression. Next, click **UnitsInStock** and then **Paste**.

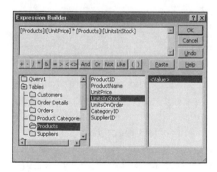

The completed formula in the Expression box.

That's it. Formulas are that easy to build. When you complete the expression, click **OK**.

Express Yourself

You can use the Expression Builder to create *formulas* (expressions that return a time, date, or another value) and conditional statements. All the operators for conditional statements (such as And, Or, Not, and Like) are available with the other math symbols just below the Expression box.

Run It!

Access pastes the expression into the grid box at the insertion point. The next step is to run the query and see whether the expression works. The Run button on the toolbar will fire up your query.

The query appears in the Query Datasheet view. At the end of the datasheet appears a new column, which contains the values created by your expression (a formula that multiplied two numeric fields).

The finished query with the new expression column.

Product Name	Unit Price	Units In Stock	Expr1
Cheddar	$5.49	38	$208.62
Brie	$6.69	23	$153.87
Swiss	$4.99	30	$149.70
Gouda	$4.99	12	$59.88
Ham	$3.99	15	$59.85
Cheese Knife	$12.99	5	$64.95
Salty Wafers	$1.99	40	$79.60

Query1 : Select Query — Record: 1 of 7

A Saved Query Is a Happy Query

When you create a query from scratch, you will have to name it if you want to save it. Click the Save button on the toolbar, and Access will prompt you for a name for the query.

The new column has a heading that reads Expr1. This stands for *expression one*. Because you probably don't want to leave this as the heading for the data column, you can return to Query Design view and edit the name that appears in this field. For example, you can select it (select **Expr1** in Query Design view, but leave the expression intact) and change it to Total, Current Investment, or something equally appropriate. Your new text will then appear as the column heading when you rerun the query or return to Query Datasheet view.

Quick-Fix Statistical Queries

Access queries also give you the ability to get quick statistical information on fields that contain numeric values. For example, this is a great way to find a total (Sum) of all the products you have in stock or find an average (Avg) of the number of support calls that you receive at your little computer store. You can also use a query to find the maximum (Max), minimum (Min), or even standard deviation (Stdev) of a certain field or fields.

Say you want a quick statistical fix on the products you have in stock. You would start a new query (from scratch) and select the **Products** table in the Show Table dialog box. In the Query Design window, you would set up the numeric fields in the table (or tables) in the grid box.

To give yourself a nasty migraine, have the query compute Sum, Max, and Min for the number of products in stock. It's really simpler than it sounds—and you most likely won't end up with a migraine (maybe a slight twitch in one eye, but not a migraine).

Normally, you would set up the field in the grid box and then tell the query to sum it (or do some other calculation—in a second, you will learn how to select the formula). Because you want to calculate three different things using the same numeric field, place the field in the grid box three times. So three columns in the Query box will be designated UnitsInStock.

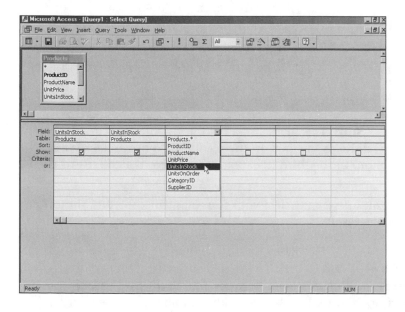

The UnitsInStock field placed in the grid box three times.

Using the Totals Section in the Query Grid Box

Now you have to let the query know what the three calculations are that you plan to perform on the UnitsInStock field. The Query Design window has been hiding the place where these formulas go. Click the Totals button on the Query toolbar.

In the grid box, below the Table row appears a new row—Total. Below each field that you have selected is a Total box; right now these boxes say Group By. Click in any of these Total boxes, and a drop-down arrow appears. Click the drop-down arrow, and you will see a list of mathematic formulas and expressions.

Selecting the formulas in the Total row.

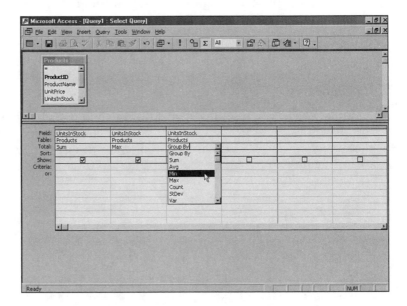

In the first field box, select **Sum**. This gives you a field in the resulting query, which gives you a grand total of all items in stock. In the second field box, select **Max**, which returns the maximum. In the third field box, select **Min**, which returns the minimum.

After you set up your query and select your formulas, click the Run button on the toolbar to see the results.

And the Answer Is...

The query resulting from the kind of statistical query that you set up will be one row of numbers: the answers to your formulas. The column headings for the query datasheet consists of two parts: The first part references the formula that you used in the Total row, and the second part of the name references the numeric field that you

188

ran the calculation on. So the first column heading (with the answer appearing below it) would be SumOfUnitsInStock, meaning that Access calculated the total units that you have in stock.

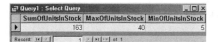

SumOfUnitsInStock	MaxOfUnitsInStock	MinOfUnitsInStock
163	40	5

The query datasheet and its calculated results.

Get the Most and Least out of Your Queries

When you set up a query in which you figure Max and Min, you might also want to show which products relate to these totals, meaning which product is the Max and which is the Min. This is very easy to do. Include two columns in the grid box for ProductName and then select **Max** and **Min** in the Group By boxes.

You can use queries like this to calculate statistical information for any field that holds numeric information, everything from the sales totals on your latest book to the standard deviation on the frequency of a certain gene allele in an isolated salamander population (and you thought I only knew software stuff). Although your sample query makes use of just one field, obviously you can place more than one numeric field (even fields from more than one table) in the grid area. Then select the formula for each field, using the drop-down list in the Total row.

Wow! These queries are really something, aren't they? Take a second to get your bearings, take a deep breath, and then move on to bigger and better things such as queries from more than one table, crosstab queries, and queries that delete or move fields. See you in the next exciting chapter!

The Least You Need to Know

➤ Queries ask your tables questions; use queries to select certain records.

➤ A query looks much like a table and appears in Query Datasheet view.

➤ The Query Wizard is a quick way to put together a simple query.

➤ The Query Design window is where you edit queries that you create with the Query Wizard or from scratch.

➤ The lower grid box area is where you designate the fields and the criteria (conditional statements) for your query.

➤ You can use queries to perform mathematic calculations on your data, such as determining a sum, a maximum, or a minimum.

Chapter 12

More Questions— Designing Advanced Queries

In This Chapter

➤ Creating incredible multitable queries

➤ Joining tables that share a common field

➤ Creating a crosstab query

➤ Placing calculations in crosstab queries

➤ Using queries that you create to create other queries

➤ Using append and delete queries

The weather was getting rough. The tiny ship was tossed about. If not for the courage of the fearless crew...oh, sorry, I was just relaxing in front of the idiot box (no relation to this fine series of books) and doing a little channel surfing. Because you're here, you must have weathered Chapter 11, "Not a Stupid Question—Designing Simple Queries." I hope it convinced you that queries are much easier to understand than you first thought. Select queries are the easiest to create and are probably the most commonly used in database management.

In Chapter 11, you created several select queries (the first was a query that selected the customers, from your Customers table, who reside in Pennsylvania—a perfect example of a select query). In this chapter, you will have the opportunity to explore other types of queries, such as the crosstab query. First, however, you will learn how to create a select query from more than one table.

As you work with select queries from multiple tables, as well as other query types (such as crosstab, delete, and append queries), all the query tips that you learned in Chapter 11 apply. Remember, if you ask the right question in the query, there probably isn't a database out there that won't give you the correct answer.

Creating a Query from More Than One Table

Let's take a look at how you create queries from more than one table. Come on, don't panic. You've already created forms from more than one table. Remember? So creating multitable queries can't be all that bad. A great use for multitable queries is to pull together information from a number of tables and then perform various query features such as sort, select, and summarize the data.

You can create a multitable query via the Query Wizard or create it from scratch directly in the Query Design window. Although this type of query isn't really the same as the select queries you used in last chapter, you will still want to use select (the default query type) to set up this multitable query. However, keep in mind that the techniques used in building this query can also be used for other query types, such as crosstab, append, and delete queries, which we will explore later in this chapter.

The key to any type of multitable query is that the tables selected for the query must be joined by relationships (yep, more of that mushy stuff). As you already know, relationships are based on common fields. The common field will be the primary key field for one of the tables and a regular field (meaning it's not the primary key) in the other table.

Selecting the Tables for the Query

Let's say that you want to create a query that will include three tables: a customers table, an orders table, and a products table. You would like this query to list, by product name, the orders initiated by each of the customers.

Creating a Query from a Query

You can use queries in the place of tables when you set up a new query, allowing you to query a query (no, I'm not trying to be funny). Think about it; this would enable you to do some pretty refined questioning of a database (seriously!). For example, you could create a select query, as you did in Chapter 11, to derive a table that holds a subset of your customers. You could then take this query table and query it for customers in a certain Zip code range or sort the customers by name or location.

This query won't create a datasheet subset of any tables involved, as your Customers select query did in Chapter 11 (the customer subset was customers living in Pennsylvania). It will combine information from the three tables so that you can see the customers, their personal information, and what products they've ordered, all on the same query datasheet.

For this whole query thing to work, relationships must exist between the tables. In our sample Fromage Boutique database, the Customers table and the Orders table are joined by the common CustNo field. So they have a relationship. The Orders table and the Products table are joined by the common ProductID field. So they're okay, too. I didn't say that all three tables must be directly related to one another. There has to be a relational hierarchy between the tables you want to include in the query.

To create this query, make sure that you have selected the **Queries** tab in your Database window (you could use the Fromage Boutique database that you've been working on throughout the book). Click the **New** button in the Database window to create a new query. The New Query box opens. Make sure **Design View** is selected and then click **OK**.

The Query Design window opens. The Show Table box also opens. This is where you select the tables you want in the query. Double-click a particular table to add it to the Query Design window. In this case, you would double-click the **Customers** table, the **Orders** table, and the **Products** table. After you have selected all the tables that you want to use in the query, click **OK** in the Show Table box. The selected tables appear in the top portion of the Query Design window. The relationships between the various tables are also shown.

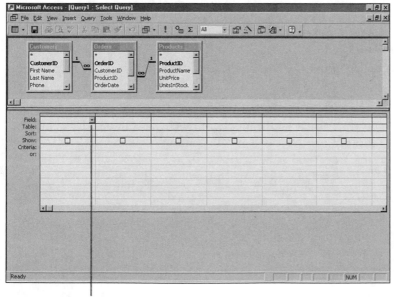

The selected tables and their relationships are shown in the top pane of the Query Design window.

Click here for a list of all the fields in the selected tables.

Selecting the Fields for the Query

It's Easy to Add Tables to the Query

 If you find that you must add another table to a query, click the Show Table button on the toolbar and select from the dialog box. When you are finished, click the Show Table dialog box close (×) button.

Selecting the fields for the query from three tables is no different than selecting them from one table. When you click in the **Field** box in the grid area of the window (the lower half), a drop-down arrow appears. Click the arrow to select from a list of field names that includes all the fields in the selected tables.

Suppose the purpose of this query is to put together a datasheet that can be used for calling your customers to let them know that their orders are in. Basically, you must include fields in the query that give you each customer's name and phone number, the date that you promised the product, and the product's name. All the fields you need for this query will be available because you've included the appropriate tables in the query.

Selecting the fields for the query.

Field:	First Name	Last Name	Phone	Promised-byDate	ProductName	▼		
Table:	Customers	Customers	Customers	Orders	Products			
Sort:								
Show:	☑	☑	☑	☑	☑	☐		
Criteria:								
or:								

Results Are Everything

After you've selected the fields for the query, you can run it by clicking the Run button on the Query toolbar.

Notice that this query gives you the results that you want (customers and their orders), but perhaps not in the format you want them. Each customer order appears in a separate row; this is kind of inconvenient when you have a customer who has placed more than one order. You could sort the query by last name, but you would still get separate entries for each order a customer has made. There is a better way to display this data—by using a crosstab query.

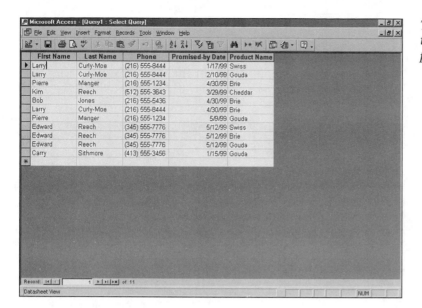

The query results list the customers and their product orders.

I'm Joining Up

You probably have the feeling that I am really pushing the creation of table relation-ships when you create the tables for your database. And you're right. A properly related database makes it easy to create multitable queries (as well as forms and reports). There might be an occasion, however, when you have not established rela-tionships between tables that you want to include in a multitable query. Believe it or not, you can create the join (the relationship) between the tables right in the Query Design window.

Creating Joins

Joining tables in the Query Design window can happen in two ways: automatically or manually (meaning that you must do it). When you add two tables to the Query Design window, using the Add Table box, and each of these tables contains the same field with the same name and holding the same data type, join lines automatically appear between the two occurrences of the same field in the two tables. For example, you can add a Customers table and an Orders table to the Query Design window; both these tables would probably include a field for CustNo (or CustomerID, some-thing very much like it). As soon as you add the tables to the Query Design window, Access automatically creates a join line between the two like fields in the two tables. However, for this automatic joining to take place, the field shared by the two tables must be the primary key in one of the tables (just as when you create a relationship in the Relationships window).

For instance, let's say you want to create a query using two tables that you have not created a relationship between, such as an Orders table and an Orders Detail table. If the two tables share a particular field, a join line will be drawn between the two occurrences of the field as soon as you place the tables in the Query Design window.

Join lines automatically appear to link two previously unrelated tables in the Query Design window.

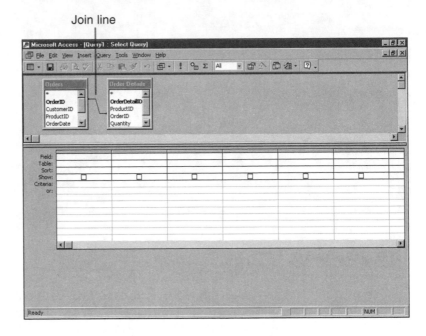

Join line

To join two tables manually (this would be necessary if the shared field used to relate the tables did not have the same name in both tables), drag one of the matching fields from a table and drop it on the matching field in the other table. This creates a join line between the two tables. The join line will look exactly like the relationship lines you create in the Relationships window to relate two tables.

After you've created the necessary relationships between the tables, you can go ahead and add fields to the query grid box and assign criteria and sort parameters to the query. When you have completed these aspects of query design, you can save the query and then run it.

Be aware, however, that the joins you create between the tables in your query are saved with the query. They do not become part of the database relationships contained in the Relationships window. This means that the relationships you create for one query are

Enforcing Referential Integrity

The relationship joins that you create between tables in the Query Design window cannot be set to enforce referential integrity. You must edit the relationship in the Relationships window.

not going to necessarily be available to you for other queries. It makes sense to create relationships that will be used to create a number of database objects (queries, forms, and reports) to be created in the Relationships window (see Chapter 8, "Between You and Me and Access: Table Relationships").

Removing Joins

You can also remove the join lines that relate two tables when you are working in the Query Design window. Use the mouse to select a join line. To delete the join, press **Delete**. The join line is deleted.

Deleting a join line in the Query Design window does not delete the relationship between the two tables for other Access objects, if the relationship was created in the Relationships window. Only the query where you deleted the join line will no longer recognize the tables as being related.

A Good Crosstab Query Will Never Double-Cross You

Wow, try to say that really fast ten times! Crosstab queries display the information in a spreadsheet-like format that makes it easier for you to view and compare the data.

Crosstab reports are perfect for summarizing numeric data from a particular field and then cross-referencing it to another field that has its data listed in the first column of the crosstab report. For example, if you want to see how many orders your customers have made, arranged by name of cheese, you could set up a crosstab to list all the customers in the first column and then give you a total (number of orders) that they have ordered for each cheese you carry in your inventory. The cheese types would be listed in the first row of the query. This configuration makes it easy for you to cross-tabulate a particular value as you visually scan the query.

Northwind Does Crosstabs!

Another excellent use for a crosstab query is to calculate the totals for the quarterly sales of a particular product. The Northwind database contains a crosstab query that displays subtotals for each quarter by product. Check it out.

To create a crosstab query, you can use the Crosstab Query Wizard, which walks you through the query creation steps, just like all the wizards in Access. After you click the **New** button in the Database window (make sure you have selected the Query tab), you will select the **Crosstab Query Wizard** in the New Query dialog box. As soon as you select your query type, click the **OK** button. Now we'll see what this crosstab stuff is all about.

The cheese orders are cross-tabulated for each customer.

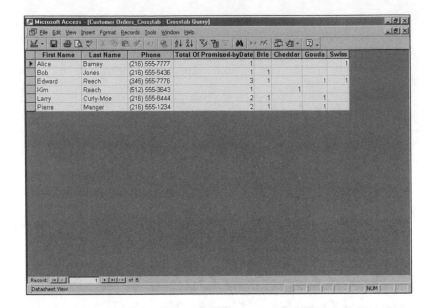

Selecting the Fields for the Query

The very first screen of the Crosstab Query Wizard would like you to designate which fields you want to use in the query. Before you can pick the fields, however, you must pick the table that holds the fields. There is one very odd thing about crosstab queries: You can't build them from more than one table. The wizard tells you this. It says that if you want to use fields from more than one table, you must run a select query first and then use the select query and its fields (which came from more than one table) to build the crosstab query.

Is this weird or what? Well, not totally. You can design queries that use other queries as the source for their fields. Queries look like tables, and most of the time they are just subsets of tables with maybe a formula or two thrown in. So there is no reason for this crosstab thing not to work. And you already have a query (the Customer Orders query that you created earlier in this chapter) that holds the fields that you want to use in the crosstab query.

For those of you who would like a quick query refresher and didn't create the Customer Orders query described earlier in this chapter, you might want to use the Query Wizard to quickly create the table for use in the crosstab query we are about to create For help creating a multitable query, check out Chapter 11, "Not a Stupid Question—Designing Simple Queries."

Pick Your Table or Pick Your Query

It seems that the very first screen in the Crosstab Query Wizard is really a crossroads with diverging paths. You must choose to base the query on a table or a query. In this case, choose **Queries**. Click the radio button to view the queries. Then you can choose the query that you want to use (**Customer Orders**).

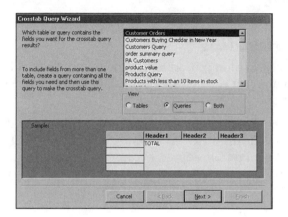

The first step in the crosstab query creation process: selecting a table or a query.

That's all there is to this step. Click **Next** to proceed.

Row, Row, Choose Your Row (Headings)

The next step in creating the crosstab query requires that you make a choice. You must tell the wizard which fields in your original query should be used as row headings in the crosstab query. To enter a field in the **Selected Fields** box, select the field and then click the **Add** button. You are limited to three row headings in the query.

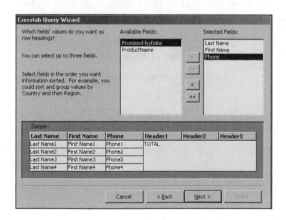

The Crosstab Query Wizard asks you to select the row headings for the query.

Because the whole point of this crosstab query is to be able to read the data from left to right and see which products have been ordered by which customer, it makes sense to use the customers' personal data as the row headings. In this case, use the Last Name, First Name, and Phone (number) fields as the row headings.

When you've selected the three fields that you want to use as row headings, you can click **Next** to move to the next step.

Choosing the Column Heading

Now the wizard wants you to pick a column heading for the query. The field that you pick will be used to create a column for each of the data values found in the particular field in the original table or query.

The query that you are basing the crosstab query on has a ProductName field listing the names of the products you sell at the good old Fromage Boutique. It makes sense to use the products' names as the column headings, because you used the customers' last name, first name, and phone number as the row headings.

Build Your Crosstab Queries from Summarizing Queries

Remember, crosstab queries cannot be built from more than one table. This is a real problem if you want to use fields from multiple tables in the crosstab. So it is necessary to build them from a preexisting query that pulls together data from a number of tables. Before you undertake the creation of a crosstab query, make sure that you have built a simple query containing all the fields (from multiple tables, if necessary) that you want to have in the crosstab.

Click the field name that you want to designate for the column heading, in this case, **ProductName**. After you've selected the field for the column heading, click the **Next** button.

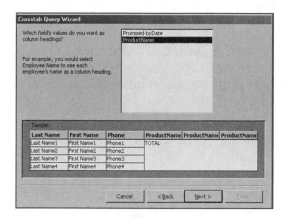

Selecting the field for the crosstab column heading.

Calculations Anyone?

Now the Crosstab Query Wizard asks whether you want to set up any calculations in the query. You can design the query so that certain calculations are carried out on the row and column intersections (just as in a spreadsheet). In this situation, you have customers who have been promised a product on certain dates, so it might be nice to see how many total orders each of them has placed. What you can do is have the query count the promised-by dates for each customer; this will give you the total number of orders that each has placed. The crosstab query can also break down the number of orders that each customer has placed for each cheese type. So the total number of orders for each customer will be found in the Promised-byDate column, and the orders by cheese will be summarized in the appropriate cheese column. Keep in mind that almost any field can be summarized mathematically. In the case of the Promised-byDate field and the various cheeses, the number of times they appear in the original query is being totaled by the crosstab query.

Notice that the Crosstab Query Wizard lists the fields (Promised-byDate and ProductName) that you did not designate as row headings for the crosstab query's column headings. When you designate the fields that will be in a crosstab, keep in mind that you will have to use them all; they must either serve as row or column headings or be summarized mathematically. Click the **ProductName** field to select it. This creates a different column in the crosstab for each cheese type. Now all you must do is click **Next** to move to the next step in the process.

Calculating Totals Using the Promised-byDate Field

The Crosstab Query Wizard makes you use all the fields that you designated when you began the query creation process. So far, you've used the Last Name, First Name, and Phone fields as row headings. You used the ProductName field as the column headings (a different column will be created for each cheese type). You have not used the Promised-byDate field in the query. No problem, the wizard is aware of this and will make use of the field in the next step of the query creation process.

Crosstab queries are great for summarizing information, especially in situations when you need a calculation done. The wizard asks which field information you want to use in calculations that will appear at the intersection of the rows and columns in the query. Because you want to see how many orders each customer has made (both total orders and orders of each specific cheese type), you want to use an Access function that counts the number of times the Promised-byDate field appears for each customer (this counts each separate order made by the customers).

This particular screen of the Crosstab Query Wizard provides several formulas, in the Function box, that you can use to calculate results that you want to appear in the crosstab query. In this particular case, select the **Count** function. This will count the orders, using the Promised-byDate field.

You can select a formula from the Functions box that will place calculated results in your crosstab query.

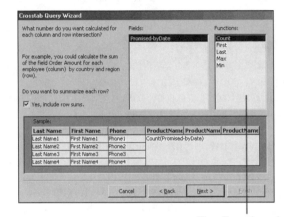

The Functions box

Make sure that **Count** is selected in the **Functions** box. Then you're ready to move to the final step in the crosstab query creation process.

The End of the Line

Clicking **Next** one last time takes you to the last step in your query quest. Name the query (type the name in the Name box) and then click the **Finish** button to view the results.

This query looks marvelous. You have row headings (First Name, Last Name, and Phone), and you have column headings (the product names), even a column that shows the total number of orders each customer has made (a result of the count formula).

You can now see how a crosstab displays its data. If you follow a particular customer's name across the query toward the right, you can pinpoint which products the customer has ordered. When it comes to viewing your data, the crosstab query is definitely an improvement over the select query.

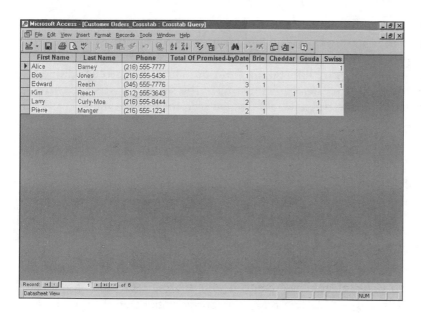

The completed crosstab query.

Using Append and Delete Queries

There are still two types of queries we should take a look at before we close the book on this particular subject. (But, wait! Don't close *this* book.) Append queries enable you to copy records from one table and place them in (or append them to) another table.

For example, you might have an Active Employees table. When an employee leaves the company, it makes sense to remove his or her record from the table. Using an append query, you can move this data to a Former Employees table. After you copy the data to the Former Employees table, you can use a delete query to totally remove his or her information from the Active Employees table. That way, the person's data doesn't clutter the active employee list, but you still know where to find this person's information if you need it.

I should reiterate the fact that running an append query only copies the data from the original table to the new table. To remove the data from the original table, you must also use a delete query.

In our case, we have a Customers table that lists customers who live in two states: Ohio and Pennsylvania. Let's say you've decided to make a separate table for the Pennsylvania customers, because you are going to open a new store in their state. This situation, then, calls for an append query to copy the data to a new PA Customers table. Later in this chapter, you will use a delete query to remove the Pennsylvania customers completely from the original Customers table.

To use an append query, you need a table that you can append the records to, and that table should have the same fields as the table from which you are removing the records. In our example, we must create a table to hold the records of our Pennsylvania customers—records we'll be taking from our current Customers table. The PA Customers table we create, therefore, must have the same fields as the current Customers table. After you create the new table, make sure that you save it.

Quickly Copying Table Fields

You can copy the fields and all their parameters from an existing table to a new table. In Table Design view, select all the fields of your existing table and copy them by choosing **Edit**, **Copy**. Create a new table and in Table Design view, paste the fields into the table. It's very easy and very fast.

To create the append query, set up a select query (from scratch or by using the wizard) for the table from which you want to copy the records—in our example, the Customers table. All the fields contained in the table should be placed in the grid box in the Query Design window. In this example, you would choose the **Customers** table and use all the fields available. The new query, however, would be a select query. This poses a problem, although an easily remedied one.

A Change of Query Identity

You must turn your select query into an append query. You can change the type of query that you are designing by clicking the Query Type button on the Query toolbar. A drop-down list appears, giving you several possibilities. Select **Append**.

As soon as you select **Append**, the Append dialog box appears and asks you to designate the table to which you want to append the records. You should type in the name of the empty table that you have created to accept the appended records. In this case, you type PA Customers, the new table for Pennsylvania customers. Then you should click **OK**. Under normal circumstances, you would probably already have a table that you are appending the records to. You would select that particular table instead of the sample PA Customers table that we created for this particular discussion of append queries.

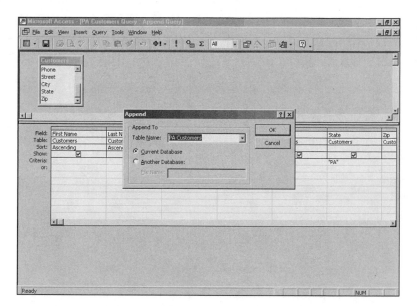

Selecting the table that will receive the records from the append query.

Notice that a new row appears in the Query Design grid box after you have selected the table that will receive the records from the append query. This row determines the fields in the new table that you will append the field information to. Because we are appending to a table that has exactly the same fields in it as the current table, the Append To row will list the same field names as those listed in the query's Field row.

Setting Up the Append Criteria

Now all you must do is set up the criteria that let the query know which records it should append to the new table. We want the Pennsylvania customers appended to the PA Customers table, so you would set up the criterion PA in the **Criteria** box below the State field (just as you did in the select query you created in Chapter 11).

After the criterion is set, click the Run button on the toolbar. Access knows that you are doing something drastic here, so as soon as you attempt to run the append query, Access tells you how many rows (records) will be appended by this query.

If you're confident that the query was designed correctly (and you should be), click **Yes** to allow the query to append the records to the new table. Remember, if the query doesn't work right, you can always go back and edit its design. If you end up with the wrong records appended to your PA Customers table, you can delete those records and start over. Access is very forgiving, so don't hesitate to experiment and learn as you work with the various database objects such as queries.

Entering the append criterion in the appropriate field column.

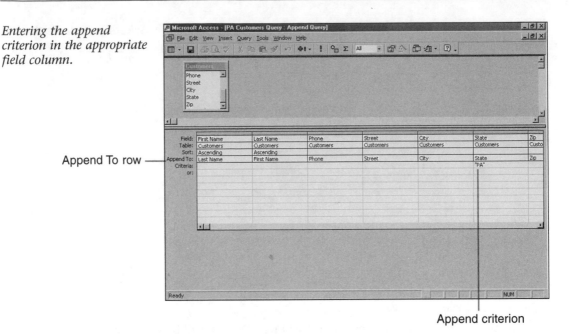

Append To row ———

Append criterion

A Query Well Run

It would be a good idea to see whether your append query actually performs as advertised. You can minimize the query, switch to the **Table** tab in the Database window, and then open the table that the records were appended to. In the example that we've been working with, a table (PA Customers) holding records for people from Pennsylvania should be the result of the query.

The append query copies the appropriate records to the table that you designate.

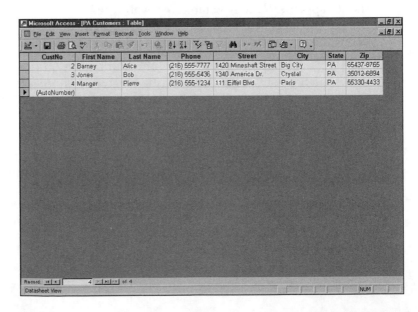

The Make-Table Query Makes New Tables Fast

Another way to quickly create a new table by using records from a current table is the make-table query. It works exactly the same way as the append query, but it creates a new table from the records selected by the query. This means that it takes care of the field creation for the new table.

Creating a Delete Query

You will find that if you open the original table (the table that you appended the records from—in this case, the Customers table), the records you appended are still there. Because you went through all the trouble to append them to a new table, you probably don't want them in the old table anymore. This is where a delete query comes in. You use it to delete the records in the old table that you appended to the new table. The great thing about setting up the delete query is that you can use the append query that you designed; the only change that you make is to let Access know that the query is now a delete query.

In our present case, you still have the append query in the Access window (you minimized it, remember?). When you restore it (click its restore button), you can change it into a delete query.

To switch an append query to a delete query, click the Query Type button on the Query toolbar and then choose **Delete**. A new row appears in the query grid box—Delete. This row can be designated as Where or From. When you are setting up a delete query for a single table, leave the Delete box as Where. When you have multiple tables, you can designate that certain fields from one of the related tables be deleted.

Deleting the Records

The last step in setting up the delete query is to set up the criteria for the deletion. Because we already had the append table set up to append the records with Pennsylvania as the state, this condition is still present in the query.

When you have designated your criteria for the delete query, you can click the Run button on the toolbar. Access lets you know how many records you are about to delete and also that the deletion is final. You can't use the Undo feature to get your records back. To make the query a done deal, click the **Yes** button.

The delete query—no turning back from this one!

Here a Query, There a Query...

As you can probably tell by now, you can do many things with queries in Access. You can select records, append records, delete records, place data in a crosstab query, and do mathematical calculations. Queries really do seem able to do it all.

The Least You Need to Know

➤ The tables that you use in multitable queries must be joined by a common field. In other words, they must have a relationship.

➤ You can create queries not only from tables, but also from other queries.

➤ Crosstab queries enable you to view your data in a spreadsheet format, in which calculations can be carried out on the row and column information.

➤ Append queries are used to copy records from one table to another.

➤ Delete queries enable you to remove unwanted records from your tables.

From Soup to Nuts—Creating Delicious Reports

I always loathed the first week of grammar school each fall. You could bet that the teacher, who was probably reconsidering her profession after a summer respite from this gaggle of screaming kids, would ask you to stand up in the front of the class and give a report about what you did on your summer vacation. I would spend hours at home writing clever (well, I thought they were clever) little stories about what I did during my summer, using nifty little index cards. I was building a database of facts for my report.

However, typically, as soon as I took my place in the front of the room and cleared my throat to begin my great oration, I would drop all my index cards into a hopeless mess.

Reporting Your Database Information

Well, fear not, those days of unorganized reports are over. Access can take the information in your tables and queries and spin reports that present your data in a format that is well designed and easy to understand. You never have to write on another index card in your life!

You've already done a bang-up job dealing with tables, forms, and queries—all database objects primarily used online. Reports differ from these other database objects in that reports are designed to be printed. Of all your database manipulations, your reports are the most likely to be seen by your coworkers (and, gasp, the boss) as printed pages.

You can create reports from single tables or from multiple tables (remember all that table relationship stuff we talked about?). You also have the same data and design control in reports as you do when you are working with forms.

Creating a Report from One Table

If you've tried to print out one of your tables, you've found that you end up with several sheets of paper that spread the fields over the pages and make it difficult to tell what data goes with what record.

SEE ALSO

> For more information about printing Access objects, see Chapter 16, "All the News That's Fit to Print."

Let's say you want to print out a readable list of your customers from a Customers table. What you need is a single-table report.

Using the Report Wizard

As you have found with nearly all the other database objects that we've explored, the easiest way to create a new object is by using a wizard, and reports are not an exception. We'll fall back on our Fromage Boutique database (or any database you care to use) as we create a single-table report from the Customers table via the Report Wizard.

After you open a particular database, the next step is to click the **Reports** icon in the Database window. You can then quickly create a new report using a wizard by double-clicking the **Create Report by Using Wizard** icon on the right side of the Database window. If you would like to see all the possibilities for creating new reports, click the **New** button at the top of the Database window.

The New Report dialog box appears, offering you a couple different ways to construct your new table. You can design the report from scratch, you can use the AutoReport command to build a quick report (columnar or tabular) using all the fields in a specific table, or you can use the Report Wizard to walk you through the steps involved in creating a new report. Using the wizard gives you some customization options that you would not have if you selected either of the AutoReport choices.

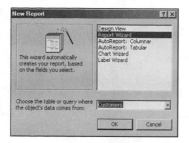

There is more than one way to design a new report.

Select **Report Wizard** and then click **OK**. The next screen is very familiar; it's not unlike the wizard screens that you've used to build forms and queries. You are asked to choose a table and specify which fields you would like in the report. The Customers table would be chosen in the **Tables/Queries** box. Because you want a report that gives all the information on customers available in the table, you will want to include all the fields. The easiest way to do this is to click the Add All button (the one with the right-pointing double chevron on it). After you've chosen the fields, you advance to the next screen by clicking **Next**.

Fast Reports with AutoReport

You can also use the New Object button on the Table toolbar to build an AutoReport for the currently selected table. It is the same feature that you used to build an AutoForm for data entry.

Are You with a Group?

The next screen wants to know whether you would like to add any grouping levels to your report. This means you can set up the information in a defined hierarchy; customer numbers, for example, can be displayed as a major heading for each record.

You can arrange the information in any order you like. In this case, it would make sense to put the customer number at the top of each record in the report and follow it with the last name and then the first name. The rest of the information for each customer will be displayed in a columnar fashion under the levels that you've set up.

To set up the grouping levels, which are just headings and subheadings in the report, select a field and then click the **Add** button. After you've chosen your levels (add CustNo, then add Last Name, and then add First Name), you advance to the next screen.

211

*Field names and the field
information can be
grouped at different levels
in a report.*

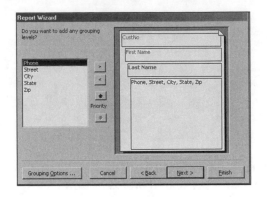

What Sort of Sort Would You Like?

The Report Wizard now asks whether you would like
to sort the records in the report by a field. You can
sort the records by as many as four fields. You don't
have to sort your records in this situation, because
you have made the customer number (the CustNo
field in our table) a first-level group. The records will
be listed in the report in order by CustNo, making
sorting unnecessary. Click **Next** to move to the next
step.

Getting Those Records in Order

If you set up a report that doesn't
group the information at different
levels, you can have the records
appear in the report according to
the sort parameters that you set.

*Your report can be
designed to sort the data
presented by one field or
a number of fields.
Reports using group levels
don't have to be sorted.*

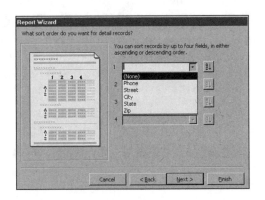

Picking a Report Layout

This report creation process has been easy so far, but now you're going to have to put on your designer's beret and decide on a layout and page orientation for the report. Several layouts are available. You can print the report stepped, blocked, as an outline (two different layouts), or in left-aligned columns (equally spaced on both the right and the left). All you must do is click the radio button for your specific choice. In this case, choose **Align Left 1**, which gives a balanced look to the printed page.

You can also choose the paper orientation for the report. *Portrait* is a regular sheet of paper in its 8.5×11–inch orientation. For *landscape*, you turn the same paper 90 degrees, and you have a page 11×8.5 inches. If you have only a few fields in your table, use the portrait orientation. If you have many fields, use landscape.

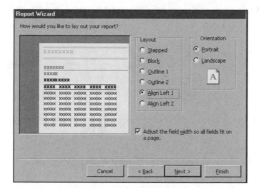

You select the layout and the page orientation for the report.

You will leave the page orientation as portrait and move on to the next step. So click **Next**.

Even Reports Have Style(s)

Now you must select a style for the Report: Bold, Casual, Compact, Corporate, Formal, or Soft Gray (who comes up with these things?). Because you are probably learning Access to help you ascend the corporate ladder of success (don't get stuck on one of its rungs), let's choose **Corporate**. After you choose your style, you can move on to the next step by clicking **Next**.

An End in Sight

Wow! You are already at the last step in the report creation process. The Report Wizard gives you an opportunity to name your report or go with the name that it has selected for it. Because you used the Customers table as the data source for the report, the wizard assumes you want to name the report *Customers*. Hey, makes sense to me!

You also must decide whether you want to preview the report or fiddle with the report's design. It probably wouldn't hurt to take a look at the report and then decide whether you want to alter it, in Report Design view (yes, it's much like Form Design view). Click the **Finish** button to take this report home!

Previewing the Report

I love previews. I mean, how many times have you left your local movie theater after sitting in the dark for two hours and lamented the fact that the previews of coming attractions were a heck of lot more exciting than the film?

Because reports are meant to be printed, Access takes you to the Print Preview window to show you the report that you created. Print Preview shows you your form exactly as it will print and gives you the chance to return to the design screen to make changes.

Using Print Preview on All Your Objects

You can also use Print Preview to look at any forms or tables that you might want to print. Seeing the various database objects as they will appear on the printed page helps you decide whether to print them. It can save you a lot of paper.

Print Preview has its own set of command buttons along the top of the window. You can click the Print button to send your report to the printer, or you can zoom in and out on the page. You can also click a button to exit Print Preview.

If you move your mouse around when you are in Print Preview, you will notice that the mouse pointer becomes a zoom controller (it looks like a magnifying glass). When you are zoomed out on your report (you can see the whole page), the zoom controller contains a plus (+) sign. This means that if you click the mouse button, you will zoom in. When you are zoomed in, the zoom controller contains a minus (-) sign. Click, and you zoom out.

You can export your Access reports from the Print Preview window directly to other members of Microsoft's Office suite of applications. You can send your report to a Microsoft Word document or analyze the data in the report, using Microsoft Excel's spreadsheet capabilities. Use the OfficeLinks drop-down button to quickly take advantage of this powerful feature.

When you are finished previewing your report, you can send it to the printer or close the Print Preview window.

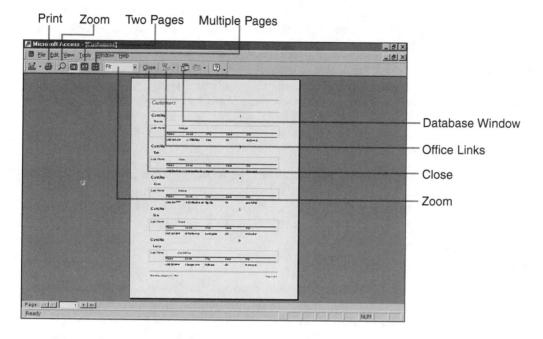

Print   Zoom   Two Pages   Multiple Pages

Database Window
Office Links
Close
Zoom

Report Design View

When you close the Print Preview window, you are taken to Report Design view. Report Design view offers you a toolbox containing the same tools that were available when you were working on forms. In Report Design view, you can delete or add field controls and labels to the report.

You can also size and move the controls and labels. For example, you might find that a report based on a table with many fields has squished the field data and the field labels on the report (looks like you should have chosen landscape page orientation). You can click a field or label and use the sizing boxes to change the width or height of a particular item.

Check This Out

Get Those Widths Right

When you initially set up the grouping levels in the report via the Report Wizard, you can change the average width of the field controls in the report by clicking the **Grouping Options** button.

Redesigning the Report

You will probably find that if you have used the Report Wizard wisely, you won't have to do a whole lot of redesigning on your report. You already know that manipulating the controls and their labels is pretty much all mouse work. From time to time, you might want to give a report a personal touch.

When you use the Report Wizard to generate the report, it automatically puts two controls in the report's footer area: the date and page numbering. Because we didn't have many records in our Fromage Boutique Customers table, the entire report fills only one page. When you have only a one-page report, it seems kind of senseless to have a page number on the page. To remove the page numbering, all you have to do is remove the appropriate control.

Because the page numbering control is in the footer area, you might have to scroll down to select it. When the control is selected, all you must do is press the **Delete** key to remove it. Whenever you make any changes to your report design, make sure you click the Save button on the toolbar to save them.

Picture This

You can also add text and other items to your report design for purely cosmetic reasons. (All the font attributes—bold, italic, underline—and border and color buttons on the Report toolbar can be used to enhance the appearance of your reports.) Because this is a report for the customers of a cheese shop, it might be nice to include a picture logo in the report design.

Adding a picture to a report is a snap (or is that snapshot?). You might have to expand one of the Report areas to place a graphic. For example, you might want to expand the report header in your report for a company logo. When you have a place picked out, click the Image button on the Toolbox (if the Toolbox is not showing click **View**, **Toolbox**). Then you use the mouse pointer to drag a rectangle onto the report (pick your spot) to hold the image.

As soon as you create this control, which will hold your image, the Insert Picture dialog box appears. This dialog box is like any other File Open or Insert dialog box; you pick the location of the item that you want to use (in this case, a picture), and then you specify which item you're talking about.

The images that come with the Microsoft Office 2000 and Access 2000 software are commonly found inside a folder, called Clipart (although this will depend on your installation; you may have to look in a subfolder of Clipart called Cagcat50). The entire path for the folder would be C:\Program Files\Common Files\Microsoft Shared\Clipart (C: is the drive where you installed Access or Office). See Appendix A, "Installing Access 2000," for all the information necessary to properly install your Office or Access software.

When you open the appropriate folder, you can also preview the images listed; all you must do is click the image. Let's take a look at the various images available with Access (and Office 2000). There should be a picture that will be perfect for our Customers report. Let's look in the Clipart folder and see whether there is a picture of some happy customers that we can use for our Fromage Boutique Customers report.

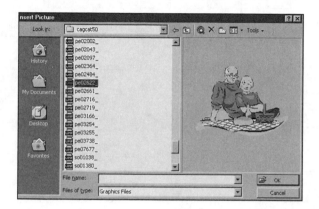

Access and Office offer a number of great graphics that are easy to insert into your report.

Scroll down through the images in the Cagcat50 folder. Notice that the images are listed alphabetically. If you scroll down far enough, you will find pe02622, a great (or is it grate?) picture of two happy customers enjoying a little wine and (hopefully) cheese in a lovely picnic setting. When you have the image selected, you click **OK**. The picture will be inserted into the control box that you placed on the report.

Many images provided with Access and Office are quite large. This means you must adjust the size of the graphic so that the whole image appears in the control box that you created for the graphic.

Changing the graphics properties so that the image fits in the control is quite easy. Right-click on the image control you've created. On the shortcut menu that appears, select **Properties** (it's at the very bottom of the menu). In the **Image Properties** box that appears, make sure you have the **All** tab selected. The fourth property parameter shown on this tab is the Size Mode. Click in the **Size Mode** box. A drop-down arrow appears. All you must do is click the drop-down arrow and select **Zoom** from the menu that appears. This sizes your new graphic so that it fits perfectly inside the control box that you drew for it. After changing the size mode, click the close (×) button to close the Properties dialog box and get it out of your workspace.

You can also change the size of the image control itself. Just grab any of the sizing handles and drag to enlarge or shrink the size of the control box. If you drag on any of the sizing handles on the diagonal corners of the control, you will be better able to maintain the height and width ratio of your graphic. You can also move the image by clicking on the control and then dragging it to a new position. Images provide a great way to dress up your reports!

You can place images in your reports by placing an image control in any of the various report areas.

The new image

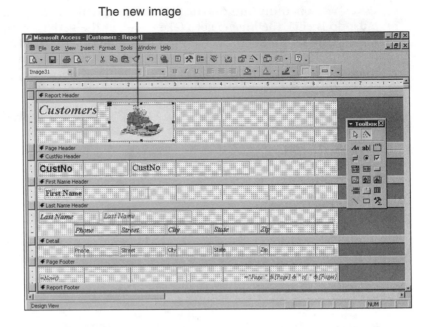

With the help of the Report Wizard, creating reports can be quite simple, and bare-bones reports can be created quickly using the AutoReport feature. Let's expand our look at reports and figure out how to create a report that is based on more than one table.

Reports Created from Multiple Tables

You can use the Report Wizard (or design the report from scratch) to generate a report that uses more than one of your database tables (and don't forget that reports can be created from queries—they provide a lot of possibilities for your reports). When you design your single-table report, the wizard asks you to specify the table and the fields that it is to use. When you build a multitable report, it's just a matter of selecting fields from more than one table.

I know this sounds really easy, but there is one catch. The tables that you take the fields from must have a relationship. If they don't, the wizard will not let you mix the fields in the report. It tells you that the tables that you are taking the fields from are not related, and it bounces you to the Relationship window.

All is not lost, however. You just establish the appropriate relationship between the tables and then start the Report Wizard again. This time, it will accept your field choices.

For example, let's say you have two tables in your database related to your products: a Products table (listing the items you sell) and a Categories table (defining the major groups that your products fall into). You want to print a report that lists the products by category.

It's easy to check or to define relationships between your tables. Make sure the Database window is open for the particular database and then click the Relationships button on the toolbar.

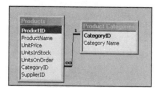

A one-to-many relationship exists between the Product Categories table and the Products table.

Because a relationship exists between these tables (as discussed in Chapter 8, "Between You and Me and Access: Table Relationships") you can go ahead and start the Report Wizard assured that you can pull fields from both tables for the new report you want to create. Inside the Report Wizard, when you reach the screen where you pick the fields for the report, you select the fields you need from both tables. This is done by selecting one of your tables—**Categories**—in the **Table** drop-down box. The fields found in the Product Categories table will be displayed in the **Field** box. To add the fields to the report, select the field or fields and then click the Add (>) button. After you've selected the fields you will use from the Categories table, select the **Products** table in the **Table** drop-down box. Select the fields that you will use in the **Field** box and add them to the report.

Techno Talk

Using a Main Report and Subreport to Summarize Data from Multiple Tables

You can create reports that show data from more than one table by creating a main report and a subreport. This is done in a similar fashion to the method that you used to create a main form and a subform. You create a report from one table and then, in Report Design view, add a control for a subreport. You can then set the parameters for the control, such as the table that should be used for the subreport and how the information should be formatted. See Chapter 15, "Pride of Ownership—Enhancing Your Reports," for more information about subreports.

Fields from both tables—
Products and Product
Categories—are selected
for the report.

Field from the Product
Categories table

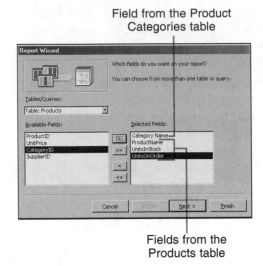

Fields from the
Products table

Boy, Is This Report Wizard Smart!

After you've determined what fields to include in the report, you can advance to the next screen in the Report Wizard. If you've chosen fields from more than one table, the wizard will ask you how you want to view the data in the report.

For example, we used fields from the Product Categories table and the Products table, so the wizard wants to know whether you want the report to show the data by category or by products. We want this particular report to list the field information by categories, which obviously means that you would tell the wizard to list it by category.

You select how you want
the combined data from
the two tables to be listed
in the report.

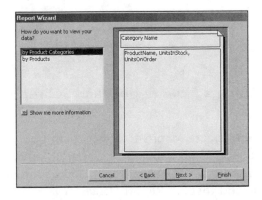

After you determine how the data should be listed, the wizard also gives you the option of grouping the information as you did in the single-table report. Because the report will list things by the main heading—Categories—you might want to select the field for the item name (ProductName, in this case) and make it one of the major heading groups.

Even though you are asking the wizard to create a report from more than one table, it still affords you all the options available for the single-table report, such as sorting the data by a particular field, and the full range of report layouts and styles.

Because you are grouping the data by headings, you won't have to sort the data, so you can skip the wizard screen by clicking **Next**. The next two screens are where you select the report layout and then the report style. Make a selection in each and then click **Next** to continue.

After you complete the steps in the report creation process (including naming the report), the new multitable report will be displayed in the Print Preview window.

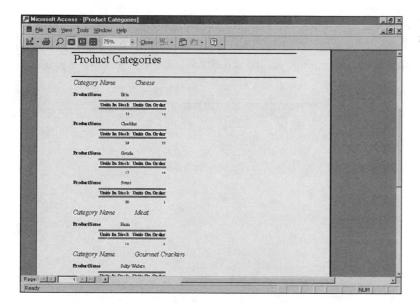

The finished multitable report.

You can zoom in and out on your report or send it to the printer. If you decide not to print, you can exit the Print Preview window by clicking the **Close** button.

Reports provide a great deal of flexibility and really are the best way to assemble your data for printing. In Chapter 15, "Pride of Ownership—Enhancing Your Reports," we'll take our survey of Access reports a little further and look at how you can easily create mailing labels, set up a report that does calculations, and place a chart in a report.

The Least You Need to Know

➤ The easiest way to create a report is via the Report Wizard.

➤ You can edit your report designs in Report Design view. This lets you fix anything that the wizard didn't take care of.

➤ You can group fields on your reports so that you get a series of headings and subheadings, making it easy to make sense of the information shown on the report.

➤ Multitable reports can also be created using the Report Wizard. This type of report makes it easy to summarize data from two or more related tables.

➤ The Print Preview window enables you to scrutinize your reports before you print them.

No Need for a Calculator— Doing Math in Reports

After the last chapter, you're probably feeling good about your ability to take seemingly unrelated data and use Access to spin a great report. Reports are meant to summarize information; it is their raison d'être—their reason for being. (Use the idiom *raison d'être* to impress friends and family; for example, *The apparent raison d'eâtre of my cat is to walk on my keyboard when I'm trying to type.*)

Placing a Total in a Report

If you buy the supposition that reports exist to summarize, it makes sense to have your reports summarize numeric information. That means it would be great to design a report that can return a total on a bunch of numbers.

Let's say that you run a design and architectural firm called Daring Designers. Let's also say that you are creating a database to help track company expenses. You would probably have at least an Employees table, an Expenses table, and a Departments table in your database. The tables would also be related by common fields (for example, the Employees and Expenses tables both would include the field Employee ID, and this field could be used to create a relationship between the tables).

Practice Makes Perfect

The Northwind database that ships with the Access software is also an excellent resource. It provides ample tables and data to practice building the various database objects such as reports. As you build your own databases, you can also use the Northwind database tables as examples of well-designed tables.

The easiest way to create this database would be to create a blank database and then use the Table Wizard to create the various tables in the database, taking advantage of the ready-made fields that the wizard provides. The Employees table should contain the fields Employee ID, First Name, Last Name, Extension, DepartmentID, and DateHired. The Expenses table should contain the fields Expense ID, Employee ID, Amount Spent, Date Submitted, and Expense Description. The Departments table should contain the fields Department Name, Department ID, and Office Location. Obviously, if you were building a database for your own business, you would set up the tables in the database and the fields in the tables to meet your particular needs.

SEE ALSO

> For more help building your tables and working with fields, see Chapter 5, "Turning the Tables: Table Design," and Chapter 6, "Going On Record: Adding and Editing Data."

The Expenses and Employees tables in your Daring Designers database.

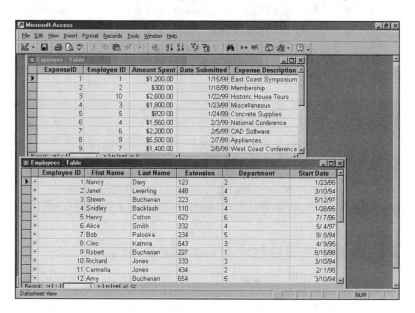

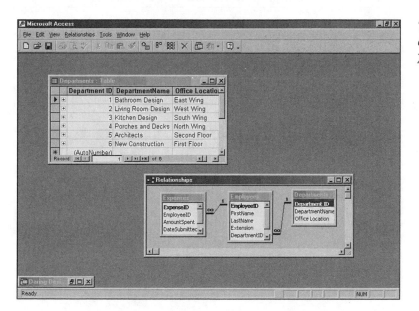

The Departments table and the relationships in your database.

When you have a proper database set up with the right tables, you can generate the reports. Your first step is to build a report (either via the Report Wizard or from scratch) referencing the fields that will supply your data—such as employee name, expense amount, expense ID, and perhaps the department that the employee belongs to. The easiest way to build this report would be via the Report Wizard. Your data would probably exist in the three tables: Employees, Departments, and Expenses. Remember that you can mix fields from different tables to design a report.

When building a report that uses more than one table or query as a source of information, you must decide how you want the data to be presented. For example, if you are building a report using information from two tables, such as the Employees table and the Expenses table, you can either set up the report to list the expenses by expense number, using the Expenses table to provide the report's view of the data, or list the expenses by employee, using the Employees table to provide the report's view of the data.

A sample of a tabular expense report that groups information by expense.

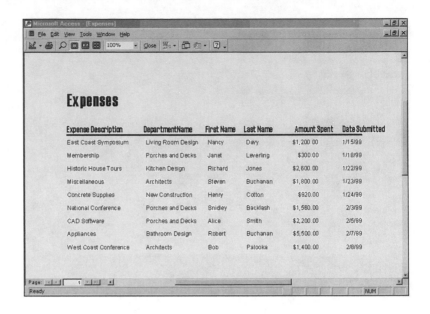

Take a Look at the Landscape

If you find that your report does not fit on the standard page orientation (Portrait) because of the number of columns in your report, switch the report's page layout to Landscape. On the **File** menu, choose **Page Setup**. On the **Page** tab of the Page Setup dialog box, select the **Landscape** radio button. This gives you much more room from left to right on the page.

When the report is built, you should switch to Design view for the report so that you can add a totals formula to the report. How and where you add that formula is our next exciting topic.

Don't Put Your Footer in Your Mouth

You already know from our earlier discussion of reports that they contain *page header and footer areas*, that is, places on either the top or bottom of each page of the report, where you can put data or other information that you want to repeat.

226

Your reports can also contain *report headers and footers*. You can use these for report names (usually the header area) or for summary information such as a totals formula (usually the footer area). The report header appears at the very beginning of the report, and the report footer, at the very end.

Information that you place in the report footer will appear only at the end of the report (the last page). Likewise, any information placed in the report header will appear at the beginning of the report. Information that you would like to repeat on each page of the report should appear in the page header or footer.

Because you want to place a formula in the report footer, the first thing you have to do is expand the footer area. It's just a matter of placing the mouse on the footer area's bottom border and then dragging the sizing tool to give you the space you need. That seems painless, doesn't it? Well, unfortunately, making a spot for the formula is much easier than putting the formula in the spot. Now you must face the tough stuff and place a new formula control in the footer area.

Adding the Totals Control

To place a totals formula in the footer area, you must add a new control to the report. In the case of the sample report (the employee expense report), it would make sense to place the totals control under the control that lists the amount for each expense.

ab| To add the new control, you click the Text Box tool on the toolbox and then drag out a new control box in the footer area. You can then click the label box for the new control and assign it a name. In this case, you might want to label the control Total Expenses.

At the Controls

You can select any of the controls in your report and drag them to new positions. Don't forget that you can also size all the label and control boxes in the report. Keep in mind, though, that reports can appear on multiple pages, so arrange your controls accordingly.

Putting the new control in the footer area to total the expenses.

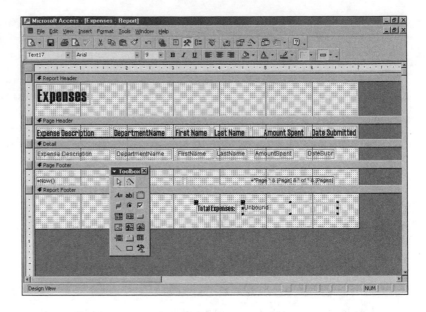

As soon as you're satisfied with the control's label and its position in the footer area, you can get down to the business of setting up the control so that it totals the expenses. Click the control to select it and then click the Properties button on the Report toolbar.

When you want to change the properties of a control in your report, make sure you have the control selected before you click the Properties button. You can also place the mouse on the control and click the right mouse button. Then select properties from the shortcut menu that appears.

The Properties box for the currently selected control will appear. Now comes the tricky part.

The Source of All Data

Okay, so we aren't after the source of all data (but it made the heading sound more mystical); we just need to tell Access the source of the data for the new control that you built. The source will be a particular field or an expression such as a math formula (you put a date expression in a report's last chapter). If you want a total to appear in this control, you must designate the field that holds the data and then build an expression to total the information.

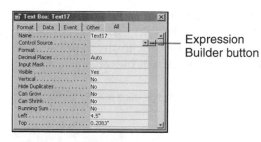

Getting ready to place an expression in the Control Source box.

Expression
Builder button

Click in the Control Source box of the Properties dialog (on the **Data** tab) for the currently selected control. A button for the Expression Builder appears. Click this button and get ready to build a formula.

Your Total Comes To...

When you're in the Expression Builder, it's simply a matter of choosing the right formula for the situation and having the formula act on the appropriate field information. The Expression Builder gives you easy access to both the formulas and the fields.

In this particular case, we want to total a group of numbers (expenses), so we'll use the sum formula. Double-click the **Functions** folder to list the type of formulas available. A subfolder for **Built In Functions** appears; double-click it, and a huge list of possibilities appears. In the third column, all the functions available in Access are listed in alphabetical order.

Check This Out

Choose from Categories of Math Functions

The Expression Builder enables you to select subsets of functions by categories (the second column of functions in the Expression Builder). When you select a category of functions, the specific formulas appear in the third column of the Expression Builder.

The Sum of It

We're going to use the sum formula, so scroll down through the third column of choices and select **Sum**. After you select a particular formula, you must add it to the expression window. You do this by clicking the **Paste** button.

The formula now appears in the expression window, followed by a pair of parentheses with <<expr>> inside them. What the Expression Builder is trying to tell you is that you must place the field name inside the parentheses if you want the expression to total the data.

You enter the field name by first clicking <<expr>>. Then you double-click the **Tables** folder (or the **Query** folder, if you are using queries to build the report, either of which would appear in the first column of information in the Expression Builder's lower pane) to select the table that holds the particular field. Double-click the appropriate table (in this example, **Expenses**).

The fields in the table will be listed in the second column of the Expression Builder. All you have to do is select the correct field (in this case, **AmountSpent**) and then click the **Paste** button to place the field name in the expression window. When you have completed your expression, click the **OK** button.

The completed formula in the expression window.

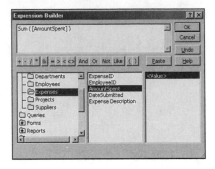

Formatting the Total

Now that you've built a superb formula for your report, it makes sense for the result of the formula to appear in the report in an appropriate format. Because you are totaling expenses, you probably want the control's contents to be formatted as currency.

Save It or Lose It

Make sure that you save any changes to your report's design. This includes adding and formatting controls.

To format the control, click the **Format** tab of the control's **Properties** box (you are returned to the Properties box when you exit the Expression Builder). Then click the drop-down arrow in the **Format** box. Several numeric formats are listed. In this particular case, choose **Currency**.

When you've completed your work in the Properties box, you can close it by clicking its close (×) button. Now comes the fun part; you get to view the changes that you've made to the report, in this case, the addition of a grand total at the end of your report.

 Click the Report View button on the toolbar (it's the first button on the toolbar). You might have to scroll down and to the right to see the new total (it appears at the end of the report because it's in the report footer, remember?). Now, wasn't that easy?

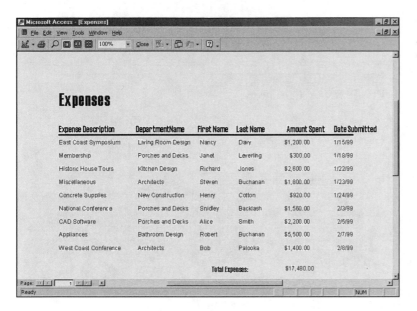

The completed report, showing the total of all expenses.

You could also place controls in the report that give you a count of the number of entries or the average of a group of numbers. All the functions necessary to summarize data via controls are found in the Expression Builder. You can also place subtotal (and other mathematic expressions) controls in the detail area of the report to figure subtotals (or other results) for various groupings of data.

Adding a Group Subtotal to a Report

Now that you have a feel for calculations in reports, we can go one step further and take a look at grouping information in a report (so that a subtotal will be performed). For example, you might have different categories of items that you stock in your store, and you would like your report to show not only the total number of items in stock (in the report footer), but also subtotals for the units in stock in each category.

Let's say that you run a cheese shop (sound familiar?) and have already run a report, using the Report Wizard, that gives specific data on the items in stock and groups them into four categories: cheese, meat, gourmet crackers, and implements (you know, those important cheese-eating aids). It should be no great shakes to edit this report so that you get a subtotal of the units in stock for each product category.

Design view of a report that displays data on items in categories.

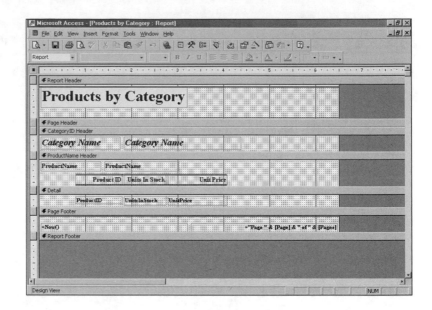

Not All Groupers Are Fish

To make this subtotal of units in stock by category work, we must find a way to let Access know that we want the information grouped. This means that Access must know that it should add the items in stock for each category, even though the category contains items that are not the same. For example, a subtotal of the cheese category gives you the number of all the cheeses, whether they are cheddar, gouda, or bada for that matter (Ouch! Bada pun).

To group this information together, we must add a new section to the report. The information in your report might already be grouped by a particular field. For example, in our sample report, CategoryID is used to group the data (note the CategoryID header in the preceding figure). So all you have to do is add another group section to the report for CategoryID—a group footer section.

You've already seen page footers, which allow you to place repeating information on each page of the report (such as the date), and report footers, which allow you to place information at the very bottom of the report (such as a total formula). Group footers allow you place a particular formula that repeats at the end of each subgroup of information that appears in your report. For example, in our report the subgroup footer contains a subtotals formula that provides a subtotal for each grouping of information (total items in stock for each category).

Then you can place your subtotal formula in the new section. Now you're probably thinking that you knew this stuff was going to get complicated eventually—but adding a new section to the report is easy.

Adding a New Report Section

Grab your mouse and let's create a new group footer section for the report. Click the Sorting and Grouping button on the toolbar. This opens the Sorting and Grouping dialog box. This dialog box is used to both sort and group information in the report (as though you couldn't have figured that out). We want to add another section to the report for the CategoryID field.

First, either select a current field or add a new field to the Field/Expression column. In this case, you would click the **CategoryID** field.

Adding Fields for Sorting and Grouping?

To add a new field to the Sorting and Grouping box, click in the first empty row in the Field/Expression column. A drop-down arrow appears in the box, allowing you to choose a field. You should be careful not to delete the fields currently listed in the Sorting and Grouping box. They were placed there when you originally set up your report and chose how the information should be grouped. If you do inadvertently delete a field listed (by selecting the entire row and pressing the Delete key), just use the technique just described to add that particular field back to the box.

A Group Properties box appears for the currently selected field (in the bottom half of the Sorting and Grouping box), showing whether a group header or group footer currently exists for the field. In our example, the CategoryID field does have a group header. It's very easy to add a group footer.

The field that you use to set up a new group header or footer should be a field that either was already used (in the original report) or can be used to group the data in your report. In the case of our cheese report, all the products were listed by category (first all the cheeses, then all the beverages, and so on.). This makes the CategoryID field the logical choice for the new footer section.

When you set up new sections in a report, another thing that you should keep in mind is where you want the new grouped information to appear. The group header will appear above the group information, and the group footer, below.

Setting the Group Properties

In the Group Properties area of the Sorting and Grouping dialog box, click in the **Group Footer** box. Then click the drop-down arrow and choose **Yes** (there are only two choices: Yes and No).

Giving the group footer a
yes vote in the Sorting
and Grouping dialog box.

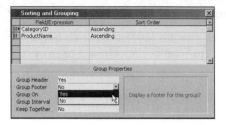

After you choose to add a new group footer or header, you can close the dialog box. The new group footer (or header) area will appear in your report.

Adding an Expression to the Group Footer Area

Now that you have a place in your report for the subtotal formula (the CategoryID footer, in this case), you might as well add your expression. You've already been through this drill once.

 Place a new control in the new footer area and then click the Properties button on the toolbar. After you select the **Data** tab of the Properties dialog box for the new control, you click in the **Control Source** box and then use the Expression Builder to build your formula.

The subtotal formula that you place in the group footer will be exactly the same as the formula that you would place in the report footer to get a grand total: the sum function and the name of the field you want to total.

Group Subtotal Versus Grand Total

Remember that, by definition, the group footer will provide only information relating to the group of data that you designated, in this case, the categories of items. This is why you can use the sum function to get a subtotal instead of a grand total.

234

In our example, we want to subtotal the number of items in stock in each category, so the formula that we would create in the Expression Builder would be the following:

> *Sum ([Products]![UnitsInStock])*

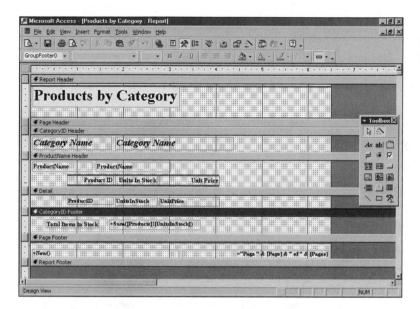

The new footer area and the subtotal expression for the report.

Viewing the Edited Report

After you've finished the editing of the report in Design view, all you must do is select the Preview button to see your changes, even the addition of a group subtotal. See how simple it is to add new sections to existing reports?

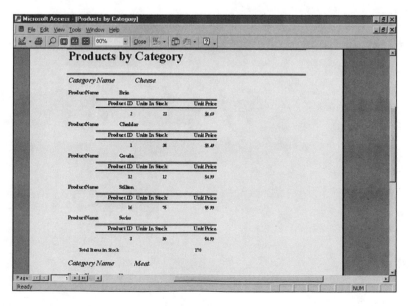

A portion of a finished report that has a group footer with a subtotal.

235

The techniques that you used in this chapter to add formulas and new areas to your reports can be used whether you build your reports via the Report Wizard or from scratch. Don't be afraid to experiment. Remember, the changes that you make to a report aren't final until you save them.

The Least You Need to Know

➤ You can place mathematic expressions in your reports by simply creating a new control and then placing a formula in the control by using the Expression Builder.

➤ The report footer area provides a good place to put a grand total for a tabular report whose numeric fields you want to summarize.

➤ Every control on a report will have a Properties dialog box associated with it. You use this box to determine the format, the control source, and other attributes of the control.

➤ You can add additional sections to your reports via the Sorting and Grouping dialog box. This box is also where you select the fields that you want to use to group information in the report.

Chapter 15

Pride of Ownership— Enhancing Your Reports

In This Chapter

➤ Adding a subreport to a report gives you two different perspectives on your database data

➤ Placing a page break in a report to divide the report and subreport into digestible bits

➤ Creating a chart

➤ Making mailing labels for your friends, family, or customers

---

Now, before you start whining about how sick you are of reports, just let me say that this is definitely going to be the final word on the subject. I mean, I could go on for another five or six chapters on reports—I love reports...oh, well, I guess I'm sick of them, too. So this is definitely going to be our last look at this highly versatile and useful database object.

Adding a Subreport to a Report

As you already know, reports are great at summarizing the information in your tables and queries. You can take this concept one step further and set up reports that contain two parts: the main report, which can list the data in great detail, and a subreport, which can summarize the information given in the main report.

Reports and Forms

Reports are very similar to forms. When you want to create a report from scratch, you add the controls to Report Design view, using the various tools on the toolbar. You can add headers and footers to your reports and also divide reports into sections. See Chapter 14, "No Need for a Calculator—Doing Math in Reports," for more information.

Drag Till You Drop

You can also create a subreport on a main report, using drag and drop. With the main report open in Report Design view, size the Design window so that you can also see the Database window. Select a report that will serve as the subreport and drag it from the database window into the area of the main report (probably the header or footer) where you want to place it. When you drop the report in the main report, it becomes an attached subreport.

For example, you might have a report that breaks down the expenses amassed by each of your employees. It might also be useful to see the information broken down by department—which would require a second report. You can take a general report on department expenses and attach it to a report on expenses for employees, and voilà! You can present the data in two very different ways in the very same report.

A Report Within a Report

This idea of a report within a report is very easy to execute. First, you build the reports that you want to combine—perhaps one specific report and one general report. You can use the Report Wizard or build these reports from scratch in Report Design view.

Once again, let's say that you run Daring Designers, and the Daring Designer database has an Employees table, an Expenses table, and a Departments table. You would use the fields from these tables to design your two reports. In keeping with our example, you would have a report that summarizes expenses by employee and a report that summarizes expenses by department.

SEE ALSO

Information on creating the tables in this database can be found in Chapter 14, "No Need for a Calculator—Doing Math in Reports." You can also get similar results, using the comparable tables found in the Northwind database, as you explore the techniques described in this chapter.

The easiest way to create these two reports would be by using the Report Wizard. The first report, summarizing the expenses by employee, would use fields from the Employees, Expenses, and Departments tables. The report summarizing expenses by department would use fields from the Expenses and Departments tables.

After you have completed the two reports, open the more general of the two reports in the Design view. The more general report will be longer, perhaps consisting of multiple pages when it is printed. The longer report will serve as the main report, and you will attach the more specific report (in this case, Expenses by Department) as a subreport.

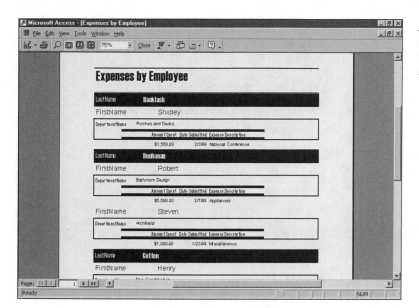

A look at the two reports that will become the main report and the subreport.

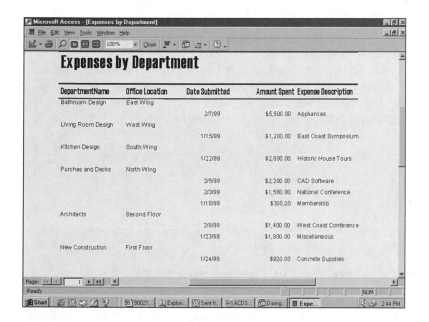

The Report Wizard

When you design a report via the Report Wizard or from scratch, you can easily change its overall format. When you are in Report Design view, choose the **Format** menu and then click **AutoFormat**. You can select from a number of formats.

Adding the Subreport Control

You've added controls to forms and reports, so creating a spot for the subreport should be no big deal. You do have to decide which section of the main report you want to use for the subreport.

You can place the subreport in any of the nonrepeating sections of the main report, such as the report header and footer, but it probably makes sense for a subreport that summarizes the information to be placed at the very beginning of the main report. Then when you print out the report, the less detailed report will appear on the first page, with the more detailed breakdown of the data following. Most people won't even leaf through the entire report. They just want to see the overall picture that the subreport provides.

Be Careful Where You Put Your Subreports

Don't place the subreports in the page header or footer sections. These areas are used for information that you want to repeat on every page of the printed report. Report headers and footers make better places for subreports.

So a good place to put the subreport is in the report header of the main report. Expand the header area to accommodate a new control that will hold the subreport. If the report label for the current report resides in the header section, you might want to drag it to the very bottom of the section. Also, if you used the Report Wizard to create the report, there might also be lines that you will want to select and rearrange in the header section.

 To add the control for a subreport, click the Subform/Subreport button on the Toolbox. Drag out a rectangle to accommodate the controls and labels in the subreport. As soon as you place the subreport control in the main report, the SubReport Wizard is activated.

Summarizing at the End

Certainly, there is also a case for placing your summary information (in a subreport) at the end of a larger, more detailed main report. That way, people leafing through all those pages can view a good wrap-up of the data in the ending subreport.

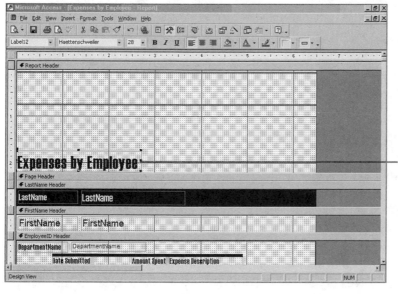

An expanded report header section, with the report title moved to the bottom of the section.

— The report title

You can add an existing report or create a new report to add to the current report.

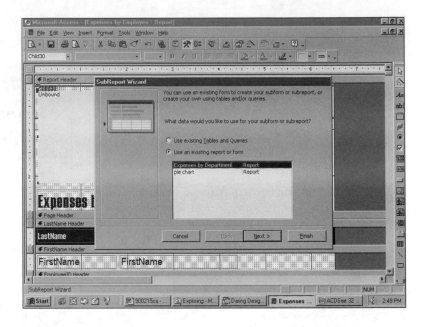

Selecting the Subreport

The SubReport Wizard gives you the option of using an existing report or building a new report for the subreport. If you created a report for this purpose, you would obviously choose the existing one and then click the **Next** button to move to the next step in the process. If you selected to build a new report by using the SubReport Wizard, complete the steps in the report-building process, and you will find that your new report has been placed in the main report.

Obviously, the fact that you can use an existing report or create a new report to use as the subreport places you in the-chicken-or-the-egg situation. If you happen to have a report that you created via the Report Wizard and it's appropriate for the subreport, select it when the SubReport Wizard gives you this option. Otherwise, you must complete all the steps necessary to build a new report that will serve as the subreport.

After you either create a new subreport or choose an already existing report as your subreport and then click **Next**, you are asked whether you want to define any fields that will link the subreport to the main report. The SubReport Wizard even offers several possibilities for this linking, such as Employee ID or other primary keys found in the tables that were used to create the reports. Because we are creating a subreport that summarizes the data found in the main report, we don't really want to link the records in the report (this linking is not unlike the linking found in related tables, where you can view related records by clicking the plus (+) symbol to the left of the current record in a table).

Scroll down through the list of fields supplied by the wizard and select **None** at the bottom of the list. Click the **Next** button to move to the last screen in the subreport creation process. Supply a name for your subreport or leave the name supplied by the wizard (it's the name you gave the subreport when you created it). Click the **Finish** button to conclude the process.

The subreport will appear in the header area of the main report. You can click on the subreport and use its sizing handles to increase its width and height. You can modify the design of the subreport at this point, using any of the tools on the Report Design toolbar.

Too Many Report Titles

When you add a subreport to a main report, the new control that you create will have a label that displays the subreport's name. The subreport will probably also have this name in the report header. Rather than have two titles for the subreport showing in the printed version of this combined report, click the subreport label and then press **Delete** to get rid of it.

Viewing the New Report

You can click the **Report View** button to see the subreport and main report as they now appear in the Print Preview mode. You can always return to Report Design view via the **View** menu if you want to make any modifications to the report design.

Adding Page Breaks to a Report

You might find that when you add a subreport to the beginning of a main report, it forces the main report well down the first page of the printed combined report. It might make sense to push the main report to a second page and allow the subreport to occupy the opening page. Adding page breaks to your reports is quite easy. It's accomplished by using the Page Break tool on the Toolbox.

To add a page break to a report, make sure that you are in Report Design view. Click the Page Break tool in the Toolbox. Place the mouse pointer where you would like to place the page break, and click the left mouse button. A page break symbol will appear on the left side of the section, showing you exactly where the page break falls.

Placing a page break between a subreport and the main report.

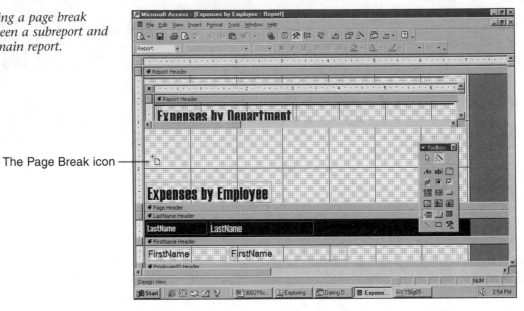

The Page Break icon —

After you've placed your page break (it will appear as a short line of dots on the report in Report Design view), you can view the report in Preview mode to take a look at the changes you've made. When you have completed the design changes to your combined report, make sure to save the changes.

Charting Your Course

You might find that even though your reports are doing a great job summarizing the information found in a particular database, you would really like to add some visual punch to your data. An excellent way to summarize data in a report and provide the reader with a pictorial representation of the information is a chart. Charts can give you a way to track information over time or look at how a certain piece of information relates to the whole. For example, say you would like to show graphically how the expenses for your various departments at Daring Designers compare. You can build a pie chart that shows the percentage of expenses by department and how they relate to the total expenses.

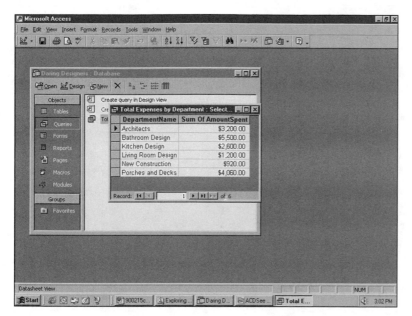

This simple query that totals expenses by departments can be used to create a chart.

When you create the chart, you can print it as a separate report page or place it on another report as a subreport. The Chart Wizard is available in the New Report dialog box to help you create your chart.

To create your new chart, open the database that contains the table or query that you want to base the chart on. For instance, in the case of the Daring Designers database, you would want to base the chart on a query that shows the total expenses by department.

After creating the appropriate query, click the Report icon on the Database window and then click the **New** button. In the New Report dialog box select the **Chart Wizard**. Select the table or query you want to base the chart on in the drop-down list at the bottom of the dialog box (in our example, the **Expenses by Department** query). Click **OK** to continue.

The first screen of the Chart Wizard asks you to select the fields, in the table or query, that contain the data that you want in the chart. Select fields in the Available Field box and add them to the Fields for Chart box. Click **Next** to continue.

Selecting the fields that contain the data you want to include on the chart.

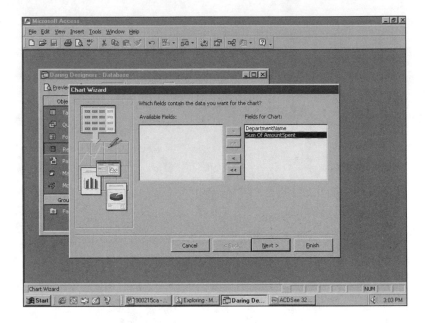

Check This Out

Selecting Fields for the Chart

Most charts that you create from your database data will be simple x, y charts, meaning that they possess two axes. Two-axis charts include line graphs, simple bar charts, and pie charts. The information on the x axis is usually textual, such as the name of an employee or a kind of newt. The y axis contains the related numeric information, such as sales in dollars or number of newts counted.

The next screen asks you to choose the type of chart you want to create. The type of chart you select depends on what you are trying to depict with the chart. For instance, bar charts are best for showing change over time. Pie charts are good for showing how the parts of something relate to the whole. Line charts are good for tracking upward and downward changes during a time period. Click the chart type you want to use (in this case, a pie chart) and then click **Next**.

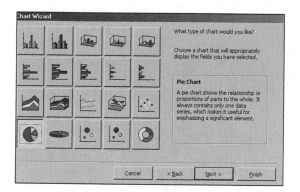

Selecting the type of chart you want to use to depict the data in your table or query.

On the next screen, the Chart Wizard gives you a chance to manipulate how the information will be shown on the chart. You are given the opportunity to place buttons that represent each field in the chart. Fields that contain data represent the y axis of the chart and should be placed on the chart itself. Usually, the x-axis field is placed outside the chart to serve as the series for the chart. For example, on the pie chart that we are creating, the Sum of Expenses field is placed on the chart (remember that we are using a query as the data source for our chart and that in the query the expenses are totaled for each department). The informational field (the button with the name of the department) is placed outside the chart.

The Preview button enables you to look at the chart before moving to the next step. When the chart looks satisfactory, click the **Next** button. The last Chart Wizard screen asks you to name

Do Not Move the Field Markers Unnecessarily

The Chart Wizard does a good job of placing the fields that serve as the various axes for your chart. Do not rearrange the fields if the chart appears to be correct. If you do, your chart will not have the correct axes values and so will not correctly portray the data in the query or table that the chart is based on.

the chart and decide whether you want to include a legend for the chart. Legends provide a way for the viewer of the chart to make sense of the data displayed. Definitely include a legend for pie charts and bar charts. Click the **Finish** button.

The completed chart will appear as a report in the Print Preview window. You can switch to the Design view for the chart by clicking the **View** button on the toolbar. Editing a chart can be kind of a hassle. If you don't like the way the chart turns out, you might find it easier to simply run the wizard again and attempt to create the chart exactly the way you want it.

After the chart is saved as a report, you can print it out or place it on another report as a subreport. As you can see, charts are a great way to summarize your table and query data.

Charts are a great way to visually depict the data in your database.

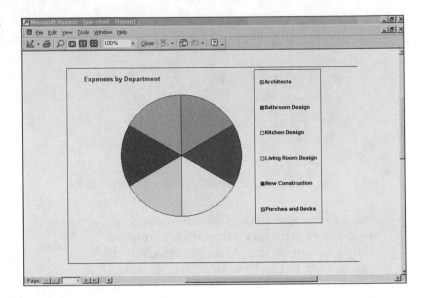

Creating Mailing Labels

You've created single-table reports, multitable reports, multireport reports (subreport and main report), and even charts. Now it's time to tackle a report type—mailing label—that on the surface might seem to be a piece of cake compared to the tables you've already created. Historically, however, mailing labels have been one of the worst nightmares of the database aficionado.

In fact, the hoops that you have had to jump through to create mailing labels, using your database, are probably the main reason that businesses have kept at least one typewriter in their offices. It is easier to type the labels on the typewriter than to create them through the database.

Well, those days of cranky databases are over, and Access provides a very straightforward path for the creation of mailing labels. Yes, you guessed it. There is a Label Wizard that walks you through the process.

To create mailing labels (which is really not-so-secret code for creating a report), you have to have a table or a query to base the report on. Obviously, because you're doing labels to go on envelopes or packages, the records in the table or query must contain all the mailing information you need for each individual.

When you have the appropriate table or query, you're ready to create the labels. Open the database that you want to create the labels from; for example, you might want to create mailing labels for the customers in your Fromage Boutique database. Make sure the **Report** tab is selected in the Database window. Click the **New** button. When the New Report dialog box appears, select **Label Wizard** and then select the table you want to use for the label data in the table drop-down box. Then you can click the **OK** button to start the label creation process.

Selecting the Label Type

The Label Wizard makes it really easy for you to select the right type of label for your report. You don't have to deal with any of that banging-a-square-peg-into-a-round-hole stuff; you select the label type by Avery number (Avery is a label brand name). The Avery number for your labels is on the box or package that the labels came in. Now aren't you sorry that you threw away that box?

A Label Is Only a Label

Avery is one of the largest label-producing companies, and its label sizes (along with other big label manufacturers like the 3M Company) have become the business standard. More than likely the labels that you use for your printer are Avery labels or clones of Avery labels (don't take this as an endorsement of Avery labels—I'm just supplying you with the facts). You will find that even the most bargain-basement generic labels may contain their Avery label number equivalent somewhere on their packaging.

For example, let's say that you want labels for a letter that you are sending to your customers. A commonly used Avery number for envelope labels is 5160—a label that is 1 by 2 5/8 inches. You would select the 5160 label number in the **Avery Number** drop-down list box. After you've selected your label number, all you have to do is select how the labels are fed into the printer—Sheet Feed or Continuous. For laser printers and inkjet printers, you use sheet-fed labels, so you would select **Sheet Feed**.

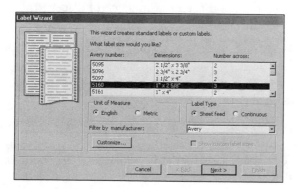

Setting the label parameters in the Label Wizard.

You can also click the **Customize** button and edit the settings for any of the label types. This enables you to use odd-shaped labels or labels that do not have an Avery size equivalent. But be careful—using labels that have an Avery number will make your life a lot easier.

After you've set your label parameters (such as label manufacturer and label size), click the **Next** button to move to the next step.

For the few who still own a dot-matrix printer, a few words should be said about creating mailing labels on one. You might have to edit the user-defined page size before you can create label reports. To edit the paper size and set the default printer, you must enter the Microsoft Windows Control Panel via the **Start** button. In the Control Panel, Double-click the Printers folder and then right-click your printer icon and choose **Properties** on the shortcut menu. In the printer's Properties dialog box, click the **Paper** tab. In the **Paper Size** box, click the Custom icon. In the User Defined dialog box, type the width and length of the label that you will use. After you have set the label parameters, click the **OK** button to exit the dialog box. Avery, 3M, and other label makers still provide tractor feed labels that can be used to print the labels that you create in Access on your dot-matrix printer.

Dressing Up Your Text

"It's better to look good than to feel good," or so Billy Crystal use to say in one of his many odd incarnations on *Saturday Night Live* (yeah, I know that was a long time ago). Unfortunately, in today's business world, appearance can be everything, so it's important that even your mailing labels look good. The next step in the label creation process is to select the look and color of your font.

Access has drop-down boxes that let you choose the font type, the font weight, the font size, and font color. You can also click check boxes to make the characters italic or underlined.

Simple fonts without serifs (such as Arial, for example) are your best bet for mailing labels. You probably should avoid italic as well. The Post Office people can get cranky when you bring in a huge pile of letters and their scanners can't discern the address on the label. They really don't like sorting things by hand.

After you've selected the various font attributes, you can click the **Next** button to continue the process.

Have It Your Way

Now you have to choose what you would like on your label (not your cheeseburger). More than likely, you will want a name and address on a label that you use for mailing. The current Label Wizard screen lists all the fields available in the table or query that you chose to build the labels from.

To add a field to the label, select the field and click the Add button. You can press the spacebar when you have to put a space between fields, such as a first name and a last name field. To drop down a line on the label, press **Enter**.

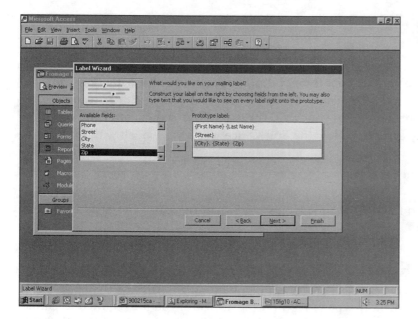

Selecting the fields for the label.

After you've selected the fields for the label, take a look at the prototype label and make sure that you have all the fields you need. If things looks good, you can advance to the next step.

Order in the Sort

Now the Label Wizard would like to know whether you would like to sort the labels by a particular field or fields. Sorting the records enables you to print the labels in a particular order. For instance, if you want to get the cheaper bulk rate on your mailing, you might want to sort the labels by zip code. Other possibilities are also available, such as sorting the labels by last name and then first name (in case you have more than one customer with the same last name).

Bulking Up

You might want to contact your local post office and find out exactly how you should format and sort your mailing labels. Different bulk mailing rates require you to do different things with your mail. For example, a comma after the city used to be widely accepted. Now the Post Office wants your labels with spaces only, no commas.

After you've selected the field or fields you want to sort the labels by, click the **Next** button to continue.

The End of the Road

The last step in the label creation process will look quite familiar. It is the final screen you get when you create any type of report using a wizard. You are required to either name the report (yes, remember, labels are a form of report) or use the name that the wizard has assigned to the report. You also have the choice of viewing the report (in this case, mailing labels) as it prints or going directly to Report Design view to modify the report.

If you chose your mailing label size correctly, you will probably find that the field information fits just fine on the label; you might want to go directly to Print Preview. More than likely, your labels look marvelous. But you might have one little problem....

But the Post Office Wants All Caps

The newest edict by that fine government institution, the Post Office, is that mailing addresses should appear in all uppercase characters. Your mailing labels probably are not uppercase. I mean, you didn't think to set up your tables in all caps, so now you're stuck.

Well, not really, you can modify the report so that the labels print out in uppercase characters. To do this, you simply add an input mask to each control in the mailing label report.

Make sure that you're in Report Design view. Then click the first control in the mailing label report. Now you have to access the Properties box for all the selected controls, so click the **Properties** button on the toolbar. Click the **All** tab of the Properties box and then place the insertion point in the **Input Mask** box.

There isn't a built-in input mask that will change your control's characters to uppercase, so you have to build one from scratch. It's actually easy. The > (greater than) sign is used to tell Access to put things in uppercase. Type a > in the **Input Mask** box. Then you have to specify the number of characters that should be made uppercase. The ? serves as a wildcard character for one text character. Type in enough question marks (after the > sign) to accommodate the longest control entry (it might be a person's name or street address).

In Case of Uppercase

You can also set up input masks for uppercase data entry in your tables or forms.

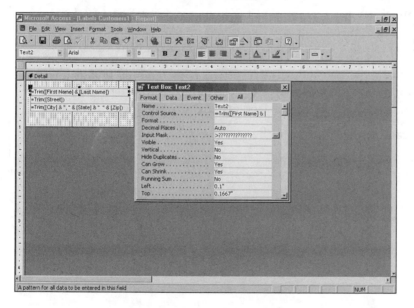

Designing an input mask for uppercase characters.

You must set up this uppercase input mask for each control in the mailing label report. Select each one and then follow the procedure outlined above. After you've set up the input mask for uppercase characters for all the controls, you can preview your new improved report. See, mailing labels can be fun.

All Out of Breath

Wow! This report saga has gone on and on and on. It just shows how important reports are to your databases. You can design great tables, set up super relationships, and create incredible queries, but if you can't print a simple report, no one will be able to appreciate all your hard work. And don't forget, reports can be a lot of fun.

The Least You Need to Know

➤ You can place a subreport on a main report, which enables you to show two different takes on the data. The subreport can be a summary of the data, and the main report can supply all the details.

➤ Depending on how elaborate your report is, you can place strategic page breaks between the various elements of the report. This enables you to control how the information prints out.

➤ You can create charts as a type of report. You create a chart based on data found in a particular table or query. Charts can be placed on other reports as subreports and provide a visual representation of your database data.

➤ The Label Wizard walks you through the mailing label creation process. All you need up front is a table that provides the data to the wizard and the Avery label number from the box of labels that you are going to use.

➤ Input masks can be used to change the way the data in your report controls print.

Chapter 16

All the News That's Fit to Print

In This Chapter

➤ Printing your database objects

➤ Selecting your printer

➤ Setting all those annoying printer properties

➤ Dealing with page setup

➤ Using the spell-checking feature

Have you ever been in a meeting where the participants are poring over a laser-printed copy of a report that they all believe to be the last word on the subject, when suddenly one of your coworkers points out an obvious error on one of the pages (at the very least, it's a typo; at the most, it's the result of a formula that doesn't even come close to the correct answer). If it's your report, you look for an open window to jump out, and if it's not, you thank your lucky stars and hope that this never happens to you.

It Might Look Good, But Is It Right?

In the realm of printouts, databases have come a very long way from the prehistoric software packages of yesteryear (which is only about three years ago). Think about it: Access enables you to design extremely professional-looking reports and forms. Even the tables and queries look good. Back in the old days, you were lucky if you could get your output into rows and columns.

Couple the desktop publishing capabilities of Access with the inexpensive laser printers and color inkjet printers available today, and it's easy to make your printed materials look like a million bucks. However, no matter how good your work looks, it's not worth a tinker's cuss (which is roughly equivalent to a wooden nickel) if the information isn't accurate.

This means that you must be extremely careful when you enter your data and extremely thoughtful and methodical when you design your mathematic expressions, reports, or queries. Knowing that exactitude is as important to you as it is to me, I'll get off my soapbox and help you tackle the real subject matter of this chapter—printing your database objects.

A Word About Reports and Your Other Database Objects

We've already spent some time discussing the printing of reports (don't tell me you skipped those interesting and pithy chapters on the subject). As I have said on more than one occasion, reports are the ideal format for printing your database information, and because of this, Access provides you with a set of very flexible report design features.

On occasion, however, you will want to print just a table or a form, maybe even a macro—nothing fancy. You merely need a hard copy. For example, you might want to send a printout of a table to a coworker for proofreading, or you might want to show off an incredible form that you designed for data entry. Access provides you with a couple of ways to put these objects on a printed page.

Quickly Printing a Database Object

The fastest way to print a database object is to select the object in the Database Explorer window. After the object (such as a table) is selected, click the **Print** button. Your database object will be sent to the printer.

Design View's Hard Copy

You can also print forms and reports in their Design views. Open the form or report in Design view, and then click the **Print** button.

Printing an object this way sends to the printer the information currently selected in your Windows setup. If you want more control over the print job, such as which printer you will print to or what paper size you would like to use, you must follow another route to printing: using the **Print** command on the **File** menu.

As you already know, headers and footers are areas where you place information that you want to appear on either the top or bottom of every page of a printout. When you print tables, forms, and queries, the printouts are automatically assigned headers and footers. The header information consists of the table or form name and the current date. The footer information consists of the appropriate page numbers.

Using the Print Dialog Box

When you choose the **File** menu and then choose the **Print** command, the Print dialog box appears.

Previewing Your Print Jobs

You can preview the printout of any of your database objects by clicking the Print Preview button on the Database or object–specific toolbar (such as the Table toolbar). Use the mouse pointer to zoom in and out on your object in the Print Preview window.

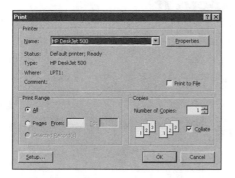

The Print dialog box enables you to select your printer and print range.

The Print dialog box enables you to select certain print parameters, such as the printer you would like to use for the current print job. It also gives you control over the print range and printer properties.

Selecting a Printer

Depending on your home or office situation, you might have your computer connected to more than one printer (especially if you are on a network). The Print dialog box has a drop-down box listing all the printers that you have access to. To select a printer other than the current printer, click the drop-down arrow and choose your printer from the list. After you choose the correct printer, click **OK** to send the print job to the printer.

Corralling Those Pages on the Range

The Print dialog box also enables you to select the range to be printed. This range can consist of a page, a group of specific pages in a sequence, or all the pages in the database object. To print a single page, click the **Pages** radio button and type the page number in the **From** box. This set of steps is also used to specify a page range, with the only additional step being the typing in of the end of the page range in the **To** box.

You can also print a set of specific records by selecting the records in the table before invoking the Print command. This is a great way to get a hard copy of important or new records that you would like to look over or verify.

Getting the Deed to Your Print Properties

The Print dialog box also gives you control over the print properties associated with the current printer. These properties range from the paper size you want to use to the print quality of the output from the printer.

When you click the **Properties** button in the Print dialog box, the Properties dialog box for the currently selected printer appears. This dialog box contains three tabs: Paper, Graphics, and Device Options.

Paper! Paper! Read All About It!

Obviously, you are going to use different paper sizes when you set up your print jobs. For example, you might have a report that you want to place on one 8 1/2- by 14-inch legal sheet of paper rather than spread it over two 8 1/2- by 11-inch sheets. Or you might have your printout set up to place names and addresses right on envelopes rather than to print out sheet-fed labels.

The Paper tab of the Properties box gives you control over paper size and page orientation.

The Paper tab of the Properties dialog box enables you to select the different paper sizes and types (such as regular sheet versus envelopes). This tab also gives you the option of printing in portrait or landscape and enables you to set the paper source.

Remember, for a standard sheet of paper, portrait orientation is 8 1/2×11 inches, and landscape orientation is 11 by 8 1/2 inches.

You Don't Have to Be Graphic...

...but your graphics have to look good. The Graphic tab of the Properties dialog box is where you set the options for how the graphic elements in your database objects print.

The dots per inch available for printing graphics vary from printer to printer. The highest setting for most older printers is 300 dpi (dots per inch). However, a number of inexpensive inkjet and laser printers now print at 600 dpi (or even higher) in both color and grayscale.

When You Go too Far—Restoring Defaults

If you really mess up the settings for how your graphics print, click the **Restore Defaults** button in the **Graphics** tab to put everything back the way it was before you starting going wild on the graphic print parameters.

The Graphics tab gives you control over the resolution (the intensity of the image produced by the dots per inch printed) of the graphic, the dithering of the graphic (how the colors or shades of gray are blended), and the intensity (the degree of lightness and darkness) of the graphic.

All the settings in the Print Properties dialog box are global settings. When you change these, you affect all the potential print jobs that you will print from all your various software packages. So be careful.

You Always Have Options

The third tab on the Print Properties dialog box is Device Options. This tab gives you control over the print quality of your print jobs and can be used to increase the speed at which the printer operates. Increasing your printer's speed from the normal setting to a faster setting (in most cases, there is only one other setting—fast) can negatively affect the quality of your print job. So you might not have as many options as you think, where print jobs are concerned.

After you set the various parameters and possibilities in the Print Properties dialog box, you can click the **OK** button to close the dialog box and return to the Print dialog box.

Give Me a Break!

You can print each record, group, or section of a report or form on a separate page by using the form or report property sheet. To access the property sheet, double-click the section selector when you are in Form or Report Design view. In the property sheet, you can select several ForceNewPage properties for the section, such as placing a page break before the section or after the section.

After you have selected your printer and the print range and have set the printer properties, you're ready to print. To send the job to the printer, click the **OK** button in the Print dialog box.

Breaking the Code—Printing Your Macro Design Information

One thing that I should probably discuss before bringing this discussion of printing database objects to a close is the printing out of your macros. You can actually print a kind of minireport that details the actions you have placed in a particular macro. Open the macro in Design view or select the macro in the Database window. Click the **Print** or **Print Preview** button.

SEE ALSO

> You can find much more information on working with Access macros in Chapter 21, "The Little Engines That Can—Making Macros."

Access will start the Database Documentor, a feature that gives you detailed information on the design of your various database objects. The Print Macro Definition dialog box will appear, giving you a set of check boxes that offer you the option of precluding certain information. There is a check box for the macro's properties, its actions and arguments, and its permissions.

The Print Macro Definition dialog box lets you decide what information should be included in the documentation report.

After you've designated the information you want to include in the macro documentation report, click the **OK** button. The results of the documentation will go either to the printer or to Print Preview.

The Database Documentor Is Always Ready and Willing

You can use the Database Documentor to detail any of your database objects' design. The Database Documentor is particularly useful for documenting the macros and Visual Basic applications (modules) that you create. To document a database object, choose the **Tools** menu, point to **Analyze**, and then choose **Documentor**.

Are You Setting Me Up?

If your database object is small—for example, a table holding only a few records or a short summary report that definitely fits on one page—you probably aren't that concerned about how the printout will be affected by such things as margins or page orientation. However, when you print a large object such as a long report or a multipage form, you might want to change the margins and select the page orientation.

To access the Page Setup dialog box, choose the **File** menu and choose **Page Setup**. The Page Setup dialog box enables you to set margins and page and column parameters for your forms and reports.

The Page Setup dialog box enables you to set the parameters for printing great-looking reports and forms.

The Margins tab of the Page Setup dialog box enables you to set the margins for your printout and also to determine whether you want the column headings in your datasheet to print out (the Print Data Only check box).

The Page tab enables you to select the paper size, paper orientation, and the printer that should be used for this particular print job. The source of the paper, such as a special feeder for labels or special paper (envelopes), can also be selected in this tab.

The Columns tab gives you control over the grid settings in a multicolumn report or form. You can select the row spacing, as well as the column size, in the final printout.

Is It Just Resting or Is It Dead?

So we've covered all our bases, and you will never have a problem printing any of your database objects, right? Wrong! A time will come when you click in all the right places and still don't get a printout. When this happens, there's a chance that something weird is going on with the printer or your connection to the printer. Yes, it could be a hardware problem. So when your printer seems to be doing something more than just resting, consult this short troubleshooting list to get your print jobs back online:

➤ Make sure the printer is on and online (I know you already checked this).

➤ Make sure there is paper in the printer or that paper isn't jammed.

➤ Make sure that you are looking for your printout at the right printer (which printer did you print to?).

➤ Check your printer cable. Is it still connected to the printer?

➤ Make sure that the printer contains an ink cartridge or toner cartridge that's actually got some ink or toner in it.

➤ Scream for your network administrator and make up a story about how that particular printout is for the big, big boss.

➤ Go to lunch and then see whether anyone fixes the printer problem while you're gone.

Spelling It Out

Because accuracy was one of the themes of the opening paragraphs in this chapter, it makes sense to take a moment and discuss the spell-checking feature available in Access. Most errors in a database are introduced during data entry, so it makes sense to try and catch these errors in the beginning.

The spell-checking feature, obviously, cannot check the numeric information that you input or help you enter proper names, but it might help you avoid embarrassing typos and misspellings. Let's take a look at how you would spell-check one of your Access database tables.

Typos Are Nasty

Although a spelling feature is not as crucial to a database as it is to a word processor, it can help cut down on your data entry problems by catching misspelled words.

Using the Spell-Checking Feature

To spell-check the information in a table, query, or form, make sure you have the appropriate item open. Click the Spelling button on the currently available toolbar or choose the **Tools** menu and then choose **Spelling**.

The Spelling dialog box appears, and words flagged as misspelled appear inside it. A list of suggestions also appears; it lets you choose a correctly spelled form of the word. You use the **Add** button to add words to the dictionary. If Access flags a name or a word that is not in the dictionary but is correctly spelled, you can either add the word to the dictionary or click the **Ignore** button to ignore the word and continue with the spell check.

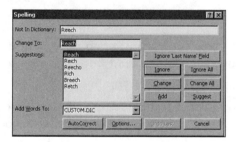

Using the spell-checking feature in Access.

In the Spelling window is also a button that enables you to bypass the current field. This is great if you want to ignore entire fields in a table and still continue the spell-check process.

Be Politically Correct with AutoCorrect

Well, not really, but Access has another great feature that will help you cut down on typos: AutoCorrect. AutoCorrect replaces common errors as you type. You can even add commons errors that you make and their correct spellings so that AutoCorrect will fix them as well. To set up AutoCorrect to work as you enter information into your tables and forms, choose the **Tools** menu and then choose **AutoCorrect**. Select the **Replace Text as You Type** box, and you are good to go!

Closing the Curtain

As we bring our little tale of printing and proofing to a close, I want to take one last opportunity to bug you about your database data. Don't print it out if it isn't right. Databases are supposed to be a collection of facts. Enough said.

The Least You Need to Know

➤ You can print any of your database objects; just open or select the object and then let fly with the Print command via the Print button on the toolbar or the Print command on the File menu.

➤ All your print parameters, both global and object specific can be set via the Print dialog box. To access this box, choose the **File** menu and choose the **Print** command.

➤ The Print Preview command can save you a lot of paper. It makes sense to preview your print jobs before you send them to the printer and kill another tree.

➤ The page margins and other page attributes for a print job are controlled by the Page Setup dialog box.

➤ Not all your print problems are software problems. Check out your hardware when you can't seem to get that database object to print.

Part 4

Expanding Your Database Brain Power

You are probably feeling really good about all the database knowledge that you've crammed in your head via this witty, yet kindly text. Your fingers dance over the keyboard as you work with your database objects; you're really using your head to design databases of epic proportions and ultimate simplicity.

Suddenly, as you work with Access, you slam up against a mental brick wall; you happen upon a feature that you have no knowledge of. Well, fear not, this book hasn't gasped out its last breath yet, and we are going to take a look at some of the more advanced features and concepts that you might have to deal with as you build your databases. Want to know how to import data from other software packages? to password protect your files so that no one can access them (except you)? and how to customize the Access application window to your own liking? Then turn the page, and expand your database brain power!

Chapter 17

OLE—Taking the Bull Out of Object Linking and Embedding

In This Chapter

➤ Understanding the ins and outs of object linking and embedding

➤ Placing an OLE field in a table

➤ Embedding an object (a picture) in a table and then viewing it in a form

➤ Placing an Excel chart in an Access report

"Woolly bully, woolly bully, woolly bully…." Oh, hi, I'm just getting in the mood for this exciting chapter on OLE. (And wondering what ever happened to Sam the Sham and the Pharaohs. You know, I think the Bangles did a cover of "Wooly Bully," and they've dropped off the edge of the earth, too!) Ever seen those video clips on the news of the annual bull run in Pamplona, Spain? It is utter chaos, people screaming and running everywhere—the same kind of hysterics that breaks out when you're sitting around the office and someone mentions the mystical acronym *OLE*.

What Is OLE?

OLE stands for *object linking and embedding,* which are two ways to take items created in any number of applications and place them into your current application—in our case, Microsoft Access. The application where these items, or *objects,* are created is called the *source application* in the case of linking and the *server* application in the case of embedding. The application that you place the object in (whether linking or embedding) is called the *destination application* (sometimes it's called the *container application*), and, of course, in our case this is (yes, you guessed it) Microsoft Access.

Database Objects Versus Linked or Embedded Objects

You are already familiar with database objects—things such as tables, forms, queries, and reports. These types of objects enable you to manipulate and store your data. A linked or embedded object is a little different. It can be a graphic, a video clip, a sound, a spreadsheet, or a chart—you name it. You can link or embed any item that originates from an application that follows the Microsoft Windows OLE rules.

Techno Talk

The Object of Your Objects

The word *object* is probably one of the most overused in the computer lexicon. *Object* is used to describe database objects (but you already knew that), certain kinds of programming, and items linked or embedded into applications. Make sure that whenever you see the word *object* used as a computer term, you determine the particular context in which it's being used.

Linked or embedded objects can be placed in your database objects. For instance, you can place an OLE field in a table and store linked or embedded photos of your employees in that particular field, or you can place an embedded or linked chart in a report to help your clients understand a complex set of statistics. Whatever you place in your database objects via OLE, you should be aware of the differing natures of linking and embedding. The big question is whether you should link or embed. There is a difference.

To Link or Embed—That Is the Question

When you link an object to your database, you are creating a connection between the source application file and Access. The object does not reside in the Access database file but is represented there by a linking code. When you have to update the file, you do so in the original source application, and the results of the update can be seen in the Access database. For instance, you can link a Microsoft Excel chart to an Access report. When you activate the chart with a double click, its source application is started (Microsoft Excel), and the file is opened in it.

The great thing about links is that you can have the same object linked to several destinations. When you update the file in its source application, the file is updated in all the places that it is linked to. Another cool thing about linking is that the object is not stuffed into the destination file (it resides outside it as a separate file, remember?), so a linked object does not greatly increase the size of the destination file. The file doesn't become bloated, making it easier to handle.

Embedding gives you the same results as linking but is kind of the flip side of the coin. An embedded object does become part of the destination file, increasing the file's size. It is basically a transplanted copy of the original file. Because the embedded file resides in the destination file, updating the original file in the original application does not update the embedded copy.

One really wild thing about embedded objects is that they are *dynamic*, meaning they can be manipulated and updated right in the destination application. When you activate an embedded object, the server application opens in a window inside the destination application. In many cases, the menu system of the server application temporarily replaces that of the destination application, so in essence, you are running the server application from inside the destination application.

A good example of this would be an Excel chart embedded in an Access report. Double-click the embedded chart, and the Access menus and toolbars are temporarily replaced by the Excel menus and toolbars. You edit the object, and when you click outside the object window, the menus and toolbars of your destination application are returned to you.

You might be asking, "When do I link and when do I embed?" The answer to this depends on the object that you want to link or embed in your Access database. Objects, such as spreadsheets built in Excel or reports written in Word, that are dynamic (the information in them is updated constantly) are best linked to Access. This enables you to update the object in the application you created it in and still have the current results linked to your database objects, such as a report or form.

Objects such as scanned photos or video clips of your vacation, which are static and not updated over time, can be embedded into your Access database. This makes the object part of the database file. For instance, you may place scanned photos in an Access table field.

OLE Ready

All the applications in Microsoft Office 2000 are totally OLE compliant. This means that you can link and embed objects between Access, Word, Excel, PowerPoint, and Office utilities such as Microsoft Chart 9.

Now that you have some of the OLE theory down, take a look at how easy it is to link and embed. You will start with an OLE field in a table.

Working in the ~~Oil~~ OLE Field

You've already worked with tables, so you know how to design the fields that hold your data. Linked and embedded objects (OLE objects) are basically the same as any other data type. You treat them no differently than a person's address or Social Security number. You build a field and place the data (in this case, an object) in it.

Say you want to build a table that will hold information on a set of vacation photos. To make it even more interesting, your photos have been scanned into your computer as Windows bitmap images.

Using Graphics of All Kinds

Graphics can come in a number of file formats. You can tell the particular format by the file's extension: Windows bitmap (.bmp), AutoCAD Format 2-D (.dxf), Computer Graphics Metafile (.cgm), CorelDRAW (.cdr), encapsulated PostScript (.eps), HP graphics language (HPGL), Kodak Photo CD (.pcd), PC Paintbrush (.pcx), and Tagged Image File Format (.tif), to name a few.

To create an OLE object field in a table, open the table in Design view. Click in an empty field row and then name the field. For example, if you were designing the field for bitmap pictures of your vacation photos, you might call the field Scan of Photo.

Selecting the Data Type for the Field

Now comes the hard part. You have to exercise your free will and make a choice. After you type in the field name, either press the **Tab** key or click in the **Data Type** box for the new field. Click the drop-down arrow and select **OLE Object** from the list.

That's all there is to it. You made a field that will hold OLE objects. Now you have to figure out how to get the objects into the field.

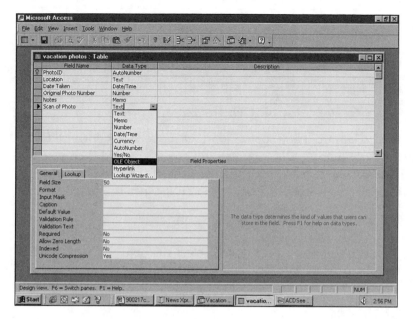

Setting the data type for the OLE field.

Insert Object Here

To insert OLE objects into a table, you must be in Datasheet view, which should make total sense because that's the table view that you use when you enter data. Make sure that you save the table design before you switch to Datasheet view. Click in the field you want to place the object in (remember that it must be an OLE field). Now you can insert the object: Click the **Insert** menu and then click **Object**.

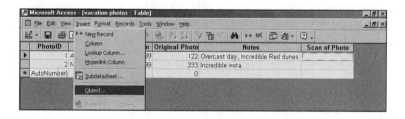

Getting ready to insert an OLE object into a table.

As soon as you invoke the Insert Object command, the Insert Object dialog box appears. A wide range of object types are available in the object list. You can probably find an object type for nearly every piece of software you have installed on your computer.

To Paste or Not to Paste

You can link or embed objects from any application that supports Windows OLE. For applications that do not support OLE, you can still copy items and then paste them into Access. These pasted items do not have the dynamic character of OLE objects; you cannot update one without pasting a revised file into the field.

Select the object type that you want to use. After you select the object type, you have to decide whether to create a new object or use an existing one.

New or Vintage Objects

The great thing about OLE is that you can use an object that already exists, such as a picture or a graph, or you can create one on-the-fly. For instance, say you want to embed a picture (a bitmap) into your table.

If you select the **Create New** radio button and then click **OK**, you are whisked into Windows Paint (or the application that creates the OLE type you've selected) and given the opportunity to create a brand-spanking-new object.

In the dialog box is also a check box that, if selected, displays the OLE object as an icon (an icon related to the server or source application) instead of a full-blown representation of itself. If you select the **Create from File** radio button, you have the opportunity to select a currently existing file to be placed in the field.

Say that you want to create the object from an existing file. Click the **Create from File** radio button. The dialog box changes. A Browse button appears that enables you to look for and specify the file to use as the object. A Link check box (if checked) allows you to link the picture object to the database table rather than embed the picture into the Access table.

When you click the **Browse** button, a dialog box appears that gives you the ability to look through the directories on your computer and select the file you want to embed or link. After you select the file, click the **OK** button. When you are practicing linking and embedding graphics in your Access tables, you can use any of the images included with your Office and Access 97 software. However, if you have a scanner, you might want to create your own images to place into the database.

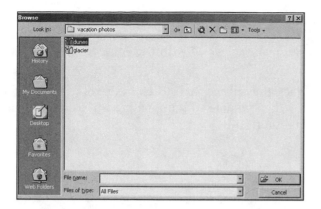

Selecting the file to embed in or link to the Access table.

You will be returned to the Insert Object dialog box. The name of the file that you selected appears in the File box. The application that the file was created in also appears above the file name if it can be readily identified via the file extension.

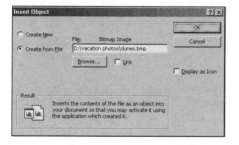

Ready to embed the object.

Click the **OK** button to embed (or link) the object. You cannot see the actual object in the table field; a file type name appears, designating it. For instance, a bitmap image would say *Bitmap Image*. An Excel spreadsheet would be tagged as *Microsoft Excel Worksheet*.

For example, in our vacation pictures database, the images are bitmap images (.bmp files), so the field contains the words *Bitmap Image*. The application associated with bitmap files in Windows is Microsoft Paint (or some other graphics package; file associations depend on the software that you've installed on your computer).

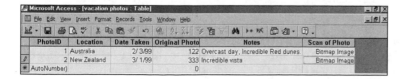

Embedded bitmaps in a sample vacation photos database.

To view the object, double-click the field. This starts the source or server application (in this case, Microsoft Paint). You can even edit the objects after you have entered the application. Any changes you make are saved with the embedded or linked object.

In the case of an embedded object, the changes are stored in the object itself, which now resides in the Access table. When you are working with a linked object, the changes are stored in the original source file.

When Linking and Embedding...

Remember that when you are working with embedded and linked objects, the embedded object becomes part of the target application (making the database file larger). The linked object remains outside the application and is represented only in the database table, form, or report.

You can edit and update the OLE objects that you link into your tables and other database objects. Click the **Edit** menu and then click **OLE/DDE Links**. A list of the current links is displayed in a dialog box. This dialog box can be used to update links if files have been moved or to replace current links with new links.

Have Your Object and See It, Too

A great way to view the objects that you embed or link into a table is to design a form for the table. In Form view, you can see the embedded objects.

When you create the form, make sure that it has a control bound to the OLE object field in the table (see Chapter 9, "It's All in Your Form," for more information). You might have to edit the size of the control box in the form to accommodate the object's size. You can do this easily by sizing the control in Design view and then switching to Form view to see the results.

Just a reminder. By using the Form Wizard, you can create your form—from scratch in Design view or by clicking the New Object button on the toolbar and selecting **Autoform**. If you select the OLE field as one of the fields for the form in the Form Wizard, you are automatically given the appropriate control. This also holds true for Autoform, which uses all the fields in the table to create the form. If you want to build the control from scratch, you should use the Bound Object Frame button in the Toolbox.

Paste Special Is Very Special

Another way to link an object to a field, a form, or a report control is to open the source application and copy the object to the Windows Clipboard. Open the destination table (or form or report) in Access and then click the **Edit** menu and select **Paste Special**. In the Paste Special dialog box, select the object and then click **OK** to paste it.

In this example, each form created for the table would display a graphic of a particular vacation photograph. As you can see (if you're viewing your objects), linking and embedding objects into tables and forms is quite easy.

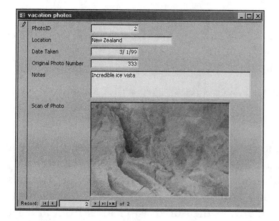

Viewing an OLE object in a form.

Placing an Excel Chart in Access

Another OLE object that you will probably get a lot of mileage out of is the *chart*, a graphical representation of your data. You already know from our discussion of objects that you can build a chart in any number of applications, such as Excel, and then embed it into an Access database form or report.

If you don't have Excel or would like to create your chart without leaving Access, however, you can create extremely professional-looking charts and graphs because of the mini-application Microsoft Chart 9.

Building Your Graphs with Chart 9

Chart 9 ships with Microsoft Office 2000 and each of the Office components (Access, Excel, PowerPoint, and Word), if you purchase them separately. When you install Access or Office, you must make sure that you also install Chart 9. (For more about installing Access, see Appendix A, "Installing Access 2000.")

SEE ALSO

> *If you prefer to create your charts from within Access, you can use Microsoft Chart 9. In Chapter 15, "Pride of Ownership—Enhancing Your Reports," see the section "Charting Your Course."*

Checking Out the Chart

Excel lends itself nicely to the analysis of data. It's not an uncommon practice to take information in an Access table and export it to Excel for analysis. (See Chapter 18, "Imports and Exports—Moving and Sharing Data," for information on exporting Access data.)

To embed a chart from Excel into an Access report, we will assume that there is an Excel worksheet based on data in an Access table and that a chart has been created. When the chart is available in Excel, it's easy to link the chart into an Access report.

Say that you've been doing a study at a lake near your house. You've been tracking the fluctuation of the water level and the turbidity of the water (how cloudy the water is) through the spring and summer. You've created a database that has a table for water level and one for turbidity. You've also created an Excel worksheet that tracks the average water level (you always measured water level from at least three sites). This Excel worksheet also contains a chart of the average water levels for April through August. The chart in Excel serves as the object.

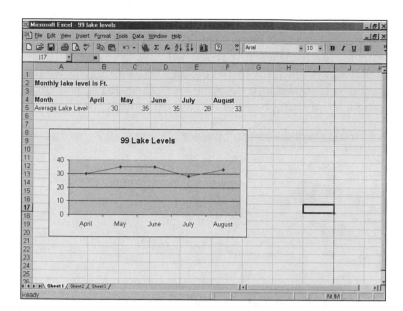

You can easily embed information from an application such as Excel (an Excel chart) into an Access report.

Techno Talk

Embedding and Linking as a Way of Life

The procedures discussed in this section for embedding an Excel chart into an Access report work for nearly any OLE object type. You can also link objects from Microsoft PowerPoint, Microsoft Word, and any other application that follows the Windows OLE rules (which is 99% of the applications that run in the Windows environment).

You would like to embed the Excel chart on average water levels into a report that you are doing in Access in the lake study database (it makes sense that the report would be in your lake study database). You could create the Access report in Design view or by using the Report Wizard. (For information on creating reports, see Chapter 13, "From Soup to Nuts—Creating Delicious Reports," Chapter 14, "No Need for a Calculator—Doing Math in Reports," and Chapter 15.) After you have completed the report, open it in Design view.

Now you can open Excel (or any application that you want to link from). Just click the **Start** button, point at **Programs**, and then select the Excel icon from the Programs menu (or the icon for the application that you will link from). Select the text, chart, or other item that you want to use as the object. In this case, you would select the Excel chart that you will embed into the Access report (in Excel, just click on the chart to select it, and a set of sizing handles will appear around the chart).

Selecting the item (in this case, the Excel chart) that you will embed into your Access report.

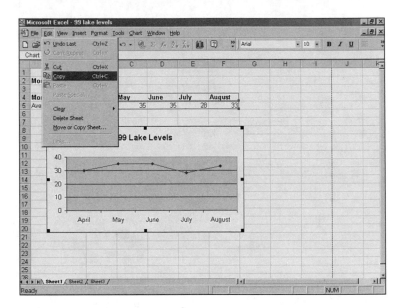

After you've selected the object that you will link, it's just a matter of copying the item to the Windows Clipboard. Surprised? Yes, linking begins with the easiest of tasks: copying an item. Select the **Edit** menu and then select **Copy**. This places the object on the Windows Clipboard. In Excel, a marquee appears around any item (such as the chart) that you've copied to the Windows Clipboard.

Now you're ready to return to the report. If you have Access already up and running and the report is in Design view, all you have to do is click the button for the report on the Windows taskbar. If Access isn't up and running, start Access. Open the appropriate database and then open the appropriate report in Design view.

Pasting the Excel Chart into a Report

Okay, you're only a couple steps away from seeing your Excel chart in the Access report. Remember that the whole point of adding the chart to the report is to graphically summarize the data. Most people relate better to graphs than to columns and columns of numbers.

You will probably want to make a place for the chart in the report header area. This places the chart (summarizing the information) right on the top of the report's first page.

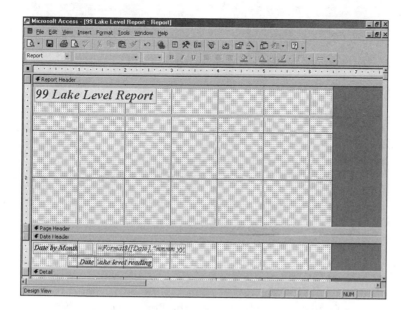

Making a place in your report for the embedded chart or other object.

Where's the Chart?

Now all you have to do is paste the chart into the report. If you are going to place the chart in a specific area of the report, such as the header area, make sure that you click the title bar for the area. This ensures that the chart will end up in the appropriate place on the report.

To place the chart in the report, click the **Edit** menu and then click **Paste**. The chart appears in your report. Notice that sizing handles appear around the chart. You can use the mouse to drag the chart to the appropriate position in your specific report area.

Using Your Imagination

When you are working with a report in Design view, try to imagine how things will look on the printed page and place your controls and objects accordingly. If you have trouble imagining things, just cheat and switch to Print Preview mode to take a quick look at how your page design is shaping up.

The Excel chart appears in the Access report.

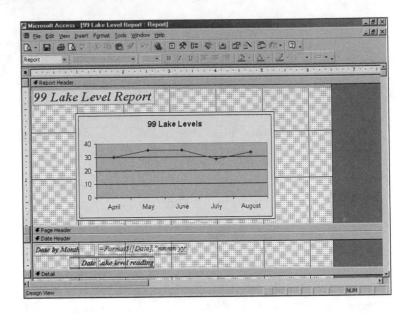

A Chart with a View

Now that the chart is embedded in the report, you can view the report in Print Preview mode. Click the Preview Mode button on the Report Design toolbar.

You can use the various buttons on the Preview toolbar to zoom in and out on your report. If you find that you would like to reposition the chart in the report, return to Design view by clicking the Design View button on the toolbar. After you make changes to the report, return to the Preview window to take a look at your work.

The report in Print Preview view shows the chart in the report as it will appear on the printed page.

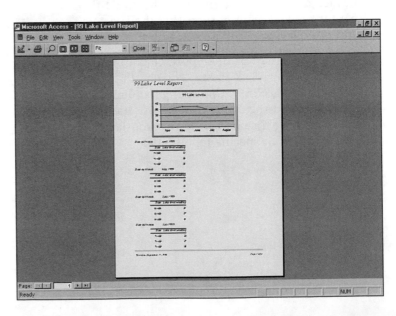

Editing the Chart

Even though you have been expending your brain cells on placing the chart in the report, I don't want you to forget the core subject matter of this chapter—linking and embedding. You can edit the embedded charts (or other objects) that you place in your reports or form, and it's just a matter of a double click.

Make sure that you are in the Design view of your report. Then double-click your embedded chart. Wait a second (watch the Access toolbar buttons), and all the toolbars will change to the Excel toolbars. You are, in effect, still in Microsoft Access, but because the embedded (and now activated) object was created in Excel, you are now provided with all the functionality of Microsoft Excel. Is this embedding stuff great, or what?

You can now edit the chart as if you were in Excel. For instance, say that you would like to change the type of chart from a line graph to a bar chart. No problem.

Click the Chart Wizard button on the Excel toolbar (remember, it's the Excel toolbar while you are editing the embedded Excel object, the chart). The Chart Wizard dialog box appears. To change the chart type, select a new type from the Chart Type list. Because you're only interesting in changing the chart type, click the **Finish** button at the bottom of the Chart Wizard.

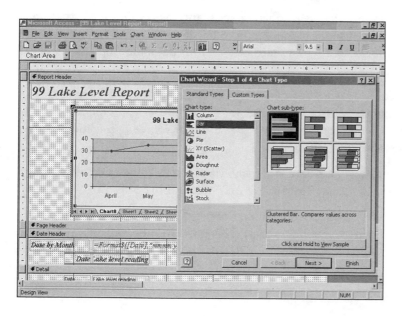

You can edit the embedded object by double-clicking it.

Whenever you edit the embedded object, make sure that you save the changes to your report. Remember that embedded objects become a part of database file. Click the Save button on the toolbar to save the edited report.

After you make changes to an embedded object, check out how the report looks in Print Preview view. If you don't like the changes that you've made or you want to make additional changes, switch back to Design view. Remember that because the object was embedded in the Access report, changes that you make to the object (the chart) won't affect the original Excel chart in the Excel workbook file.

You as Matador

As you can see, you can use OLE for many things in your databases. You can link or embed various objects in your tables, and you can place objects in your reports or forms. The OLE capabilities of Access enable you to create very complex and rich database objects. Although you might not get rich from your databases, your data will certainly be visually compelling—no bull!

The Least You Need to Know

➤ OLE objects are items, such as graphics, graphs, and even video clips, that are created in other applications. Access adheres to all the OLE rules, so you can link or embed just about anything into one of your database objects.

➤ Linking and embedding are pretty much flip sides of the same coin. An embedded object resides inside your database file, making it bigger, and a linked object remains outside your database file. Whether you embed or link, you can create the file from scratch via the server or source application, or you can use a previously existing file.

➤ A great way to portray your data is visually, via a chart. You can create a chart in Microsoft Excel and then embed it in an Access report or form.

➤ Your charts (or other embedded or linked objects) can be quickly edited by double-clicking on the embedded chart. This starts the server application, programs such as Microsoft Excel. You can then edit the object in its native application.

Chapter 18

Imports and Exports—Moving and Sharing Data

In This Chapter

➤ Importing an Excel worksheet into Access

➤ Analyzing data by using the Analyzer Wizard

➤ Normalizing a flat file database by splitting the data into multiple tables

➤ Sharing Access data with other applications, such as Microsoft Word and Excel

By now, you probably have a pretty good feel for the internal workings of Microsoft Access and understand how to use the various database objects to manipulate your data. Unfortunately, not all the data that you end up working with starts out in nice neat tables. You might have to deal with the dreaded data from the outside— information that you desperately want to get into Access, but that currently resides in a file originating in another software package.

You Always Externalize Everything

It's not uncommon to find that a large amount of data has been squirreled away in a format not conducive to database management. You might even have a list of important contacts or other information stuck somewhere in a text document or a worksheet. Fortunately for you and millions like you, Access can rescue your data. No longer will it be trapped in the land of the flat file.

Importing External Data

Importing data into Access is not as difficult as you might think. The first thing you must do is make sure you know where the external file resides on your computer. Then it's just a matter of clicking the right menu selection.

Let's say you have a worksheet file that contains a list of transactions you made at your business, a cheese shop (surprise!). The worksheet details a number of orders that you made for customers. Because a worksheet is not a proper database, however, there is a lot of duplication of information. Each time customers make an order, you have to retype all their personal data, such as address and phone number.

A worksheet used to track orders.

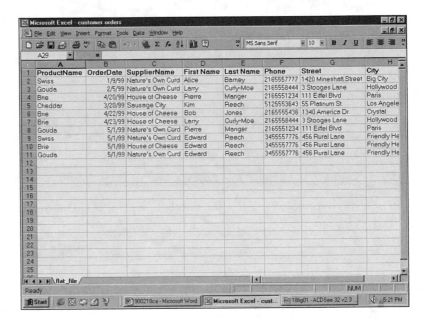

Notice that the worksheet mixes information such as customer name and address with data regarding products and suppliers. This is the curse of the flat file database. When you work in Access, however, you don't have to retype customer information each time you place a new order, because orders, customers, and products all reside in separate tables. So it makes sense to take the worksheet data and import it into an Access table (or tables).

Repetition, Thy Name Is *Flat File*

That you have to repeatedly enter the same data over and over in a worksheet used to track orders is a perfect example of a flat file database. It does not supply you with the option of creating separate tables for categories of information and then relating them for queries and reports, as Access does.

Getting External

To import external data, open a new database or an already existing database. Click the **File** menu and then point at **Get External Data**. Now you are given two choices: Import (choose to import the worksheet data) and Link Tables (to link to the worksheet).

If your system seems to be busy for a very long time as it tries to import the worksheet, you can halt the process by pressing **Ctrl** and **Break** simultaneously. After you break out of the import, you can attempt the import again. However, to free up resources for Windows, close any applications that you might not be using.

When you import the data, it is placed in an Access table that has no link or connection to the original Excel worksheet file. If you make changes in the worksheet, they won't affect the data in the table. If you link to the worksheet, however, you are dealing with the flip side of the coin. A link between the worksheet and the table means that if you update the information in the worksheet, it will be updated in the table as well (by virtue of the link). In the example we walk through in this chapter, we will import the file rather than link to it.

Think About Your Link

Remember, a link means that there is a source application (in the worksheet's case, Excel) and a destination application (Access).

More than likely, you will not use the worksheet again (especially if you are going to all the trouble of importing the data into Access), so in the example, you forgo the link and choose the **Import** command. As soon as you choose Import or Link, an Import dialog box appears and asks you to identify the file that you want to import. Make sure that you change the Files of Type box in the Import dialog box to **Microsoft Excel** by clicking the drop-down arrow. Otherwise, the Import box won't show you any file types other than Access.

*Selecting the worksheet
file to import.*

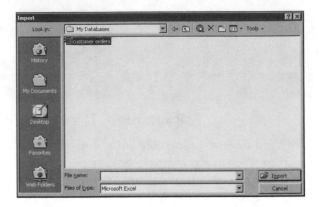

After you select your file (by using the Look In drop-down box to locate the file on your computer), click the **Import** button. Access starts the Import Spreadsheet Wizard, which helps you convert the spreadsheet to an Access table.

Running Your Own Import Business

The Import Spreadsheet Wizard walks you through the import process. The first step is to let the wizard know which of the sheets in the Excel workbook that you are importing is the sheet you want to create a table from (if you have only one worksheet in your Excel workbook, you won't get this wizard step). Just click the particular sheet and then click the **Next** button. (You can also create the table from a named range of cells in the Excel worksheet, but this requires that you have named ranges in the worksheet.)

In the next step of the process, you tell the wizard whether the first row in your spreadsheet contains column headings that can be used for field names when the data is placed in a table. The answer is probably yes because most worksheets use headings to identify the data types in each column. The worksheet for customer orders that we are using in this example does have the field names in the very first row of the worksheet, so you click the **First Row Contains Column Headings** check box.

After you click in the check box, the next screen asks one question: Do you want your data in a new table or an existing table? If you want to use an existing table, use the drop-down list to choose the table. If you are creating a new table from the data (as we are in this example), make sure the **In a New Table** radio button is selected. After you've made your decision, click the **Next** button.

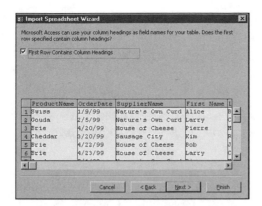

Letting Access know whether the first row of the spreadsheet contains column headings.

Fielding the Import

The Import Wizard's next screen enables you to determine which fields you want to include in the import. Each column heading in the original spreadsheet is considered a field unless you specify otherwise. You can also change the field names for the fields and let the wizard know whether a particular field should be indexed. Finally, you can also use this screen to change the data type for each field.

Changing the field parameters is easy; a copy of the original worksheet is shown on this screen. Just click a particular column heading and then specify each parameter for the particular field. After you've determined which fields you want, advance to the next step in the process.

Turning the Key

You already know from your work with tables that each table requires a primary key that uniquely identifies each record. The next screen in the Import Wizard asks you to either select a field to serve as the primary key or let it create a new field for this purpose. You can also choose to have no primary key, and if you choose that option, you will have to add a primary key to the table in the Design view after the import process is over. Every table needs a primary key.

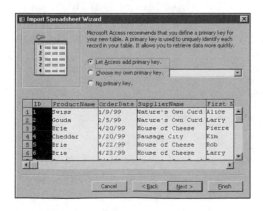

The Import Spreadsheet Wizard helps you set a primary key for your new table.

287

Say you decide to let Access create the primary key. It will create a new field, called ID, and assign a number to each record. Then you can click the **Next** button to move to the next step.

That's All, Folks

The last step in the import process is to name the new table that will be created from the spreadsheet data. Because our example deals with customer information, let's be hypercreative and call the table *Customers*.

The final screen of the Import Wizard also gives you two check box choices. You can check a box to start the Table Analyzer, which helps you decide whether the new table should be broken into several smaller tables. Also, you can check a box to display help on working with the new table when you exit the Import Wizard.

If your worksheet contains redundant data, such as the sample spreadsheet that you've talked about, you probably will want to run the Table Analyzer immediately and get the data in proper shape. Otherwise, the new table will be just as unwieldy in Access as it was in your spreadsheet software package. Whatever you choose to do, click the **Finish** button on the last screen of the Import Wizard.

Freud Would Have Been Proud—Analyzing Your Table

Whether you immediately invoke the Table Analyzer as you finish the import process or analyze your table at a later time, you will find that most spreadsheets that you import into Access need some work before they can serve as proper database tables. The process of splitting a table's data into related tables (necessary because of the duplication of field information) is called *normalization*.

What's Normal?

Because I'm not the best person to decide what is (and isn't) normal, I'm glad that the Table Analyzer exists. You can use the Analyzer to walk through the steps necessary to normalize a table. What is great about this whole process is that you can split a document such as a worksheet (a flat file database) into smaller, related tables. Then you can use the related tables to generate forms, queries, and reports—just as you would if you had created the database from scratch.

Working with the Table Analyzer Wizard

Normalizing a database with the Analyzer helps you understand how tables in a proper database should be structured. You want a lot of small tables that hold discrete subsets of data and then are related to other tables by a particular field.

Using the Table Analyzer Wizard to normalize an improperly designed table is very straightforward. Click the **Tools** menu and then point to **Analyze**. To begin the process, click **Table**.

Understanding the Problem

The first dialog box that appears in the Table Analyzer Wizard takes a look at the potential problems caused by a poorly designed table or imported spreadsheet. Examples are displayed, showing you why duplication of data in a database table is not a good thing. After you've taken a look at the examples provided in this dialog box, you can click **Next**.

Understanding the Solution

The next dialog box in the wizard explains what the normalization process is and how it can potentially solve the problems in your table. Again, examples are offered to help you understand the process that will take place. When you're satisfied that your table needs to be normalized, click the **Next** button. (You probably feel that your coworkers should be normalized, too, but the wizard can't do everything.)

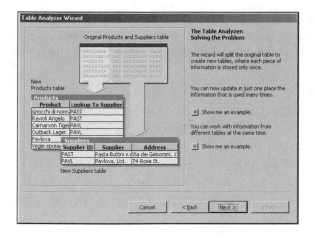

The Table Analyzer Wizard explains the normalization process and then walks you through the steps to normalize a selected table.

Check This Out

Brand New Tables

New tables are created during the normalization process, but the original table also still exists after you analyze it. You can delete it if you no longer need it after normalization.

Selecting Your Table

Now that you've decided to go ahead and try this normalization thing, the wizard would like you to identify the table that will be processed. It asks you to identify the table that contains fields where values are repeated. Just click the appropriate table (in our example, it would be the imported spreadsheet) and then click the **Next** button.

Who Makes the Decisions Around Here?

The next stop in the table normalization process is the decision of how to split the fields in the table. New tables will be created by the process, and you have to decide which fields go where. You yourself can split the fields, or you can let the wizard help you out.

If you do let the wizard decide, you have a chance to adjust the field locations. At least the first couple times you do this normalization thing, it would probably make sense to let the wizard take the lead. After you decide whether you will let the wizard place the fields in the new tables, you can proceed to the next step in the normalization process. Just click the **Next** button.

Group(ing) Therapy

The wizard will take a look at the fields in the original table and do its best to group them into new tables. You will find, however, that the wizard is not infallible and probably cannot pull all the fields out of the original table and place them in appropriate new tables.

For example, say that you have a spreadsheet (which you imported into Access) that tracks orders for your cheese shop. The spreadsheet includes a field for the product ordered and a field for the product supplier. The other fields in the original spreadsheet relate to the customer, such as name, address, and so on.

The wizard probably won't have any problem creating a customer table from these fields or identifying when a second table for suppliers should also be created. However, the wizard might not break fields related to product out of the Customers table and create a third table for products.

A Real Drag

The grouping of fields will probably require some input from you and depends on the complexity of the original table. Creating the new tables is a real drag: A quick drag of the mouse pulls a field out of a current table. Dragging a field into the group box creates a new table and also the appropriate relationship with the table that you drag the field from. You can then rearrange the fields in the tables any way you like; just drag a field from one table to another.

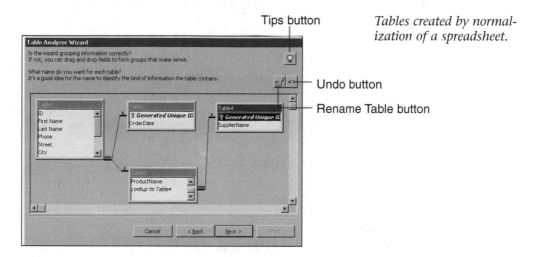

Tables created by normalization of a spreadsheet.

You can also drag the relationship lookups that the wizard has created, so that the tables have the appropriate kinds of relationships. You might even drag inappropriate relationships and create new tables that have yet to be totally defined by the normalization. (The lookups created by the Table Analyzer are really just relationships between the tables; for a refresher on relationships, see Chapter 8, "Between You and Me and Access: Table Relationships.")

For example, you would want a relationship between a newly created Suppliers table and a newly created Products table, but neither of these tables would have a direct relationship with a Customers table (customers are usually related to orders). So you would probably want to drag the relationship lookup out to create a new table and eventually turn it into your Orders table.

To get a usable database out of a spreadsheet or other flat file database, you usually have to put your database thinking cap on and do quite a bit of field rearranging and table creating. The tables that the wizard creates are only the starting point for turning a flat file database such as the spreadsheet into a relational database that will get the job done. Now you know why I harangued you so much about the importance of table relationships in Chapter 8, "Between You and Me and Access: Table Relationships."

Name That Table

When the new tables are created by the Analyzer Wizard, they are given temporary names such as Table1, Table2, and so on. You will want to give the tables more meaningful names, and the Grouping dialog box provides you with an easy way to do this. Select the table that you want to rename. Click the **Rename Table** button. Type in the new name and then click **OK**.

Naming one of the newly created tables.

Hot Tips on Table Creation

A Tips button in the Grouping dialog box gives you a list of things to keep in mind as you work through the table normalization process.

The Analyzer Wizard Grouping dialog box also gives you an Undo button, which you can use to undo your last action. If you name a table and change your mind, or if you move a field and want to put it back, just click **Undo**.

After you create the tables that you need and arrange the fields the way you want them, click the **Next** button.

Finding Your Keys

When you deal with database tables, there is no way to get away from the concept of the primary key (just like there no way of getting into your car if you can't find your keys). Every table needs one; it supplies the unique identifier for each record in the table. The Analyzer Wizard knows this, so the next step in the normalization process is to make sure that each new table created has a primary key.

You can specify a field in a table as the primary key by selecting it and then clicking the **Set Unique Key** button. If a table does not contain a field that would be appropriate for the primary key, you can create a new field in the table by clicking the **Add Generated Unique Key** button. This Table Analyzer dialog box also equips you with an Undo button and a Tips button.

In our example, the Customer List table has an ID field, but it has not been designated the key field. To make it the key, click the field and then click **Set Unique Key**. After you've made sure that each table has a primary key, you can click the **Next** button.

One Last Check (Actually, Two)

As soon as you click **Next**, the Table Analyzer takes one last look at your new tables and tries to determine whether the fields that you've grouped together make sense as a unit (meaning a table). If it finds a table that might contain unrelated fields, a message pops up to let you know.

You must decide whether to continue with the splitting of the fields. If you want to continue, click **Yes**. If you want to backtrack and take another crack at arranging the fields in the new tables, click **No**.

The Analyzer also checks the new tables for any typos in field data that might have been duplicated (such as a customer who has a number of orders, but you misspelled his or her name in one order). If you don't have any repeat field data with different spellings, the only indication that this takes place is a short onscreen message when the final splitting of the fields is analyzed. If you do have misspellings or other typos, Access walks you through the data and gives you the chance to choose from a drop-down list of corrections or to leave the data as is. After you correct any typo issues, click **Next** to continue.

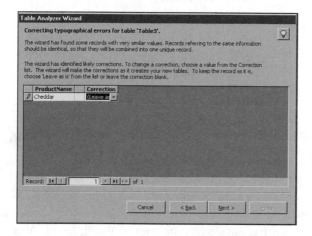

The Analyzer will even help you resolve typos in your data.

Pass Go and Collect a New Query

You've breezed through the Table Analyzer, and you're sitting pretty at the finish line. The last choice in the table normalization process is whether to create a query from the new tables that duplicates the grouping of information in the original table. This is an excellent idea and enables you to have all your original information in the query; it gives you the option of deleting the original table (which you don't need anymore).

After you decide about the query (I vote yes, let the wizard build the query), click the **Finish** button to end the normalization process. If you say yes to the query, Access will build and display it onscreen.

The query is given the name of your original table, and the original table's name is changed to include *_old* to identify it. You can now delete the original table. The new tables created from the normalization process can now be filled with appropriate fields and data and then used to create forms, queries, or reports.

Exporting Data from Access to Other Applications

Now that you have a feel for how easy it is to pull data into Access, we should take a look at the flip side of the coin and see what it takes to put Access data into other applications. Two obvious uses of Access data are spreadsheets and word processing documents.

For example, you might find that the data you have in a table or in a query would be better off in an Excel spreadsheet, where you could use all of Excel's number-crunching capabilities, or you might want to create a form letter in Microsoft Word and mail it to a number of your clients. The names and addresses are in Access, and you have to know how to get them into your Word documents.

An Important Message Regarding Importing and Exporting

Importing and exporting data to and from Access is easiest when you are using other Microsoft products. This is not a commercial for Microsoft, just a fact. The Microsoft Office Professional suite includes a very well-integrated set of applications, so your imports and exports will be more successful and less time-consuming when accomplished using the Office software components: Word, Excel, Access, and PowerPoint.

Copycat or Cutup

You can copy or cut data from Access and paste it into other applications such as Microsoft Excel and Microsoft Word. Copying the data makes a duplicate of the information and places it on the Windows Clipboard. Cutting data from a table or query removes it and places it on the Clipboard. To copy or cut data from Access, open the database object (most likely a table or query) that holds the information. Select the data that you want to copy or cut.

You can select a record by clicking on the record selector, you can select an entire field column by clicking on the field selector. If you want to select the entire table, click the **Select All** button in the upper-left corner. (There is an easier way to place an entire table or query into Excel, so hold that thought.)

After you've selected the data, go ahead and paste it into the other application. Start that application, if you don't already have it running, via the **Start** button on the taskbar. When the application is running, choose the spreadsheet (in the case of Excel) or document that you want to paste the information into.

In Excel or Word, you can click the Paste button on the toolbar or click the **Edit** menu and then click **Paste** to place the Access data into a spreadsheet or a document. When you paste the data into Excel spreadsheets, the text formatting that you assigned to the information in Access is carried over into Excel. Access information pasted into Word appears in a table format.

Paste or Paste Special

You can paste Access data into Word so that it does not create a new table. Click the **Edit** menu and then click **Paste Special**. Choose **Unformatted Text** in the **Paste** dialog box and then click **OK**. The text will be placed in your Word document as regular text.

Drag and Drop Can Be a Real Delight

For those of you who are adept with your mouse, you can also drag and drop Access tables and queries into Microsoft Word and Excel. To place an Access table in Word, open both the applications (Word and Access) so that they are side by side on the Windows desktop. (Click the Restore button on each application window, and then you can drag each window to a new location, using its respective title bar.)

For example, let's say you want to place the Customers table in Access into a document in Word. No problem. Open the appropriate Database window (Fromage Boutique) and then drag the table icon (the specific icon for the table, it includes the table's name) into the appropriate place in the Word document.

You can drag an Access
table and drop it right
into a Word document.

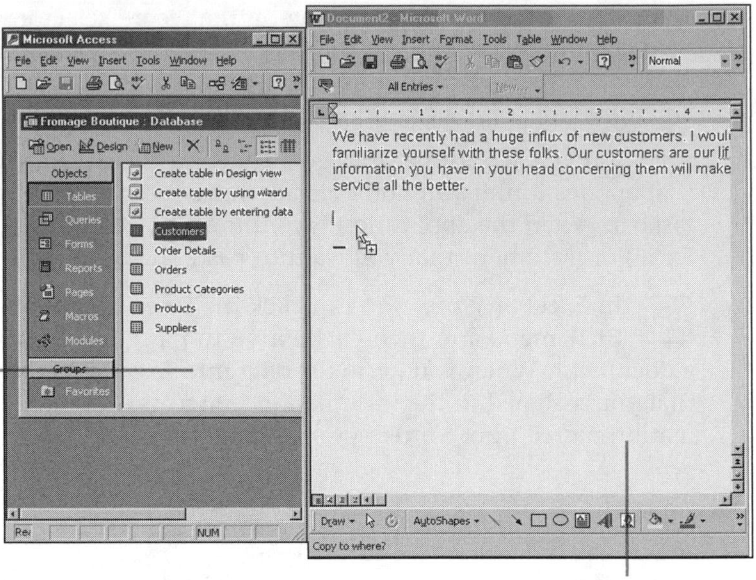

Access window

Word window

OfficeLinks Is Not Corporate Golf

Although copying and pasting takes care of some of your data transfer needs, you will likely want to involve Access data in some fairly big data export deals such as data analysis in Excel or a mail merge in Word. Yeah, I know, learning one piece of software is hard enough, and now you're expected to be familiar with a couple others. Such is life in our technological age. Before you run outside and shake your fist at the sky, screaming for a return to a simpler time when there was no personal computer, let me tell you that moving major chunks of Access data into Excel or Word is very easy.

The Access toolbar provides a drop-down button that can whisk your data into Excel or Word: the OfficeLinks button. Click it, and you are given three choices: Merge It with MS Word (with Word), Publish It with MS Word, or Analyze It with MS Excel.

Merge It

When you select **Merge It with MS Word** from the **OfficeLinks** drop-down list, the currently selected table or query in the Database Explorer is used to supply the data for a Microsoft mail merge. The Microsoft Mail Merge Wizard appears and enables you to link the selected data (in a table or query) to a currently existing form letter or other Word document. You can also choose to create a document from scratch.

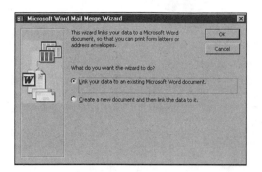

You can use the Microsoft Word Mail Merge Wizard to get your table or query data in shape to use in a form letter or other duplicate document that you created in Word.

Merging Data with Word

A mail merge is just the merging of the information in your database records, such as names and addresses, with a form letter or an envelope. A letter or an envelope is produced for each record in the database table or query. The actual creation of the letter or the envelope is done in Microsoft Word.

If you choose to use an existing Word document, a dialog box opens, enabling you to select the specific document. Select the document and then click **OK**. Word opens, and a link allowing data exchange between the Access table and the Word document is created. Field codes to be placed in the Word document are based on the field names in the Access table or query.

If you decide to create a Word document from scratch, a new document is opened in Word, and the same data exchange link is made to the table or query. Both avenues provide you with a quick way to take Access data and place it in a form letter (or envelopes) or even mailing labels, with a minimum of hassle.

Publish It with Microsoft Word

The Publish It with MS Word OfficeLinks choice takes the data in the currently selected database object and places it in a new Word document as a text file. This is a great way to take report information and place it in Word. Having the data in Word in a text format gives you greater flexibility in presenting information from Access in a written report or other summary document.

Analyze It with Microsoft Excel

When you click **Analyze It with MS Excel**, Excel is opened, and the currently selected table or query is placed into a worksheet. The worksheet created by this method will have the same name as the table or query in your Access database.

An Access table providing lake level readings has been imported into Excel, using the Analyze It with MS Excel command.

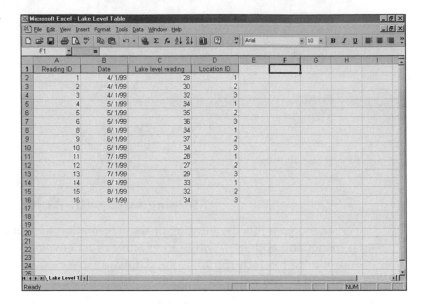

Excel offers an incredible array of mathematic functions and charting possibilities, so it's definitely a good idea to use the Analyze It feature when you have a query or table in which you will have to do a lot of mathematical massaging to get the answers you need. When your table or query in Excel is in a worksheet format, you can even use Excel's powerful Pivot Table feature, which gives you a way to view data from various perspectives and then chart it.

A pivot table in Excel looks very much like a crosstab report in Access. It enables you to group the data in rows and columns and then pivot on certain categories of information. For example, a pivot table detailing monthly sales by regional sales office could pivot so that the data is shown by individual salesperson, regional office, or even time (by month). In essence, the purpose of an Excel pivot table is to give you various views of the same worksheet data.

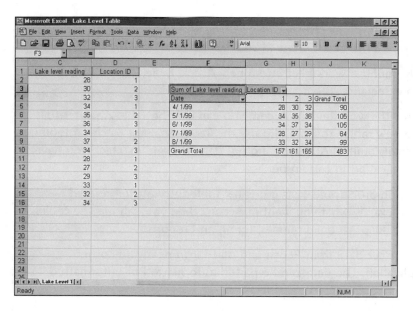

An Excel Pivot Table enables you to view your data from different field perspectives. You can quickly create one in Excel, using the Pivot Table Wizard.

Techno Talk

Pivot Tables Are Not for Fine Dining

Pivot table views are not unlike some of the groupings that you create when you work with Access reports. You can view data as a summary of certain information, or you can break it down to be more specific. This is the special talent of the pivot table—views of the same data in a crosstab format that ranges from the very general to the specific. The Pivot Table Wizard in Access helps you create pivot tables. However, because of Excel's greater number-crunching and charting capabilities, it might make more sense to export the information to Excel and work with it there.

This Data Door Swings Both Ways

As you can see, Access is quite flexible when it comes to importing and exporting data. As you become more familiar with the capabilities of Access and the other software packages you use on a regular basis, you might find that you haven't always placed information in the correct place. These easy-to-use importing and exporting features enable you to get that data in the right format, whether it is an Access table, an Excel worksheet, or a Word document. Putting information where it is best suited will save you time as you work with it and give you that extra hour at lunch for shopping or hitting a bucket of balls at the golf range.

The Least You Need to Know

➤ You can easily import a worksheet into a new Access table, using the Get External Data command.

➤ When you have the worksheet in Access, you can use the Table Analyzer to normalize the new table. You can also use the Table Analyzer to check tables that you originally built in Access or another database and in which you have found data duplication in certain fields.

➤ The normalization process breaks the original table into smaller, related tables, which is exactly what you want in Access. Then you can use the tables and their relationships to build queries, forms, and reports.

➤ You can copy or cut data from Access and place it in nearly any other Windows application. The data can be pasted as formatted or unformatted text.

➤ The OfficeLinks button on the database toolbar is your ticket to easy exports to Microsoft Word and Excel. You can set up a mail merge with Word (using Access data), place Access objects in Word as text files, or place a table or query in Excel as a worksheet.

Chapter 19

Keeping Your Databases Running Smoothly

In This Chapter

➤ Using the Performance Analyzer to fine-tune your databases

➤ Documenting your database objects

➤ Compressing a database

➤ Repairing an ailing database

➤ Repairing the Access application

Society is obsessed with the notion of excellence. No matter what your vocation is, you're urged to strive to be the best, to be part of a winning team. Also, every trade has specialized tools to assist its practitioners in their quest for excellence. Astronomers have incredible tools, such as the Hubbell space telescope, to help them search for new galaxies. Body builders use scientifically formulated diets and specially engineered equipment to stay pumped up. Database gurus, well, they use a bunch of great tools that Access offers for keeping their database objects in tiptop shape.

An Award-Winning Performance— The Performance Analyzer

One way to keep your databases running well is to use the Database Performance Analyzer. This Access tool can be used to optimize the performance of any database objects in a particular database. You will find that if you are careful setting up your database tables, they probably will not have to be analyzed for performance. (Tables are best analyzed by using the Table Analyzer rather than the Performance Analyzer, and if your tables are that suspect, you do not pass go and collect $200 but must return to Chapter 5, "Turning the Tables: Table Design" and take another look at the information it provides.)

The other objects that you create, based on those tables—such as forms, queries, and reports—benefit the most from the Performance Analyzer's optimization process. The main benefit of the Analyzer is increased speed. If you optimize a query, report, or macro, it will do its job faster.

To use the Performance Analyzer, open the database that you plan to optimize. Click the **Tools** menu, point to **Analyze**, and then click **Performance**.

See Them All

You can view all the objects in the database at once by selecting the **All Object Types** tab in the **Performance Analyzer**.

And the Object Is...

It might take a moment for the Analyzer to set up things. The first dialog box that appears, and the first choice that you must make, deals with the object that you want to analyze. A tab for each object type enables you to view the objects that you have created in each category (table, form, report, macro, and so on).

When you've decided what type of object you want to optimize, click the appropriate tab on the Performance Analyzer dialog box and then click the check box next to the actual item you want to analyze. For example, say you want to optimize a report that you built. Click the **Reports** tab and then click the check box next to the actual report.

The first step with the Performance Analyzer is to choose the objects you would like to optimize.

You can also select all the objects in a particular category by clicking the **Select All** button on the right of the particular object tab (such as Reports). When you've chosen which objects you want to optimize, click the **OK** button to continue.

Diagnosis and Treatment—Optimizing an Object

The Analyzer scrutinizes the selected object, and if you watch the screen closely, you can see that it also takes a look at all the objects associated with the one that you are currently analyzing. For example, when you analyze a report, the Analyzer takes a look at where the data for the report came from (the tables or queries).

If the Analyzer has no suggestions for optimizing the currently selected object or objects, it gives you a message that reads "The Performance Monitor has no suggestions to improve the objects you selected." Click **OK** to close this message box.

If Access lets you know that it doesn't have any suggestions, you can pat yourself on the back. This means that the objects you chose to analyze are well built. However, improvements can't hurt either, and in many cases, the Performance Analyzer might provide you with a list of recommendations.

When the analysis is complete, you are presented with the Analyzer's recommendations for optimization. A dialog box appears, giving you a list of possible fixes that will improve the performance of the particular database object. For instance, let's say you run the Performance Analyzer on a table in a database. The Analyzer will look at the fields in the table and advise how you might restructure the table or change the data type for fields in the table.

Absolutely Perfect

If your database object is well constructed (because you followed all the tips in this book), the Office Assistant will tell you that the Analyzer has no tips to offer you—congratulations!

The Analyzer offering advice on a table.

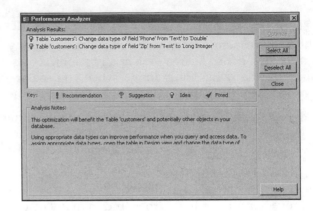

When the Analyzer's Optimization box appears, the optimization tips come in three flavors: recommendations, suggestions, and ideas. Each optimization tip is represented by an icon. Recommendations are represented by an exclamation point, suggestions by a question mark, and ideas by a light bulb.

To view the details on a particular optimization, click it, and the information will be displayed in the Analysis Results box of the Performance Analyzer dialog box. It wouldn't hurt to mention the fourth icon in the Optimizer key: Fixed (represented by a check mark). A little later in the chapter, I will discuss the Fixed icon and how you get it in the Optimizer window.

The Performance Analyzer doesn't supply you with information on how to optimize Access itself or the computer system that you are running it on. Increasing a computer's memory always increases software performance, but you can also do other things to keep your software and hardware working in harmony. For example, use the Windows system tools, such as the Disk Defragmenter and Scan Disk, to keep your hard drive operating optimally.

Give It to Me Straight

Each optimization tip type has its own idiosyncrasies. Recommendations are the most straightforward and usually result in a performance gain if you implement them on the object. Suggestions usually have some kind of potential tradeoff associated with them, and you should look closely at the Analysis results before implementing them.

Suppose you were trying to optimize a particular report. A typical recommendation or suggestion provided by the Analyzer would probably suggest changing the way that the data is compiled for the report. Usually, you would require the report to pull data from several related tables. A possible recommendation or suggestion to optimize the report would be to construct a query that pulls the data together in one place. Then, when you build the report from the query, the report would run optimally.

Any Ideas?

The third type of optimization tip is the idea. Ideas provide you with more general information (unlike recommendations or suggestions). For instance, the analysis of a macro or module might result in an optimization idea regarding the inclusion of a certain type of code statement at the beginning or end of the macro or module. Any time, however, that you work with macros and modules, compiling issues arise, so ideas don't give you the whole story and require a little more research and thought before you can carry them out.

Make It So

After you view the details of each optimization possibility, you will use some and reject others. Recommendations and suggestions can be performed through the Performance Analyzer. Select the recommendation or suggestion and then click the **Optimize** button in the Performance Analyzer dialog box.

The Analyzer creates the recommended or suggested object or carries out any other steps detailed in the recommendation or suggestion. When the Analyzer has carried out a recommendation or suggestion, it places a check mark next to the tip to let you know.

Only the Lonely

You must perform ideas by yourself. (I guess you could have a couple friends gather around your computer for moral support.) Click the idea and view the suggestions the Analyzer gives you in the Analysis Results box. When you have a handle on what you have to do, you can close the Performance Analyzer dialog box via the **Close** button and begin the optimization on the particular object.

Optimizations performed by the Analyzer (and by you, if you implement an Analyzer idea) might not appear to obviously increase the performance of your database. However, they do speed up the inner workings of the various database interactions and provide a more stable database for your use.

Other Performance Enhancers

You can optimize your database objects in other ways besides relying exclusively on the Performance Analyzer. You are already familiar with the Table Analyzer (it was used to help normalize your database table in Chapter 18, "Imports and Exports—Moving and Sharing Data"), which is an excellent way to improve the overall database management capabilities of a database. Tables are the building blocks for all your other database objects; for this reason, they should be constructed carefully. The other database objects can also be tweaked to improve performance as follows:

➤ To optimize queries, use the Group By command on as few fields as possible.

➤ If you create a crosstab query, use fixed column headings.

➤ To optimize a form, avoid overlapping the controls it contains.

➤ Use bitmaps and other graphics sparingly in your database forms.

➤ In reports, avoid sorting and grouping data on expressions you create via the Expression Builder.

➤ Base a subreport on a query rather than on several tables and limit the subreport to only the fields that are absolutely necessary to impart the information.

Documenting a Database Object

After you have honed your objects with the Performance Analyzer and your own database construction savvy, you can use the Documentor to print out a detailed report on a particular object. The Documentor report tells you everything you need to know: the date the object was created, the date it was last modified, details on its makeup (the fields in the table, the controls in a form, or the actions in a macro), and even information on who has permission to delete, read, or change the object.

To start the Documentor, click the **Tools** menu, point to **Analyze**, and then click **Documentor**. The Documentor is very much like the Performance Analyzer; it provides an opening dialog box that enables you to specify the object type and the particular object that you want to document. Click the appropriate tab to select the object category. Then click the check box for the specific object that you want to document.

The Documentor provides a detailed report on the attributes of a particular database object.

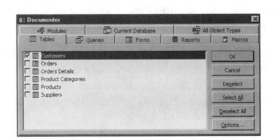

After you've made your selections, click the **OK** button. The Documentor will take a look at the object and build a report detailing its attributes.

Techno Talk

Getting the Complete Scoop on Your Tables

The anatomy of a table documentation report includes the date of creation, the date of the last modification and information on each field, including field type, size, and whether the field has a Display Control (if it does, the documentation would supply information on the source field and the source table).

And the Answer Is...

The documentation report appears in Print Preview view. This gives you a chance to take a look at it and decide whether you want to print it. After you've given it the once over, click the **Print** button to send the report to the printer.

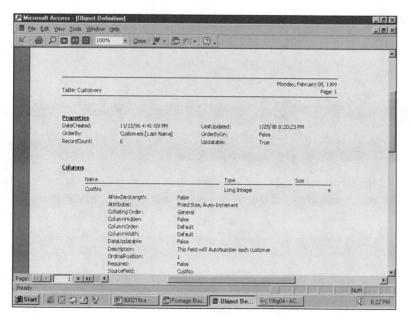

A documentation report for a table gives information ranging from the attributes of each field in the table to the relationships that the table has with other tables in the database.

Object documentation reports present detailed information on how to improve a particular object or how to build a new object based on the attributes of the one you've documented. You can even impress your friends and colleagues (maybe even your boss) by providing them with the documentation reports of some of your better built objects. Let them learn more about Access by seeing a real genius at work.

A Quick Weight-Loss Plan for Your Database

Even though you optimize your database objects, your database can still become flabby over time. If you delete tables from your database, the file becomes fragmented and uses the space on your hard drive inefficiently. This can cause your database to run more slowly.

Access, of course, provides a diet plan for the overweight and sluggish database. You can compact the database, which defragments the file and frees up disk space. It also (yes, you guessed it) improves the performance of the database.

Get Ready with the Mouse, Take a Deep Breath, and Compact

To compact a database, close the current Database window. Your menu selections dwindle to File, Edit, View, Insert, Tools, Window, and Help.

Caution: Database in Use

If you work in a multiuser environment (a network where a number of people can use the database file), make sure that no one is currently using the database you want to compact.

Click the **Tools** menu, point to **Database Utilities**, and then click **Compact Database and Repair Database**. The Database to Compact From dialog box opens, enabling you to specify the database file that you want to compact.

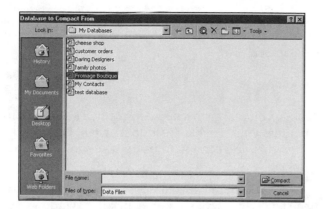

Selecting the database you want to compact.

Click the database that you want to compact (this might require you to switch to another directory or drive) and then click the **Compact** button in the lower corner of the Database to Compact From dialog box. Access opens a new dialog box, Database to Compact To, and asks you to specify a database name to save the compacted database under. Because you are compacting the database to save disk space, it makes sense to allow the compacted file to overwrite the fragmented, flabby file. So click the same database name that you selected in the Database to Compact From dialog box.

After you select the appropriate database name, click the **Save** button in the Database to Compact To dialog box. If you use the same database file name, you are asked whether you want to replace the original file. Sure, you don't want that old couch potato lying around; click **Yes**.

Access compacts the database and saves it under the current name. Now your database will run better, take up less disk space, and look good in a bathing suit (both male and female databases go to the beach, so don't try to catch me on that gender-insensitive stuff).

My Database Has Fallen, and It Can't Get Up

No matter what kind of shape you keep your databases in, they can become damaged. For instance, if you're working on a particular database and one of your coworkers just happens to kick your computer's electrical plug out of the socket, the database could sustain damage. Unfortunately, this damage is not always obvious.

In most cases, Access can detect whether a database is damaged when you try to open it or compact it. At that time, it prompts you regarding whether you want to try to repair the problem. It would make sense to fix the database immediately because the problem will only worsen.

You might, however, run across a situation in which you are using a database that is acting totally wacky, but Access doesn't detect that the file is damaged. No problem, you can still try to repair the database.

Let's Back Up a Bit

Before you try to repair a database, you make a backup copy of it. The repair process can be risky business, and sometimes your database just doesn't pull through. It makes sense to have another copy that you can use to try to save some of the data if the repairs don't work out.

You can use the Windows Explorer to copy the database file. All you have to do is close the database file and then start Windows Explorer. (Click the Windows **Start** button, point at **Programs**, and then click **Windows Explorer**.) Select the database file in the Windows Explorer window and then click **Edit** and then **Copy**. To stick a copy of the file into the current directory, click **Paste**, and the file will be named *copy of (your filename)*.

All Users Shut Down, Please

Make sure that no one in a multi-user environment is currently working on the damaged database. If you want to repair it, the file must be closed by all other users.

The Database Doctor

Now you can scrub up and get ready to operate. Remember that this process is designed to repair a database file that has become corrupt because of hardware considerations such as a faulty drive or the loss of power while you were working on the database. Do not use this feature on a database that is functioning normally.

To begin the repair process, make sure the database is closed. Again, your menu choices become limited, as they did when you compacted the database.

Click the **Tools** menu, point to **Database Utilities**, and then click **Compact and Repair Database**. Attempt to compact the database. If Access finds a problem with the database, it tries to repair it. Access will churn up your hard drive a little bit and then report on the status of the repair. In most cases, you will be told that the repair was successful. Congratulations! (If things don't work out, you always have the backup).

Access in Intensive Care

Access 2000 (like the other Office 2000 applications) now has the capability to detect and repair problems with the Access software itself. Occasionally, you might receive a message that says the Access software cannot find a particular file or is having problems completing the process that you have requested with a particular command.

You can attempt to fix problems with the Access software by using the new Detect and Repair feature. Before you attempt to repair problems with Access, make sure that you have your Access or Office 2000 CD-ROM in your CD drive.

To detect and repair problems with the software (you shouldn't do this unless you are experiencing problems with Access that seem related to the software, not just your database), select the **Help** menu and then select **Detect and Repair**. The Detect and Repair dialog box will appear. This dialog box lets you know that an attempt will be made to detect and repair any problems associated with the Access software itself.

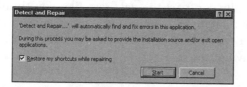

You can use Detect and Repair to try to fix any problems that you are experiencing because of corrupt or missing files associated with the Access software.

When you are ready to go for broke and try to repair Access, click the **Start** button. You will be asked to wait while the installation program attempts to fix any problems with the Access software. An indicator lets you know the progress of the installation.

Shut Down All Office Applications and Reinstall

If Detect and Repair doesn't seem to remedy the problems you are having with Access, you might try to reinstall the application completely. When you place your CD-ROM in your drive, you are greeted by the Microsoft Maintenance mode installation window. You can click the **Repair Office** button to reinstall all the Office software, or you can uninstall everything (click the **Remove Office** button) and then do a completely fresh installation. Sometimes this seems to get your applications (such as Access) back on their feet.

When the Detect and Repair feature finishes, you will see a message that says "Microsoft Office 2000 setup completed successfully." You can try to run the Access software and, hopefully, any problems that you were experiencing will have been remedied.

The Care and Feeding of Your Database Files

Obviously, there is more to database management than the creation and manipulation of your database objects. You should take the time to optimize the performance of your objects, as well as occasionally compact the database file. You should also put together a backup schedule for your database, using some kind of backup utility. Keep in mind that *without data, there ain't no database*. Maintain and protect your files and your database, and your business will prosper.

The Least You Need to Know

➤ You can enhance the performance of all your database objects, particularly queries, reports, macros, and modules, by using the Performance Analyzer. It provides you with optimization tips that help you improve the design of your objects.

➤ Analyzer recommendations and suggestions can be carried out automatically to improve the object's performance. Ideas require you to become involved hands-on in the object optimization process.

➤ The Documentor provides a detailed report on the design parameters of a specific database object. The report can be printed and tells you everything from the date of creation to specifics about each component (such as a field or action) that makes up the object.

➤ Over time, your database file can become fragmented. Use the database utilities and compact the database file to free up disk space.

➤ There is always a slight chance that a database file can become damaged. The Repair command can be used to fix the problem. Before attempting to repair a database file, however, make sure that you make a backup copy of the database.

➤ If you are experiencing problems that seem to be associated with the Access software itself, try to use Detect and Repair to fix the problem. This reinstalls portions of the Access application.

Chapter 20

What's the Password?

In This Chapter

➤ Assigning a password to your database

➤ Dealing with the various user levels you can assign to a database

➤ Assigning users to security groups

➤ Using the Security Wizard to set up all this security stuff

You've seen that Access provides numerous tools for building, managing, and fine-tuning your databases. Because of the valuable data residing in your databases, you might also want to take steps to secure them. This is especially true if you are an aficionado of tabloid news and daytime television talk shows. You are, no doubt, convinced that your coworkers are either aliens from another planet or extremely dangerous maniacs, and you are obsessed with protecting your databases from them.

Choosing a Database Security Blanket

Access provides a couple methods for securing your database files. You can add a password to any of your databases. Then when you open the database, you are prompted for the password—a simple and straightforward method of protection. It's kind of like sticking one of those club things on the steering wheel of your car. Just don't lose the key (or the password).

If the simple password approach doesn't work for you, you can beef up security to a higher level of paranoia by defining user levels. User-level security works by placing users into various groups, each with a different level of access to the objects in the database. User-level security is not unlike the methods used to grant permissions on a computer network.

Adding a Database Password

Opening from the Toolbar

You can also use the **Open Database** button on the toolbar to open the database file and gain access to the Open dialog box.

To add a password to your database, make sure that the database is closed (if you are on a network, all other users must close the database as well). Now this might seem a little odd because you just closed the database, but the first step in adding the password to the database is to open the database. Click the **File** menu and then click **Open**. When the Open dialog box appears, select the database file you want to add the password to.

Now comes the tricky part. In the Open dialog box, click the drop-down arrow to the right of the Open button. A menu will drop down. Select **Open Exclusive** on the menu. This means that you want exclusive rights to the database file. The database will open in the Access window.

After you select the database that you want to password protect, make sure that you click the Open drop-down arrow and select Open Exclusive.

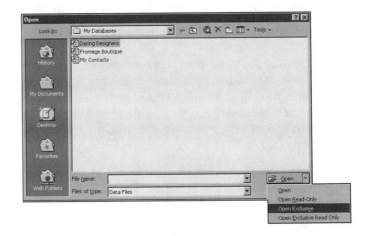

Calling Security

Now that you've opened the database by using the exclusive rights parameter, you can set up the password for the file. Click the **Tools** menu, point at **Security**, and then click **Set Database Password**. The Set Database Password dialog box appears.

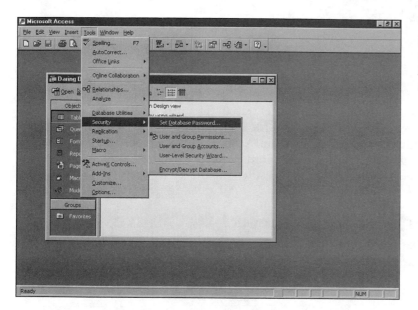

When you have the database open, use the Tools menu to find the Set Database Password command.

The purpose of the Set Database Password dialog box is to enable you to type in a password and then verify it by typing it in a second time. In the Password box, type your password. The password will appear as a series of asterisks (it's supposed to be a secret, remember?).

Now you have to verify the password. Press the **Tab** key to move the insertion point to the Verify box. Retype your password.

If you make a typo while verifying your password, Access alerts you when you click **OK** in the Set Database Password dialog box. Just click **OK** to close the Microsoft Access box, and type your password into the Verify box.

After you verify your password, click the **OK** button. Now the database is password protected. When you or any other user attempts to open the database, a dialog box will appear, demanding the password. One thing that you should keep in mind is that if you forget the password for the database, you are basically doomed; you won't be able to open it.

Case-Sensitive Passwords

Passwords are case sensitive, so you might want to limit the characters in the password to lowercase. That way, you don't have to remember what is uppercase and what is lowercase (it's hard enough remembering the password).

Type the password for the database and then type it again in the Verify box.

But, hey, your memory is probably like a steel trap (a nonrusty steel trap), so there is no chance that you would forget the password. Even if you do, I know that you're smart enough to write the password down and keep it in a safe place. Take a look at what happens when you try to open a password-protected database file (meaning, close your database and let's see what happens when you try to open it).

Opening a Password-Protected Database

When you open a password-protected database, the Password Required dialog box appears. Type in your password and then click **OK** to open the database file.

Access needs your password to open the protected database.

If you type an incorrect password, or if someone tries to get into the database without knowing the correct password, Access states the obvious: "Not a valid password."

Access won't open the database until you type the correct password.

Your only recourse is to click **OK** and try the password again. If you type it correctly (it's case sensitive, remember), you open the database.

Guess the Secret Word and Win 200 Dollars

If this heading conjures up an image of Groucho Marx and a duck, you certainly weren't born yesterday. You should know that this database password stuff isn't going to work if you don't keep your password a secret. There is also the additional burden of being the keeper of the database. After you password it, you own it. You have exclusive rights to the file.

Junking the Password

You can remove, or *unset*, a password for a database file. First, you must open the database and select the **Open Exclusive** choice from the Open drop-down list in the Open dialog box. You will be prompted for your password to open the database. After the database is open, click the **Tools** menu, point to **Security**, and then click **Unset Database Password**. Enter the correct password in the dialog box that appears and then click **OK**. The database will no longer require a password when you open it.

If this idea of exclusivity scares you, there are other ways to protect and limit access to a particular database file. You can set security levels for each user of the database. Of course, please understand that setting user levels is necessary only if you are sharing a database with others on a network. If you are running a database on a standalone PC, you don't have to worry about security (if you do worry about security on a standalone PC, even a password isn't going to protect your files after you've opened them).

Another thing to remember is that if you work in a multiuser environment (that is, a network), you probably have a network administrator who will grant you network security rights, as well as database rights. However, even if you are not in charge of the databases and their security, it doesn't hurt to know how the various security levels are assigned.

Assigning User Levels to a Database

The process for setting up user levels is fairly straightforward. Someone has to be in charge, and an Administrator account must be created. The *administrator* is the person who assigns the access levels to all the other users. It's starting to sound like some futuristic police state in a sci-fi movie, with Big Brother watching, isn't it?

Joining a Group

Security levels in your database will be defined for groups; each group can have a different level of access to the objects in the database. The default groups already defined in Access are User and Admins (people in the Admins group are obviously considered administrators for the database and have more rights to the database than other groups). To begin securing a database, you assign the users to a group. The Admins group will have complete access to the database. The User group will have limited access to the database.

For example, you might assign only yourself and one other person to the Admins group, which will have full access to the database and its objects (an administrator's level of use). People assigned to the User group will have limited access to the database and its objects. The whole matter is as simple as that. One word of caution, however: If you share this database with others on a network (the whole point of password protecting it), make sure that you discuss the fact that you want to add security to this shared database with the other users. Otherwise, you might be accused of setting up a database police state and probably won't get any more lunch invitations from your coworkers.

Open the database that you want to work on. To assign yourself and other users to a group, click the **Tools** menu, point to **Security**, and click **User and Group Accounts.** The User and Group Accounts dialog box provides you with all the tools to assign individuals to the various groups.

The User and Group Accounts dialog box enables you to create user and group accounts for your databases.

Group Therapy for Users

The User and Group Accounts dialog box has three tabs: Users, Groups, and Change Logon Password. The Users tab is where you assign new users to the groups. For instance, say you want to include yourself in the Admins group. In the **Users** tab of the User and Group Accounts dialog box, type your name in the Name box and click the **New** button.

The New User/Group box opens with your name in it. All you have to do is press **Tab** and then give yourself a personal ID (PID) in the Personal ID box. Your PID is used to identify you in the user list. The PID must be at least 4 characters (a maximum of 20) and is case sensitive. As you did with database passwords, pick something you can remember and keep it in lowercase. After you've established the PID for you or other users, you can assign the user (or yourself, if you are the user we are talking about) to any of the groups that appear on the User tab. Just select a particular group in the Available Groups box, and then click the **Add** button. Your user is now a member of that group and the group name will appear in the Member Of box.

Creating New Groups

The Groups tab is where you create new groups. For instance, say you want to create a group that has access to almost all the objects in the database (such as a human resources department), but you still do not assign them all the rights that the Admins group has. Just click the **New** button and then assign the group a name (such as Human Resources) and a PID, as you did for a new user. When you return to the User tab, the new group will appear in the Available Groups box.

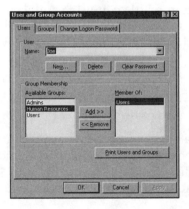

The Users tab of the User and Group Accounts dialog box enables you to create user accounts for a database and then assign them to user groups with various levels of access to the database objects.

I haven't yet explained the Change Logon Password tab. It is used to create a new password or change an old password for a particular user. When new users are initially assigned to the various groups, the Logon Password is blank, so a proper password must be set up.

After you've established the user and group accounts for the database, you are ready to move to the next step in the process—assigning the various security levels for the database objects. Access makes this stage of the game easy on you; it's just a matter of invoking the Security Wizard and letting it take care of the details.

Learning to Share

This whole database security thing is necessary only if you are going to share the database with other users. Users who can access a database over a network are assigned to a workgroup. The workgroup parameters are held in the Access 2000 Registry in Windows. Sounds confusing, doesn't it? You should probably do a little in-depth research in the Access 2000 Help system before pursuing multiuser security levels.

Using the User-Level Security Wizard

If you find all this talk of groups and users a little confusing and would rather be walked through the process of creating security group and user accounts for a particular database, you can use the User-Level Security Wizard. The User-Level Security Wizard, like all wizards in Access, helps you create groups and assign new users to these groups by guiding you through a series of screens.

To use the User-Level Security Wizard, you must have a database that has not been previously password protected. I repeat—no password!

If you have password-protected your database, open the database by using the **Open Exclusive** choice in the Open dialog box. Provide your password, and the database will open. After the database is open, click the **Tools** menu, point to **Security**, and then click **Unset Database Password**. Enter the correct password in the dialog box that appears, and then click **OK**.

Okay, now we're sure that we have a database that's definitely not password protected. To start the Security Wizard, click the **Tools** menu, point to **Security**, and click **User-Level Security Wizard**. The first screen of the Security Wizard explains that it will make the current database secure and that it will also create an unsecure copy of the database (this gives you a fallback plan if the secure database has a problem). The wizard also explains that a workgroup information file will be created that includes the names of users and groups who will have access to the database. Click **Next** to continue.

The next screen of the Security Wizard asks you what file name you would like for the workgroup information file that will be created for this database. A workgroup ID (WID) will also be created; this is a unique string of alphanumeric characters and is generated randomly by the wizard. You should make sure that you write down the workgroup information file name and the WID that is created. You will need this information if you ever want to edit the information file. You can specify the file name for the workgroup information file or use the file name generated by the wizard. Click **Next** to move to the next step in the process.

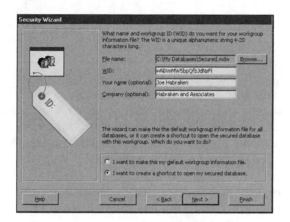

A workgroup information file and a WID are necessary for you to secure your database.

The next screen of the Security Wizard provides a tabbed dialog box that has a tab for each object type in a database (tables, queries, forms, and so on). Click one of the tabs, such as Tables, to view the tables currently contained in the database. Each table has a check box next to it, which is currently selected. This means that the particular object will be secured. If you don't want to secure a particular object (such as a table, form, or report), click the appropriate object tab and then click the object's check box to preclude it from the security setup.

After you determine which objects you will secure and which objects you won't, click the **Next** button to move to the next step in the security setup process.

Rounding Up All the Objects at Once

You can view all the objects in your database by clicking the All Objects tab on the Security Wizard's Object dialog box.

The Security Wizard enables you to select which objects in the database you would like to secure.

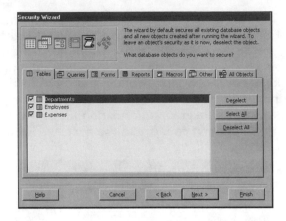

On the next wizard screen, you are asked to provide a password for your VBA project. This simply means that if your database contains any Visual Basic modules (this includes Visual Basic code that was used by Access to create forms and reports for the database), they will all be secured by this one password. To make a long story short, enter the password that will be used to secure the programming code in this database. You will use this password if you have to add any Visual Basic modules to the database in the future. (Make the password easy to remember or write it down; it might be a while before you actually build any Visual Basic modules for your database.)

Some Basics About Visual Basic for Applications!

Visual Basic for Applications (VBA) is a programming language used extensively to customize the applications in Microsoft Office. In Access, Visual Basic can be used to create custom interfaces and program Access modules used to automate certain processes. If you plan on eventually creating high-end, specialized databases, learning some Visual Basic probably makes sense.

After you type in the password, click **Next** to move to the next step.

Getting Your Groups

The next screen asks you to select from a list of optional security groups that can be added to the workgroup information file. This gives you a number of groups with pre-assigned access levels to the objects in the database. For instance, you can click the check box next to the New Users Group. Users whom you place in this group can add and read data in the database, but cannot change any objects in the database or delete data.

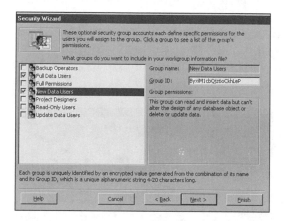

You can choose to add a number of optional groups to the workgroup information file.

After you select the optional groups (which you can add users to later and take advantage of the different permission levels in these groups), click **Next** to move to the next step. On the next Security Wizard screen, you are given the option of assigning certain permissions to the default User group (the group that automatically contains all users of the database), or you can choose not to assign this group any permissions at this time. If you give permissions to the User group, basically anyone with a copy of Access can get in and fiddle with your database. You might want to select the **No, the Users Group Should Not Have Any Permissions** radio button (it's selected by default) and then click **Next** to continue with the process.

The next screen gives you the opportunity to add users to your database. Each user must be assigned a password and a unique PID. To create a new user for the database, click **Add New User** in the left pane of the wizard's screen. Then all you have to do is type a name in the User Name box and place a password in the Password box. The PID is automatically generated.

When you have entered the user and his or her password, click the **Add This User to the List** button. You can add as many users as you like, using this series of steps. When you are finished adding users, click the **Next** button.

Picking a Group or Picking a User

The next screen enables you to add users to your various groups, and it provides two ways to do this. You can select a particular user and then choose a group to add the user to, or you can choose a group and then select users to include in the group. Although it might sound confusing, it's very straightforward. When you select the **Select a User and Assign the User to Groups** radio button, a list of all the groups appears with check boxes at the bottom of the wizard screen. A drop-down box lists all your users. Simply use the drop-down box to select a user and then click the check box next to each group that you want the user to belong to. When you choose the **Select a Group and Assign Users to the Group** radio button, the groups are listed on the drop-down list, and the users are listed with check boxes in the pane. After assigning your users to the appropriate groups, click **Next** to continue.

The Security Wizard enables you to assign your users to the various user groups.

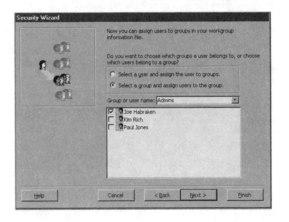

May I Have Permission to Go Now?

This whole Security Wizard thing sure seems to take a long time, doesn't it? Well, hang on, we're on the last step. On the final Security Wizard screen, you are given the option of naming the new database that will be created by the Security Wizard. Remember that the wizard creates a secured duplicate of your database. This means that the original database still exists under the original file name. After you determine the name that you want to use for the secure database duplicate (the default is *secure* followed by the name of the original database, such as *secure daring designers*), click **Finish**. You've created a secure database with user groups, user accounts, and various levels of permissions.

It's a Clone!

The Security Wizard actually creates a secured clone from your original database (called secured.mdw; it will be stored in the same folder as the original database), which is not modified. If this security thing doesn't work out, you always have the original file to fall back on.

When you open the new database (the secured clone), you are asked to log on, using your username. The database then opens. The various permissions that the users who open the database will have totally depends on the permissions they were given during the Security Wizard setup of the database. If you have to add new users or change the permissions for a particular user by including them in a group, you can use the User and Groups Permission command described earlier in the chapter.

Final Notes on Security

When you assign user levels to a database, the file is *encrypted*. This means that you will have a heck of a time getting to your data if something goes wrong or if the security levels are not assigned properly. This is why the Security Wizard duplicates the original file.

One good reason for assigning user levels to databases is to protect the macros and modules built for the database. As you know, modules and macros can be used to dramatically change a database's interface and capabilities. By protecting modules and macros, using user levels, the chance of someone inadvertently changing the code and therefore ruining the module or macro is reduced to nil.

The need for passwords and user levels should be dictated by the value of the data in your database. If you are working with extremely sensitive, highly proprietary data, it would make sense to use a database password or assign user levels in a multiuser environment.

However, if you are working with a database that holds data that someone could find in the public phone book, don't bother worrying about security. You have to decide for yourself how important your data is. Whatever you do decide, don't let it keep you up at night.

The Least You Need to Know

➤ You can make a database your own by assigning a password to it. When you open the database file, you will be prompted for the password.

➤ You assign a database a set of user levels, which gives the various users different levels of access to the database objects.

➤ User access levels are established by groups. Each group has a different level of access to the database.

➤ The Administrator (an account that is created for a database) has the ability to assign the various security levels to the groups.

➤ You can use the Security Wizard to set up group and user accounts for a database.

➤ Don't become involved in database security unless you have to. You must decide whether your data is important enough to warrant dealing with user levels and passwords.

I THINK I CAN...
I THINK I CAN...

Chapter 21

The Little Engines That Can—Making Macros

In This Chapter

➤ Designing simple macros

➤ Creating macro actions

➤ Using macros to take the drudgery out of some repetitive Access tasks

➤ Chatting for hours about all the great stuff macros can do

In my youth, I was always amazed at the incredible products you could find in a box of Cracker Jacks. There were fake tattoos, yo-yos (okay, really small yo-yos), and secret decoder rings. With the ring, you (and any of the millions of kids around the country that had the ring) could write and decode secret messages, just like spies in the movies. (Of course, when you decoded the message in the Cracker Jack box, it usually said "Buy more Cracker Jacks.")

Macros Revealed

Access has its own secret code that can greatly enhance your ability to manipulate data in your databases: macros. Macros exist as lines of code that can be used to complete specific database tasks for you. Macros are the easiest way to automate some of those things that you do over and over. A *macro* is basically a string of actions that are fired off in sequence when you run it. This lends itself to many possibilities.

Access makes it easy for you to create macros and provides a lot of help. Before you create a new macro, you must have the Database window open for the database you want to use. Click the **Macro** icon in the left pane of the Database view to select it. Now comes the moment you've been waiting for. Put away that Cracker Jack toy and click the **New** button to begin your exploration of macros.

Designing a Macro

When you click the **New** button, the Macro window appears. This window is a little different from the Design windows that you used for some of your other objects, such as forms and reports. The top half of the Macro window consists of two columns: the Action column and a Comment column. The Action column holds the commands that make up the macro. The Comment column enables you to make optional notes related to each action that you place in the macro. The lower half of the Macro window displays the arguments contained for each action. For example, an action that opens a certain form will display the form's name in the Action Arguments Form Name box. Obviously, other information concerning the action will also appear in the Arguments box and these are best seen by constructing a sample macro.

Let's say that you have a database with a customers table and a customers form. You use the form primarily as a way to enter data easily into the table. A simple macro can be constructed that will open the customers table, open the customers form, and then tile the two database objects on the screen. This might sound difficult, but the simple action macro is easy to create.

Getting In on the Action

To add an action to a macro, you click in the first row of the **Action** column. A drop-down arrow appears in the box. When you click the arrow, a list of built-in macro actions is displayed. Now, think this macro through. You want a macro that tiles two windows on the desktop—a table window and a form window. There's just one small problem here. You've probably noticed that when you open a database object, such as a table, form, or query, the Database window also stays open on the desktop. The first action in this macro, then, should be a command that minimizes the Database window. That way, when the table and form are opened by the macro, the desktop will be empty (except for the minimized Database window, which will no longer be an issue). To place this action in the macro, you click the drop-down arrow, scroll through the actions list, and select **Minimize**.

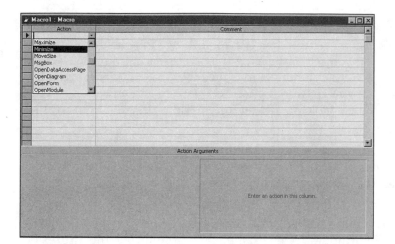

Placing an action in the Macro Action column.

Techno Talk

Be Responsible for Your Actions

The actions that you place in a macro can be previously created macros instead of actions from the drop-down list. This enables you to link a large number of actions together in one macro; each action consists of a macro that can consist of a number of actions. Because you have probably tested each of the previously created macros, this method enables you to quickly build a powerful macro from known actions.

After you select the action, a description of it appears on the right of the Action Arguments box. This particular action (Minimize) minimizes the currently opened window when the macro is started. Because you start this macro from the Database window, it minimizes the Database window (which is good because that's what you want it to do).

After you place an action in the Action column, you can click in its **Comment** box to add information regarding the particular action. For example, you might enter a comment for the Minimize action so that you remember that it will minimize the Database window when you activate the macro.

Macros Can Be a Drag

Actually, in the case of macros, being a drag is a good thing. You can set up actions that open a specific database object by dragging the object's icon from the Database window into the Macro Actions column. Sounds incredible, doesn't it? It certainly simplifies the example that you are working on. You want to add an action to the macro that opens a Customers table, so all you have to do is drag the right icon into the Macro Design window.

To see the objects in the Database window and the Action column in the Macro window at the same time, you have to tile the two windows. Click the **Window** menu; then click **Tile Vertically**. This arranges the windows side by side, making it easy for you to drag the object icons to the appropriate place.

To create an action that opens a particular database object, select the appropriate object tab in the Database window. In the example, you would click the **Tables** tab. Now all you have to do is drag the icon for the particular table (Customers) to the Action column (that's right, just drop the Table icon under the Minimize action).

When you release the mouse, a new action appears in the Action column. This action opens the object that you dragged into the Macro window. In this case, you dragged in a table icon, so the Action will read *Open Table*. In the Action Arguments box, the Table Name appears, as well as the view for the table and the data mode, which in this case is Edit.

The new action and its associated arguments.

New action—

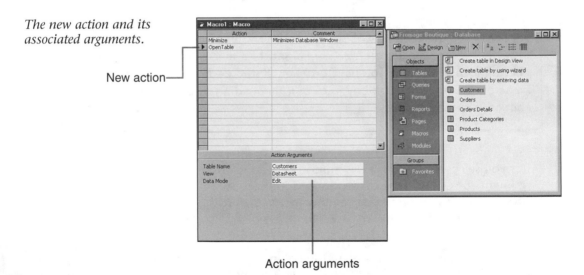

Action arguments

You can place as many open object actions into the macro as you need. In our example, you also want to open the Customers form, so you drag the icon for Customer form into the Actions column below the previously placed action. After you've finished dragging objects from the Database window to the macro, you might want to maximize the macro window so that you have more room to work on subsequent commands.

Creating Macro Actions for Menu Commands

So far, you've seen how to create an action that minimizes a window and an action that opens a particular database object, but this macro thing won't get you very far if you can't add actions that fire off different menu commands. Access has you covered. First, you might want to maximize the Macro window by clicking its Maximize button. Then, to add a menu command to the Action column, click the drop-down arrow in the **Action** box. Scroll down the list of actions to **RunCommand** and select it.

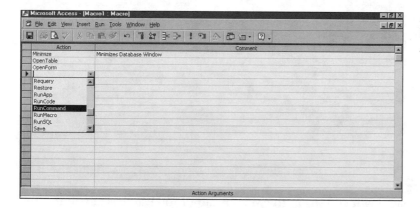

Placing the RunCommand action in the Macro Action column.

When you have the RunCommand action selected, you have to set the action arguments so that the right command is fired off by this part of the macro.

Setting Action Arguments

The action arguments give a particular action its specificity. For the RunCommand action, you have to tell Access where to find the particular command that you are talking about. This information consists of the menu bar where the command resides and the specific command itself.

Click in the **Command** box in the **Action Arguments** box (it's in the lower half of the Macro design box). A drop-down arrow appears, displaying a list of all the Access menu commands. You want the command **Tile Horizontally** (normally found on the Window menu), so scroll down the command list until you find it. When you find it, click it.

That's all there is to it. You specify the command (Tile Horizontally), and then you're ready to roll.

Now that you have a macro that will actually do something, it's important to save it. Click the **Save** button on the Macro toolbar. Type an appropriate name in the Save As dialog box and then click **OK**. After you save the macro, you can close the Macro Design window.

A new macro with a lot of action. Make sure you save it.

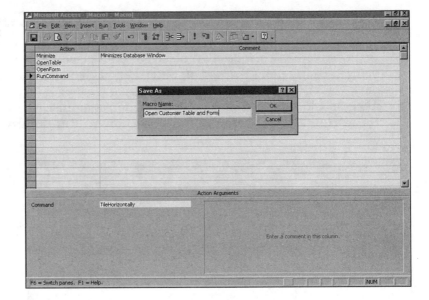

Playing a Macro

Your newly created macro will appear on the Macros tab of the Database Explorer. To play a macro, you select the macro in the Database window and then click the **Run** button at the top of the Database window or double-click the macro name. In the case of your sample macro, you will end up with the Customers table and the Customers form tiled horizontally on the desktop.

You can design macros that are much more sophisticated than this example. Whether you build simple or complex macros, it sometimes helps to scribble your ideas on a piece of paper so that you can start to assemble the chain of events you want to take place when the macro is played.

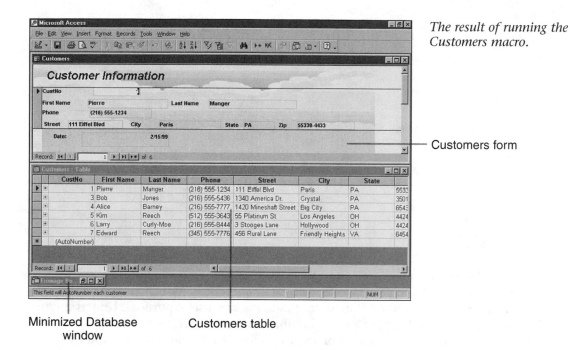

The result of running the Customers macro.

Customers form

Minimized Database window

Customers table

A Word About Modules

Access offers another programming object for the advanced Access user: modules. Although macros might seem straightforward to even the casual user of Access, modules are another story entirely. Creating modules is the pinnacle of database geekdom and requires a strong knowledge of the Microsoft Visual Basic programming language.

Modules are groupings of Visual Basic code that enable you to rewrite the way an application looks and is used. For example, modules could be employed as the building blocks for a point-of-sale system that uses the power of Access to create invoices and manage inventory. The actual users of this system would be using a custom interface (menus, dialog boxes, and so on) and might not even be aware that they are using Access to do the job.

The Northwind database, which ships with Access 2000, includes several modules. Open Northwind and then click the Module icon in the Database window to see the list of modules. (Northwind also has macros that you can look at.)

In Design view, open one of the modules, such as the **Startup** module, by clicking the module to select it and then clicking the **Design** button on the top of the Database window. The Module window's toolbar includes specific tools for creating modules.

The Visual Basic code contained in the Startup module.

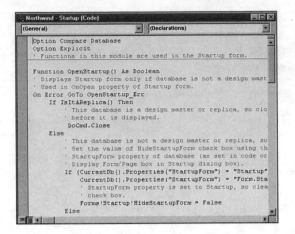

```
Northwind - Startup (Code)                          _ □ ×
(General)                    ▼  (Declarations)            ▼

Option Compare Database
Option Explicit
' Functions in this module are used in the Startup form.

Function OpenStartup() As Boolean
' Displays Startup form only if database is not a design mast
' Used in OnOpen property of Startup form.
On Error GoTo OpenStartup_Err
    If IsItAReplica() Then
        ' This database is a design master or replica, so clo
        ' before it is displayed.
        DoCmd.Close
    Else
        ' This database is not a design master or replica, so
        ' Set the value of HideStartupForm check box using th
        ' StartupForm property of database (as set in code or
        ' Display Form/Page box in Startup dialog box).
        If (CurrentDb().Properties("StartupForm") = "Startup"
            CurrentDb().Properties("StartupForm") = "Form.Sta
            ' StartupForm property is set to Startup, so clea
            ' check box.
            Forms!Startup!HideStartupForm = False
        Else
```

If you find yourself in need of extremely customized databases, modules are definitely the way to go. However, you have to learn a fair amount of Visual Basic for Applications to be able to code modules that serve any useful purpose. Understanding how macros work and having a very good handle on the other object types in a database (tables, forms, and so on) are prerequisites for creating (and understanding) modules in a database.

The Least You Need to Know

➤ Macros enable you to greatly streamline and enhance your database management chores. Before embarking on an intense journey of discovery with macros, you will find it well worth your while to fully understand the ins and outs of the more common Access objects, such as tables, forms, queries, and reports. Working with software should never be regarded as drudgery, so always consider the possibilities of these "little engines that can" as you design and redesign your databases.

➤ Macros provide a way to automate repetitive tasks that you perform during database management.

➤ Macros consist of sets of actions that you define in the Macro Design window. These actions can be used to fire off a string of commands when you invoke the macro, or the actions can be designed to invoke a command only when a certain condition is met, such as the completion of a form or report.

➤ The building of efficient and useful macros requires a good understanding of the other database objects and many Access commands and features (but don't be intimidated; half the fun of working with software is discovery).

➤ The next step in database programming is the creation of Access modules. Modules enable you to customize how Access works and looks. To create modules, you need an understanding of the Visual Basic for Applications programming language.

Chapter 22

Have It Your Way—Customizing Access

In This Chapter

➤ Adding buttons to a toolbar

➤ Creating a button for a macro

➤ Viewing more than one toolbar

➤ Creating a new toolbar

➤ Setting other options in Access

One of modern society's greatest contradictions is its high regard for the individual. Everyone loves the person who stands out from the crowd and doesn't run with the herd. This is quite perplexing because by definition, a society *is* a herd—sorry, *group*— of people who operate under a set of standards. We go to great lengths to broadcast our individuality, from our car license plates (you just have to love those vanity plates) to how we order our burgers at the local fast-food joint (remember, "Hold the pickles, hold the lettuce, special orders don't...").

Well, in the spirit of rugged individualism, Access provides you with the ability to customize certain aspects of the Access application window. You've learned all sorts of ways to optimize the objects that you create in Access. Why not set up the user interface (the toolbars and some of the other defaults) so that you can work quickly and efficiently. So, saddle up, Pilgrim, it's time to individualize.

Access 2000 Personalizes for You

In Access 2000, you've probably already noticed that the toolbar and menu system actually adapt to your command usage and show the menu selections and toolbar buttons that you use most often. This is called personalized menus and toolbars, and this feature is embraced by the other Office applications, such as Word and Excel. The personalized menus show the commands you've used most recently at the top of a particular menu. If you hold the menu open for a second or so longer, you will get a complete list of the commands available on that menu. The toolbars work in much the same way. The most recent commands used will appear on the toolbar (in cases where the commands shown on the toolbar exceed the space the toolbar has available to show commands).

Adding a Button to a Toolbar

As you've worked with each database object described in this book, you've probably become familiar with the commands available on each object's individual toolbar. In some cases, however, frustration might have raised its ugly head, such as when you couldn't find a particular command on a toolbar and had to go to the menu system to get a particular job done.

Well, don't let it get you down, tenderfoot, because you can easily add buttons to any of the Access toolbars and proclaim your individuality to all (well, to all who see your Access workspace, which is probably just a couple coworkers and the guy who sweeps the office floors and peaks over your shoulder when you're working late). You can even create buttons that run macros you have designed. Take a look at how to customize a typical toolbar—the Table toolbar. (The steps outlined here for adding a button to the Table toolbar work for any of your toolbars.)

I'm Missing a Button

When you open a table, the Table toolbar appears (so open a table—for example, the Customers table in the Fromage Boutique database). It contains a set of buttons designed to help with the maintenance of your tables; there are sort buttons, filter buttons, a whole bunch of buttons. But what if you want to use a particular command, and there's no button for it? You can always fall back on the menu system to fire off your command, but it would, of course, be easier if you could just click the toolbar.

The Secret Order of the Right-Click

Access makes it quite easy for you to add a command button to a toolbar. Place the mouse pointer on any toolbar; that's right, any toolbar. Now you get to perform a mouse manipulation that many desire but few have mastered: Click the right mouse button (pretty easy, huh?).

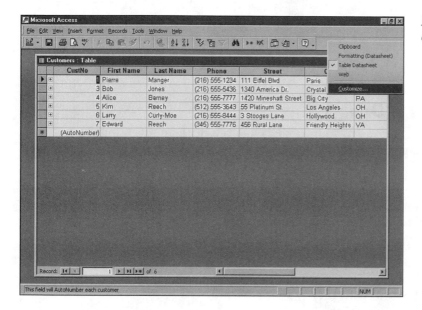

Right-clicking a toolbar to access the toolbar menu.

To add buttons to a toolbar currently showing in the application window, click **Customize**. The Customize dialog box appears.

The Customize dialog box has three tabs: Toolbars, Commands, and Options. The Toolbars tab enables you to select the toolbars that you want to show in the Access workspace. The Commands tab is where you add, to a specific toolbar, buttons that represent the various Access commands. The Options tab controls the size of the buttons on the toolbars, whether ToolTips show, and whether you want the menus to do special things when you open them (menu animations). More importantly, the Options tab contains a check box labeled Menus Show Recently Used Commands First. This check box is selected by default and provides the adaptive menu feature that customizes your menus on-the-fly. To turn off the adaptive menus, deselect this check box (just click on it to clear the check mark from the box).

Because you want to add a button to a toolbar, click the **Commands** tab. Now you can concentrate on the buttons you want to add to a particular toolbar.

339

The Commands tab offers buttons for just about every command you could imagine.

Life Isn't Always a Drag

In the case of adding buttons to your toolbars, life is a drag; adding a button is as simple as a quick drag of the mouse. But first, let's take a look at what the Commands tab is all about.

The Commands tab is made up of two areas: a Categories box, listing the various categories of Access commands, and a Commands box, displaying a group of buttons that relate back to the currently selected category in the Categories list.

For example, the first category in the Categories list is File. The buttons displayed in the Commands box are for commands that relate to files. There's a New button (for starting a new database) and an Open button (for opening an existing database); both commands are used to deal with files.

Buttons for Every Occasion

Each category in the Categories list relates to a particular database function. For instance, the Toolbox category includes all the buttons that normally would be found on the Toolbox. The object categories, such as All Tables, All Queries, and All Forms, enable you to make buttons for specific objects in your database.

Although the name of each button is present in the command list, you might want more information on a specific button and its associated command. No problem, just click the button and then click the Description button in the Commands tab. You get a great thumbnail sketch of what the particular button will do.

Sewing On the Button

The process of getting the right button and therefore the correct command on a toolbar is very straightforward. Select the category of commands that you want to use in the Categories list. A list of buttons will appear in the Commands box. Decide which button you want to add to the toolbar and drag it onto the toolbar, preferably placing it in an open space.

For example, if you are working with the Table toolbar a lot, building your tables, but you would like to quickly check the relationships that you've created between your tables, you might want to stick the Relationships button on it so that you have quick access to the Relationships window.

Click **Tools** in the Categories box. Then scroll down the Commands list until you see the Relationships button. Drag the **Relationships** button onto the toolbar, and that command will be available whenever you need it.

That's all there is to it. The button, and therefore the command associated with it, will be available on the toolbar. You can add as many buttons to a toolbar as you like. However, if you add too many to the toolbar, not all the buttons will be visible at the same time in the application window. You will have to scroll the toolbar to the right or the left to access all the buttons.

Deleting Buttons

*To delete a button from a toolbar, open the Customize dialog box via the shortcut Toolbar menu. Click and drag any toolbar that you want to delete from the toolbar. The button disappears. When you complete your deletions, click the **Close** button to close the Customize dialog box.*

Adding a Macro to a Toolbar

You can also add buttons to your toolbars that open or run objects you have created. You can create a button for a table, query, form, and even a report. However, you might find that macros are the best choice as far as buttons for objects go; one click of a macro button and all the actions in the macro are fired off.

To add a macro or other object to a toolbar, click the object category in the Categories list, in this case, All Macros. A list of the macros that you have created for the currently opened database will appear. Simply drag the macro onto the toolbar. The ToolTip for the new button (which looks like a scroll) will read *Run Macro*, followed by the name of the macro.

An Icon for Every Object

Each database object has a particular button icon associated with it. Tables use the datasheet icon, queries use the double datasheet icon, forms use the form icon, reports use the notebook icon, and macros use the scroll icon.

After you finish adding buttons to a toolbar, click the **Close** button in the Customize dialog box. The buttons that you add to a toolbar are saved with the toolbar and will be available whenever that particular toolbar appears in the application window.

Tying It On with the Toolbars

An alternative to adding buttons to your toolbars is to display more than one toolbar at a time. Each toolbar is specific to a task, such as creating and maintaining tables or designing and running macros. It might be easier for you to just give yourself access to more than one set of commands (via multiple toolbars) rather than try to create the ideal toolbar by dragging a lot of unrelated commands onto it.

You already know that to get a list of available toolbars, you right-click any currently visible toolbar, click **Customize**, and then make sure that the Toolbars tab is selected on the Customize dialog box.

A list of all the toolbars available in Access appears in the Toolbars tab of the dialog box. To place any of these toolbars in the application window, click the toolbar's check box.

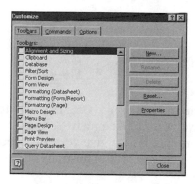

The Toolbars tab of the Customize dialog box gives you access to all the available toolbars and various toolbar-related commands.

Checking Your Buttons

Command buttons are also available in the Customize dialog box. The New button enables you to create a new toolbar. The Rename button enables you to change the name of a toolbar that you created. The Reset button returns the selected built-in toolbar to its original state (it gets rid of all the extra buttons you've stuck on it). The Properties button gives you access to the Properties dialog box, which enables you to tie a particular toolbar to a particular database object. For instance, you can have a special toolbar appear when you open a particular form or table. The Close button closes the dialog box.

Creating a New Toolbar

So you've tried everything: You've added buttons to an existing toolbar, you've stuck more than one toolbar in the application window, but these just didn't work for you. Well, when all else fails, you can create your own personal toolbars.

Blank Utility Toolbars Await Your Commands

You will find that two Utility toolbars are listed with the other Access toolbars. The Utility toolbars are empty toolbars that you can modify for a particular purpose. For example, you might want to make your own utility toolbar for use when you work on forms or reports in Design view, giving you easy access to the design commands you use most often.

Click the **New** button on the Toolbars tab. You are asked to name your new toolbar.

Access asks you to name
your new toolbar.

Type a descriptive name for the toolbar and then click **OK**. The new toolbar will appear in the application window. It won't look like much. To flesh it out, you have to add buttons to it. You can assign commands that give your new toolbar a very specific use, or you can make it a more general, jack-of-all-trades toolbar.

Deleting Custom Toolbars

You can also delete custom toolbars that you no longer need. In the Toolbars tab, click the toolbar you want to get rid of. The Delete button will become active. Click the Delete button to delete the table. Don't worry, Access does not allow you to delete any default toolbars. When you select them in the Toolbar dialog box, the Delete button does not become active.

Positioning the Toolbars

You can drag any of the toolbars to new positions in the Access window. Click the handle portion of the toolbar (it's on the far left and is designated by two parallel lines) and then drag the toolbar to where you want it. For instance, you can take one of the horizontally displayed toolbars and place it vertically along the left or right side of the application window.

You can also drag a toolbar onto the workspace window, creating a floating toolbar. Floating toolbars actually move out of your way as you work in a particular object window. This enables you to keep working and negates the need for dragging a floating toolbar out of the way when it obscures something you have to see in a table, form, or other database object. You can quickly view additional buttons for a floating toolbar by clicking the triangle in the upper-left corner of the floating toolbar's title bar (in some cases, the Add Buttons triangle appears on the far left of the floating toolbar).

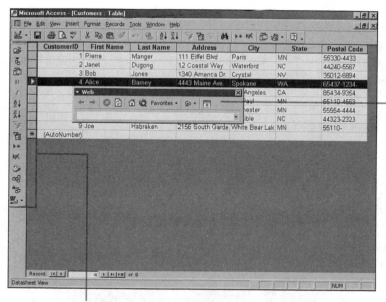

You can place your toolbars anywhere in the application window.

Floating toolbar

Custom toolbar displayed on left side of Access window

As you can see, the toolbars are very flexible helpmates as you build and maintain your database. Having the commands that you use most often one click away can make the entire database process much easier to deal with.

Techno Talk

Creating Custom Menus

You can also create custom menus in Access via the Commands tab of the Customize dialog box. You can drag a new menu to the menu bar and then add various commands to it. The Access Help system provides additional information on creating and editing custom menus.

Setting Options in Access

Customizing your toolbars is one step on the route to having Access act your way. Another group of Access parameters that you can customize to your own liking is options. These options range from what items are displayed in the application window (and how they are displayed), such as the status bar and the toolbars, to what happens in a table when you press Enter. To open the Options dialog box, click the **Tools** menu, and then click **Options**.

The Options dialog box breaks down these customizable items into eight categories: View, General, Edit/Find, Keyboard, Datasheet, Forms/Reports, Advanced, and Tables/Queries. Each category has its own tab on the dialog box.

If you set options that you don't like, click the **Cancel** button in the Options dialog box. This will return you to the application window with no harm done.

When the Options dialog box is open, you can access a particular category of options; just click the appropriate tab.

The Options dialog box gives you control over a number of Access settings.

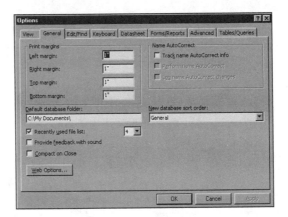

It's All up to You

Most options that you set in the options categories are set by either check boxes that you select, drop-down boxes in which you select from a list, or text boxes where you type the needed parameter. Taking the time to sort through the following options can help you set up Access to run the way you prefer:

View This tab enables you to select whether to show the status bar and other application window items, such as hidden objects. It also controls how the Macro Design window is displayed and certain attributes of the Database window, such as opening objects with a single click or double click of the appropriate icon.

General   This tab lets you set the print margins for your objects: left, right, top, and bottom. You can also choose the default database directory in this tab.

Edit/Find   This is where you set the default behavior of the Access Find/Replace feature. You select the type of search (fast search or general search) and also what types of actions require confirmation from you during a Find or Replace operation, such as changes in records or deletions.

Keyboard   This tab handles the effects of certain keyboard actions. You can decide whether the mouse pointer should advance to the next field after you press Enter or what happens in a table when you press the arrow keys.

Datasheet   Setting the color and appearance of your datasheets is the purpose of this Options tab. It gives you control over the font, the background color, and the style of the gridlines. You can also choose various cell effects such as Flat, Raised, and Sunken.

Forms/Reports   You set the default form and report templates using this tab. You also set selection behavior for controls (how much of the control you have to touch to select it.

Advanced   This tab lets you set parameters involved with object linking and embedding. You can also decide how Access should open databases: in either an exclusive or a shared capacity.

Tables/Queries   This tab gives you control over the default field size and the default field type in your tables. You can also set query parameters such as Show Table Names and Output All Fields.

A Little Help from My Friends

When you are working with the tabs of the Options dialog box, you can get limited help on each option available to you. Click the Dialog Help (it looks like a question mark) button at the top (on the right) of the dialog box, and then click the mouse pointer on any area of the dialog box.

For example, let's say that you are on the Datasheet tab and aren't sure what the Show Animations check box is for. Click the dialog box **Help** button, and then click the **Show Animations** check box.

Access gives you a brief description of the area that you clicked. Getting immediate help on a specific option makes it much easier for you to choose your settings.

*Using the dialog box
Help button to get help
on specific items in a
dialog box tab.*

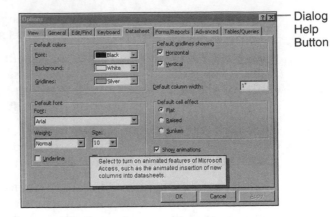

Dialog
Help
Button

Stepping Out of the Crowd

So go ahead and express your individuality. It makes good sense to take the time to customize and individualize Access so that you are comfortable with its look and feel. Database management consumes many hours, so being at ease with the interface will make the trials and tribulations you are going to face a little more palatable.

Besides, you certainly wouldn't want anyone to accuse you of being just a face in the crowd. Step out and whip database management on your own terms!

The Least You Need to Know

➤ *You can customize any of the Access toolbars. You can add buttons and delete buttons; right-click any of the toolbars to access the Toolbar menu, and then click* **Customize***.*

➤ *You can create toolbar buttons for any of the macros you design. This gives you quick access to their actions.*

➤ *You can create your own toolbar from scratch, if you like, and populate it with a customized set of command buttons.*

➤ *You can place additional toolbars in the application window via the Toolbars dialog box. When you have your toolbars in the application window, you can drag them to pretty much any place you like.*

➤ *The Options dialog box is your one-stop shopping for the control of the Access window's look and feel. Click the particular tab where you want to change the settings and have it your way!*

Surf's Up, Dude—
Access on the
Internet

As far as small talk goes, the Internet is red hot. You can't enter an elevator or stand in the checkout line at the grocery store without overhearing conversations about how cool it is to cruise the Net and surf the Web. Although the Internet and probably its most used component, the World Wide Web (WWW, or Web), are categorized in the mental junk-food category along with television, they are actually powerful and useful avenues for the movement of information.

This book has harangued you time and time again that good database management is all about taking care of information (data). It's only natural that Access databases would give you the option of taking advantage of the biggest information reservoir in our planet's history—the Internet.

If you think back, you will realize that you already dabbled with the Web in Chapter 3, "Help, I Need Someone…." Microsoft supplies Help menu choices that directly connect you to software support and information sites on the Web. Remember the mechanics of connecting to the Web: Access pulls in Microsoft Internet Explorer to give us a hand in dealing with the actual Web pages. As you embark on a survey of other ways to use the Net and the Web with Access, you will find that Internet Explorer continues to play a part in the process.

Weaving a Database for the Web

Access 2000 takes full advantage of the Net. In fact, a Web toolbar provides you with buttons that help you quickly open Internet Explorer and go to one of your favorite Web pages or search the Web. You can, in effect, use the Access Web toolbar as your command center for interacting with the Web as you work within Access.

You will also find that you can easily make your database objects Web ready. You can save your various Access objects in HTML format and then display them on a Web page. Saving a particular object in HTML format provides you with only a snapshot of the object, enabling you to place a static copy of your product list or a special report on a Web page.

But hold on, there is more. You take advantage of a new breed of Access object called the *data access page*. These Web-ready pages enable you to create data entry forms and other items for the Web that are interactive. For instance, you could create a data access page that can be used by your customers to enter their personal information via your Web page. The coolest thing about the data access page is that the information placed on the form is entered into your Access database. You, in effect, create an online data entry form with just a few clicks of the mouse.

We're not finished with the Web integration features Access has to offer you. In your tables, you can place a special kind of field, a hyperlink, that will whisk you (or another user of your database) to a particular site on the Web. Let's take a close look at how Access makes it easy for you to swim and not sink (maybe even surf) on the Web.

Access 2000 makes it much easier to create online data entry forms and other Web-ready objects than previous versions of Access.

Going Hyper with HTML

Web pages consist of text, graphics, and other items tagged with Hypertext Markup Language (HTML). The purpose of HTML tags is to format the information for viewing with a Web browser (such as Internet Explorer). Using HTML to design a Web page is no different from using a word processing package such as Microsoft Word to design a flyer or brochure. Items in a brochure, for instance, are tagged to be bold, a certain font size, or a certain color. Also, a brochure may include linked graphics tagged to show their directory location on your computer.

Access Cracks the HTML Code

Basically, then, HTML tags for the Web operate in the same general way as the word processing tags for a print document. The problem with Web documents in the past, however, was that you had to learn HTML to set them up; you had to know what the codes did. You know, it was programming.

The great thing about Access is that it HTML-codes your database objects when you save them as Web-ready items; you yourself do not have to do the tags. You get HTML-formatted database objects with just a few clicks of the mouse!

HTML Is Easy with Office 2000

All the components of Microsoft Office 2000 offer you this quick HTML conversion for Web documents. Microsoft has also developed a Web design tool, Microsoft FrontPage. It is a component of the full-blown version of Office. FrontPage helps you to design your own Web pages with little (or almost no) understanding of HTML. Wizards and templates are used to build very sophisticated home pages and Web sites for business or home use.

Exporting an Access Report to HTML

Okay, let's give this HTML thing a try and see what happens. Say that you're building a Web site for your business, and your business just happens to be a cheese shop (this cheese shop analogy is really getting ripe). Now, you want to create an HTML object that will tell your customers (when they're browsing your Web page) who they should contact if they have questions about any of your product lines (the lines are Cheese, Meats, Implements, and Gourmet Crackers).

Your employee information and your product category information would reside in tables in your database, so the best way to get together the information that you need for your Web site would be to generate a report from the tables. Reports also look nicer than tables and queries, so when you convert your report to HTML, it will end up looking better than a table or query would.

A report generated to show employees and the product lines they manage.

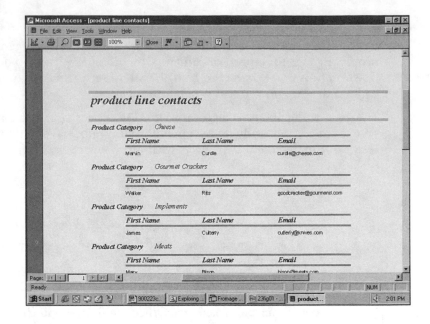

Doing the Export Thing

After you have created a report or other object, it's easy to convert it to HTML. You are going to take the object and export it to the HTML file format. Make sure that you have the object open (such as a report) that you would like to export into the HTML format.

The rest of the job is pretty much mouse work. Click the **File** menu and then click **Export**. The Export dialog box appears, and this is where you save the report or other database object in HTML format. There are several steps in the process, but they are straightforward, so don't despair.

The Export Report As dialog box is your avenue to create Access HTML objects for your Web pages.

Save In box

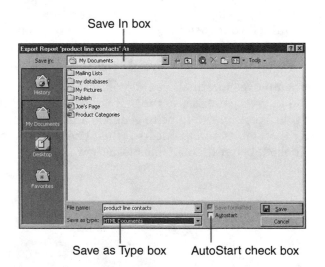

Save as Type box   AutoStart check box

In the Save In box, you designate where you want to place the file. That is, where on your computer's local drive or on a network do you want this new file to end up? After you designate the exported file's resting place, you have to make sure that the file is saved in HTML format. This is done in the Save as Type box. Click the drop-down arrow for this box, and then select **HTML Documents**.

AutoStart Your HTML Engines

After you designate the type of file you want the export to give you (HTML, in this case), you are almost ready to click the Save button. But hold on a second. Access offers you a nice perk in the Export dialog box. Because you are going to save this report in the HTML format, Access figures you might want to take a look at it as it would appear on the Web, and Access is probably right. Clicking in the **AutoStart** check box automatically opens the new HTML object in Internet Explorer after the Export process is completed. Notice that the Save Formatted check box is automatically selected when you choose HTML as the file format (it is also grayed out and unavailable as an option). This makes sense because you want this new file to be laid out as a formatted report in the HTML format. Remember that you want the report to appear in its pristine published form on your Web page.

Internet Explorer 5 is an integral part of Microsoft Office 2000. Make sure that you install Explorer from your Office 2000 CD-ROM when you are prompted to do so at the beginning of the installation process. You should take advantage of the powerful Web capabilities of Access and the other Office components.

Dressing Up Your HTML Objects with Templates

Now you can take this export business to the next step. Click the **Save** button. The HTML Output Options dialog box will appear. This dialog box enables you to specify whether you would like to use an HTML template to enhance the look of your object. These templates can provide you with navigation buttons to move through a multipage report, or they can make sure that special graphics, such as a company logo, end up in the header section of the report. Access offers you a number of ready-made HTML templates to take advantage of. After you select a template (or decide not to use one), click the **OK** button.

Where Are My HTML Templates?

Your HTML templates should be in the Access folder, which resides in your main template folder for Microsoft Office. Use the browse feature in the HTML Output Options dialog box to find and select your templates. The typical path for the templates (the final location will depend on how you installed Office and Access) is C:\program files\microsoft office\templates\1033\web.

The HTML Output Options dialog box lets you choose a template to dress up your new Web-ready object.

Explorer Takes Center Stage

After you end the Export process, your computer will probably take a couple seconds to process your new HTML file. Then, amazingly, Internet Explorer will open up and show you the fruits of your labor (this is because of AutoStart, remember?). In this example your report has been saved as a Web page. The great thing about this whole HTML export thing is that the new objects that you create can be incorporated into existing Web sites, providing easy-to-update information for the people who use your home page on the Web.

Your new HTML object appears in the Internet Explorer window.

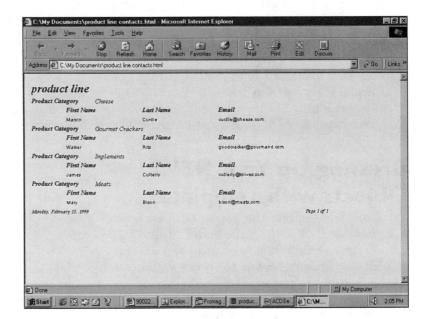

Your Web Page at a Standstill—Static HTML

Exporting Access objects as HTML is a great way to put information on your Web site. However, you have probably noticed that saving a report (or other object) as HTML via the Export command only creates a fixed view of the object. It's kind of like a photo of the information, and the new HTML object cannot be updated. In fact, if you wanted to show new data in your HTML report or table, you would have to run the report again or edit the table in Access and then use the Export command again to show the updated information on your Web page.

This type of HTML is called *static*. It is the easiest way to make an Access object Web ready. A table in static HTML is not unlike a picture taken 20 years ago of your college roommate. You have to take a new photo to update his image to his new look (because he's probably put on 20 pounds and lost most of his hair).

Creating Dynamic Web Objects in Access

Static HTML objects are okay for situations in which you just want to show a particular object on your Web site. It's pretty much the same as printing a hard copy of a report or other object. You can show it to people, but you can't update it. Access provides a feature that enables you to create more dynamic Web objects, particularly data access pages that can be used on your Web page to add data to a particular database.

For example, you can place a customer response form on your Web page. When a customer or potential customer accesses your Web site on the Web, he or she can enter personal data to receive a catalog or answer survey questions related to your business, among other things. The great thing about the data customers enter on your Web site is that it is automatically placed into one of your Access databases. The data access page placed on the Web site is directly tied to the Customer or New Customer table in your database.

A Short History Lesson

I probably should make it clear how fantastic the new data access page object provided by Access 2000 really is. If you ever tried to build a Web order form using previous versions of Access, you already have an appreciation for how much easier your life has become with the advent of data access pages.

A number of steps were required to create an online data entry form tied to a particular database. You first had to create an ODBC (open database connectivity) data source in the Windows Control Panel. The ODBC data source tied a particular data source driver file to the database (any typical Access database) that would be receiving the data placed in the Web form.

After the ODBC data source was created, a currently existing Access form had to be saved as a dynamic HTML file (.asp file), which would then be placed on a Web page. Although this explanation of the entire process takes only a couple paragraphs, believe me when I say that it burned up some brain cells to work through all the steps required. Well, fortunately for you (and me), you can throw this all out the window because when you create a data access page using the Data Access Page Wizard, all the hard stuff is taken care of for you, and you end up with a Web-ready data entry form.

Creating a Data Access Page

Creating a data access page in Access is no different from creating any other object. In fact, Access provides a Data Access Page Wizard, which makes it really easy for you to create a Web-ready data access page for any of your databases.

Let's say you want to create a data access page for new customer information. You will eventually stick this Web-ready object on your Web site, and when a potentially new customer wants to provide mailing and contact information (so that you can send a catalog of your products by regular mail), he or she can just fill in the form on your Web site.

Open the database that you want to create the data access page for. Then make sure that you select the **Pages** icon on the left side of the database window. To start the data access page creation process, double-click the **Create Data Access Page by Using Wizard** icon in the right pane of the Database window.

Double-click the Data Access Page Wizard to start the process of creating a Web data access form.

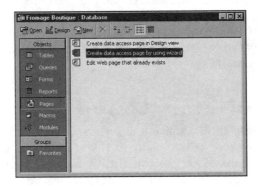

Working with the Data Access Page Wizard

On the first screen of the Data Access Page Wizard, you are asked to select the fields that you want to place on the access page. Notice that this is not unlike creating a form using the Form Wizard. What you have to keep in mind, however, is that you are creating a data entry form for your Web page. This means that people who access your Web site will be doing the data entry, not you. Include only the fields that you want them to enter. For instance, you wouldn't want to include a CustNo or Customer ID field on the data entry form, because your customer table is probably already set up to automatically assign a number to each new customer added to the table.

Use the table drop-down list to select the table or tables that the page will be based on. Then add the fields to the page as you would if you were creating a form or report.

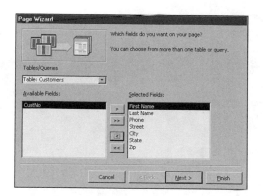

Selecting the fields for the data access page.

After you've selected the fields for the page, click the **Next** button to continue. On the next wizard screen, you can add grouping levels to the page by selecting a field or fields (just as you can in a form or report). After you've selected the field group levels, click **Next** to continue.

SEE ALSO

> *You will find that creating a data access page in Access either using the Page Wizard or creating the page from scratch in Design view is very similar to creating a form or report. Check out Chapter 9, "It's All in Your Form," for background information on creating forms and Chapter 13, "From Soup to Nuts—Creating Delicious Reports," for a primer on creating reports.*

The next wizard screen enables you to set sorting parameters for the page, based on a particular field or fields. Select the **Sort** drop-down arrow to select the field (or fields) you want to sort the data by. Then click **Next** to continue.

On the last wizard screen, you are asked to provide a name for the page. You can call it pretty much anything you like. In the case of our example, we are creating a data access form for our Web site to get information on new customers. We could call this page New Customers. After you've entered a name, click **Finish**.

That's all there is to it. The new access page will appear in the Access window. You will find that it looks a lot like a form and contains a navigation toolbar that enables you to move through the current records in the database table (or tables) that you based the page on.

You can edit the page just as you would any other Access object. Click the **Design View** button on the Access toolbar to switch to Page Design view.

You can move, edit, or add fields to the page as you would to a form or report. Make sure that you save any changes you make to the page in Design view. After you close the new page (either in Page or Design view), you will find that your new data access page is listed in the Page pane of the Database window.

The completed page in
the Access window.

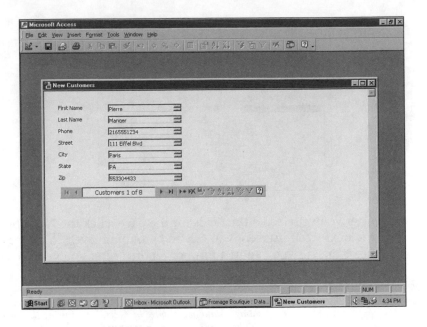

Saving an Existing Form as a Data Access Page

You can also save an existing form as a data access page. After you've created the
form, select it in the Database window of your particular database. Select **File** and
then **Save As**. In the Save As dialog box, click the **As** box (at the bottom of the
dialog box) and select **Data Access Page** as the file format. This saves the form
in the .asp file format.

Viewing Your Access Page in Internet Explorer

Now comes the fun part. You get to view your new page in Internet Explorer (as a vis-
itor to your Web site would) and enter data into the access page. The most amazing
part is that when you return to the database table the page is based on, you will find
that the data entered in Internet Explorer resides in the database table. What a fantastic way to quickly build a customer or contact list or even have customers place
orders on your Web site!

To view (and test) your new data access page in Internet Explorer, make sure that the page is open in the Access window; then click the **File** menu and select **Web Page Preview**.

Internet Explorer will start and open a window on your desktop. Your new data access page will appear.

Enter a new record, using the fields in the data access page. Notice that when you click in a particular field with the mouse, the insertion point appears. Type in the appropriate data.

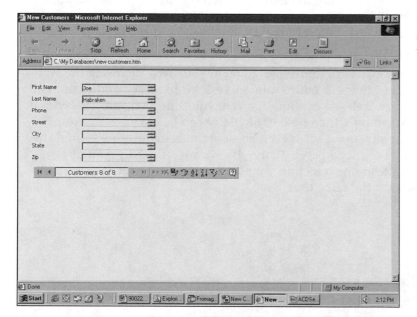

The data access page in the Internet Explorer window.

When you have completed entering the data, close the Internet Explorer window. Now comes the real test. Return to the Access window and take a look in the table that the access page was based on (you know, the place where you got the fields for the page). You will find that a new record has been entered into the table, using the data that you entered on the page in Internet Explorer.

As you can see, pages are a great way to take your databases online and allow visitors to your Web site to add information to your Access database. This online stuff is fantastic!

Taking It Home with a Home Page

You now have a feel (I hope) for the fact that you can create two kinds of Web objects for your Web pages: HTML static objects and .asp files that provide you with active data access pages. Obviously, these two Web objects help you build Web sites that contain information derived from an Access database (such as a report saved as an HTML file) or enable you to actually receive data from the Web site (using a data access page) and have it placed in the appropriate database.

After you have created files in Access that are Web-ready, you have to assemble them with the other files that you will use to build your Web site. Microsoft FrontPage (which ships with the full-blown version of Microsoft Office 2000) is an easy-to-use tool that can help you "chain" the various Web files together into a well-designed personal or corporate Web site.

An alternative to using Microsoft FrontPage is to build your Web site using the various tools provided in the Microsoft Office suite (Access, Word, Excel, and so on) and then publish the files to a Web server, using the Web Publishing Wizard. This wizard is included with the Microsoft Office 2000 CD-ROM or can be downloaded from Microsoft's Web site (http://www.microsoft.com—use the search feature to find the Web Publishing Wizard download page). To use the Wizard efficiently, you place all the files for your Web site in one folder on your hard drive. Then you can process everything in the folder at the same time.

Building a Web Site Takes More Than a Hammer

Creating Web sites that look good and work correctly takes a fair amount of understanding of the HTML language. You also have to develop some basic Web design skills so that you can lay out a Web site that makes sense to the users who access it on the Web. Spend some time getting familiar with HTML, and take advantage of programs, such as Microsoft FrontPage, that can do a lot of the design work for you. Also, spend some time on the Web, and check out how the sites you like best have been designed.

Basically, the Web Publishing Wizard is a tool for getting your Web files onto a Web server (so that others can access your Web pages with their Web browsers). All you need is the URL address (such as www.*mywebsite*.com) and the FTP address (such as ftp.mypages.com) for the Web server that you will upload your files to. (Actually, both addresses point to the same location, but when you transfer the pages to the server, you use a method called FTP—File Transfer Protocol—which enables you to upload content.) If an Internet service provider supplies you with Web server space for your Web page, make sure that you get the correct site addresses from your provider.

After you have this information and your Web files assembled in a particular folder, select **Start**, then **Programs**, then **Microsoft Web Publishing**, and finally, **Web Publishing Wizard**. The Web Publishing Wizard opens. Follow the prompts to get your Web files onto the Web server.

Going Hyper with Hyperlinks

Wouldn't it be great if you could set up a field, in a table or form, that would whisk you to a site on the Web? Well, you can; you set up your field as a *hyperlink*. Hyperlinks chain or connect two items, such as documents. For instance, when you click a hyperlink, you are taken to the next document, picture, or other item. You might have a field in a database table that lists important documents related to your business. Clicking on the hyperlink field would take you to the actual document, which could reside in Microsoft Word.

Hyperlinks and OLE objects have certain aspects in common. They both can be used to get to information that resides outside your current database table or form. Hyperlinks, however, do not truly link or embed themselves to your database fields, as OLE objects do. Hyperlinks are just a quick path to another place or item.

Hyperlinks to the Web

In your database tables, using hyperlinks that reference sites on the Web is a great way to tie your Access databases into the Information Superhighway. Let's say that you work at a computer consulting firm and that one of your jobs is to keep track of the companies that supply technology training resources (like this wonderful book). No problem, you can set up an Access database that lists all the various technology resources. The table would probably include the name of the company, a contact person, and other pertinent fields.

Wouldn't it be great if you could set up the technology resource table with a field that, when clicked, would take you to the particular company's home page? Well, sure it would, and this is a great way to explore how Access uses hyperlinks to connect to the Web.

A table for technology resources cries out for a hyperlink field.

Creating the Hyperlink Field

Creating the link is very easy. All you have to do is open your table in Table Design view. Create a new field for your hyperlink, and then make sure that you set the field type as (yes, you guessed it) Hyperlink.

Getting back to our example again, you have a table for your technology resource companies (after Macmillan and Microsoft—okay, so I had to mention them because they publish my books and create the software I write my books about). After you are in the Edit view, create a new field. Let's say you call it `Web Site`. You would type this into the Field Name box. Then you press **Enter**, and that takes you to the Data Type box. Click the drop-down arrow that appears in the Data Type box, and select **Hyperlink**.

Setting the field type as Hyperlink.

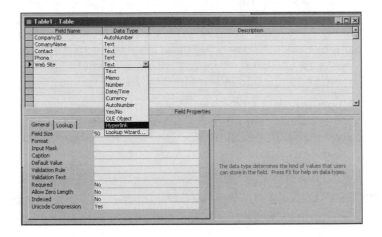

Setting up the data type (Hyperlink) is the easy part of the process. After you return to the Datasheet view of the table, you have to specify the actual document or place (such as a Web site) that you want the hyperlink to take you to.

Specifying the Web Address in the Hyperlink Field

The information that you place in the Hyperlink field in the table specifies the document, spreadsheet, graphic, or Web page that you would like the field to take you to when you click it. Hyperlinked items can reside on a local drive, a network, or the Web. In our example, we want the field to take us to the Web support site of a software company listed in our vendors table.

Web sites on the Web are located by their URLs. *URL* stands for *uniform resource locator*, and URLs serve as the addresses for all the sites residing on the Web. For instance, Microsoft's Web site has the URL `http://www.microsoft.com/`.

URL Back Story

You will find that URLs ending in com are sites related to companies. Sites related to an educational institution have a URL ending in edu. Government site URLs end in gov.

Let's say that we want one of the fields in our table to connect us to Macmillan Publishing's home page. All you have to do is type `http://www.mcp.com` in the field.

The Hyperlink field contains the Web site address.

Notice that when you place the mouse pointer on the field, a small hand appears. This means that the hyperlink is ready to go.

If you hate typing long URLs into your Hyperlink field, you can use Internet Explorer to give your fingers a rest. Open a particular Web site, using the Web toolbar in Microsoft Access. You can pull the site right from your Favorites list. This will open Internet Explorer and display the Web page. Select the URL that appears in the Explorer's Address box. Then press the Ctrl key and the letter *C* simultaneously (Ctrl+C). This copies the address to the Windows Clipboard. All you have to do then is return to the Hyperlink field in your database table and paste the URL into the field, using the Edit and Paste commands.

Surfing via Your Hyperlink

When you have the hyperlink addresses entered into the table, all you have to do is click a particular field (the one with the hyperlink in it), and it will open Internet Explorer and take you to the correct Web site. This provides you with a database table connected to a wealth of information concerning a particular product, a company, or some other piece of knowledge that you like to locate quickly.

363

Access and the Global Network

By now, you have a feel for the incredible possibilities that Access offers you through its connectivity with the Internet and the World Wide Web. These features, such as HTML and hyperlinks, tie you into an enormous global network that is just swimming in information.

Not only does Access tie you into this huge information loop, but it also gives you the tools to publish your own information in a Web-ready format. Move over, Buck Rogers, because Access is going to help blast us right into the twenty-first century—the information age and beyond!

The Least You Need to Know

➤ Saving your database objects in HTML format enables you to quickly create Web-ready objects for a home page.

➤ Creating access data pages enables you to place dynamic Access objects right on your Web pages. These data access pages can be used by visitors to your Web site to add data to your various Access database tables.

➤ Hyperlink fields can be used to quickly jump to a document, spreadsheet, or site on the World Wide Web.

➤ The Hyperlink field type is created in Design view of your table.

➤ You enter the location or Web address of the hyperlink destination in Datasheet view of a table.

➤ Access offers an excellent connection to the Web and all its incredible informational resources.

Installing Access 2000

A Very Easy Installation

Installing Microsoft Access 2000 and the other components of Microsoft Office 2000 couldn't be any easier. As a matter of fact, when you insert the CD-ROM into your CD drive, the installation software automatically starts itself.

My CD-ROM Is Dead!

If for some reason the auto-run feature on the CD-ROM does not load the installation software, you can do it manually. Click the Windows **Start** button and then click **Run**. In the Run box, type D:\setup.exe. (Make sure that you designate the drive letter of your CD-ROM in the place of the D shown if your CD drive is not labeled D.) Then click **OK**. The Office installation program should load.

Name and CD Key, Please

The first Office installation screen welcomes you and asks you to provide your name, your organization name, and the CD Key for your Office CD-ROM (the key is usually on a sticker on the bottom of the jewel case that the CD came in). Type the information in the appropriate box and then click **Next** to continue.

The opening screen of the Microsoft Office installation asks you to identify yourself and provide the CD Key for the Office CD-ROM.

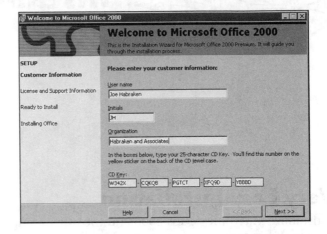

Terms of Endearment

The next Office installation screen asks you to read the Office 2000 end-user agreement (end-user, that's you). After you have read the agreement, click the **I Accept the Terms in the License Agreement** radio button. Then click the **Next** button to continue.

Ready to Install

The next screen is where you actually start the installation process. You can do a typical installation or do a custom installation. The easiest way to install the software is to click the big **Install Now** button. This will place Office 2000 (or Access 2000, if bought as a standalone product) on your computer's C: drive in a folder called C:\Program Files\Microsoft Office.

The typical installation will install the most common Office 2000 components, such as all the applications (Access, Word, and so on) and other tools, like clip art.

Be advised that Internet Explorer 5.0 will also be installed as part of the Access (or Office) installation. This means that all previous versions of your Internet Explorer software will be replaced. Don't let this fact send you screaming from the room, however; the Internet Explorer 5 upgrade does import your history lists and bookmarks. You will also find that the new version of Outlook Express included with Explorer 5 will import your address book and mail folders.

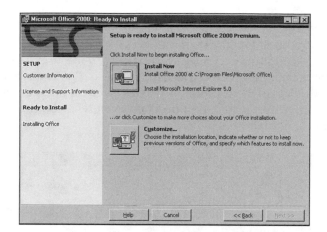

The easiest route to an Office 2000 installation is the big Install Now button.

Installations May Vary

If you purchased Access as a standalone product or if you are doing the software installation from disks, the procedure for installation might differ slightly. For help, take a look at the *Getting Started* booklet, which is in the box with your software.

If you choose to do the typical installation already discussed, your CD-ROM will churn for a while, and then Office 2000 will be installed on your hard drive. You will also be told that your computer will be restarted, but this signals the end of the installation. When your computer restarts, you can start using the Office 2000 applications—even Access.

Getting a Custom Installation

If you would rather do a custom installation and make sure that all the components you typically use are installed on your computer, you can take that route. Although the typical installation is certainly a sure-fire method of getting your software up and running quickly, the custom installation allows you to make sure that all the bells and whistles included in Office are installed. To do a custom installation, click the **Customize** button on the Office installation screen.

Location, Location, Location

If you choose the customize option, the next screen asks you where you would like to install the software. That is, what location or folder do you want to use to put all this stuff on your hard drive? The default location for the installation is C:\Program Files\Microsoft Office. You can change the location as needed. Notice that on this particular installation screen, the Office installation program even tells you how much free space you have on each drive.

Determining where you would like to install the Office software.

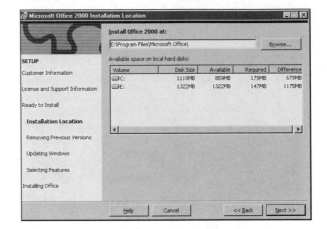

When you specify a location, the installation program creates the folder for you, if it doesn't already exist. To continue with the installation, click the **Next** button.

Any Older Versions Installed?

The next step in the installation process is the detection of previous versions of Office software. If the installation software detects previous versions of Office components on your computer, it will list them on the installation screen. You are advised to remove these components (you can remove them by canceling the installation process, placing your CD-ROM for the older version of the software in your CD drive, and then using the Remove feature to remove the software from your computer).

If you don't want to remove older versions of Office components, that's okay. They should be able to coexist with the newer versions. Just make sure that when you specify a location for the installation of Office 2000, you pick a folder other than the folder that the older software lives in. This should keep both versions happy.

When you've sorted out this older version conundrum, click **Next** to continue with the installation.

Internet Explorer 5—Love It or Not

In the next step of the installation process, you are told that Internet Explorer 5 will be installed on your computer. It is an integral component of Office 2000. You can select (using the drop-down arrow) to install Internet Explorer 5 in a standard installation or minimal installation. The standard installation includes Microsoft Outlook Express and other Explorer tools. If you are short on hard drive space and do not use Outlook Express as your email package, you might want to go with the minimum installation, which does not include Outlook Express and so does not require as much space. Choose your installation preference and click **Next**.

Definitely a New Look

On the next screen, you get a look at the new software selection interface for specific component installation. The new Microsoft Installation Interface shows an icon for each Office product, such as Access, available on your CD-ROM. A plus symbol (+) next to a particular software application enables you to open and view all the components for that application. Click one of the plus symbols, and a cascading list shows you all the components under a specific category (such as Microsoft Access for Windows).

After you have seen all the options for a particular software component, you can click a particular option and then choose from a menu how you want the component installed: Run from My Computer (meaning it is installed on your PC), Run from CD (the component is run from a CD, so make sure that you keep it in the CD-ROM drive), and Installed on First Use (the component is not installed from the CD until you use the component for the first time).

When you do the typical installation, a number of features such as additional wizards and other special components are not installed to your computer (the Run From My Computer choice). They are instead marked with a 1, meaning they will be installed on first use. One thing you should understand about first use installations is that you should keep your Office 2000 CD-ROM nearby. When you try to use a particular feature, Access might ask you for the CD-ROM so that it can install the feature.

If you have the hard drive space, you might want to mark some of the components listed to run on first use as Run from My Computer so that they are installed during this initial installation of Office.

Components can be marked as Run from My Computer, Run from CD, or Installed on First Use.

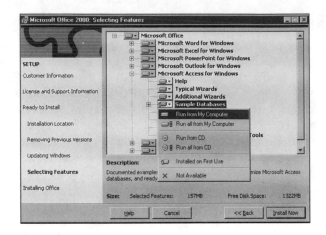

Finishing the Installation

After you choose the components you want to install and how you want to install them, you are ready to complete the installation. Click the **Next** button, and the Office installation software copies all the files from the CD-ROM to the place you've designated on your local drive. When the installation is complete, Office lets you know. All you have to do is click **OK**, and then you're ready to start doing some serious computing.

Icons for your Office components will be placed on the Program menu activated by the Windows **Start** button. Office also provides you with the Office toolbar that can be used to start any of the Office components.

Final Notes on Software Installation

When you begin using your software, you might find that you would like to add components that were not installed during your initial run-through with the software. This doesn't pose a problem. Just reinsert the CD-ROM into the CD-ROM drive. A window will automatically open. Click the **Add or Remove Features** button and then select components that you want to install (or remove). You complete the installation of the new components by following the prompts, as you did when you initially installed your software.

After you install the software, I think you will agree that Office 2000 and its components (you know, Access, the subject of this great book) are incredible productivity tools that are easy and fun to use. Good luck with all your computing!

Speak like a Geek: The Complete Reference

action argument   An argument that gives a macro action its specificity. For example, for a particular command such as the DoMenuitem, you must set an action argument that tells the macro which menu item to do or select.

action   A specific command or other macro that you place in the macro design box. When you run a macro, all the actions in the macro are fired off in their appropriate sequence.

administrator   The owner of a database who has been assigned user-level security. The administrator assigns the rights and maintains the various groups associated with the database.

alphanumeric character   A letter of the alphabet or another non-numeric symbol.

AutoForm   A form that uses all the fields in the table as it displays the data one record at a time. You click the **New Object** button on the toolbar to create an AutoForm.

best fit   Double-clicking on a column divider in a datasheet widens the column to the left of the mouse pointer to accommodate the longest entry that has been entered in it.

bitmap image   A file format for graphics. It is the standard format for the Windows environment.

bound control   A control in a form or report tied to a particular field in the associated table or query. The opposite of the bound control is the unbound control.

chart   A graphical representation of numeric data in a table, query, form, or report. Charts for Access objects can be created using the Graph 5.0 program that ships with Access and the other members of Microsoft Office software package.

child form   A subform that is inserted into a parent form as an object in Design view. Each of the forms, the child and parent, must be forms based on related tables. The child form typically shows records in a datasheet format.

combo box   A box that provides a drop-down list of choices in a table form, or report, and also gives you the option of typing in an entry not found on the list.

command button   A button that can be placed on a form to invoke certain commands such as printing. Command buttons can also be tied to macros.

compact   To defragment a database file to increase its performance. Compacting a database file also frees up disk space on your hard drive.

control   A dynamic box in a form or report that calls data from a specific field in a table or uses a formula designed in the Expression Builder to calculate an answer.

control format   The way a control is set up to display its contents, such as with a certain number of decimal places or as currency. Control formats are set in the control's Properties box.

criterion   A conditional statement that you devise for a query.

crosstab query   A query that displays its results in a spreadsheet-like format, presenting the data in rows and columns. This type of query works well when you want to follow a certain field, such as *name*, across the crosstab to view items associated with a particular person or thing.

Database Documentor   An Access feature that can provide a detailed report on any of your database objects. The report includes date of creation and specifics on such things as the fields in a table, or the actions in a macro.

database object   An item that can be part of a database. Objects can consist of data manipulation and viewing containers such as tables, forms, and reports, or mini-software programs that you create using macros and the Visual Basic application language that comes with Microsoft Access.

data access page   A Web-ready data input form that is created as an access page, a new object type included in Access 2000. The data access page is created using fields from a table or tables and then used as a data input device on a Web page. Data entered into the access page on the Web is incorporated into the appropriate table or tables in your database. See *HTML* and *World Wide Web*.

data file   A file for an Access 2000 database. Each Access database is saved with the file extension .mdb.

detail area   The main area of the design window for forms and reports. The detail area is where the controls representing fields or calculations are placed when a form or report is being designed.

dialog box   Boxes that gather information from or present messages to the user.

drag and drop   The easiest way to move a selection a short distance. Select an item and then drag it to the new location.

Dynamic HTML   A concept that enables Access objects (tables and forms) exported as .asp files to be used to receive new data via the Web. Data input received through these objects updates the associated table in an Access database. See *HTML*.

export   To move data out of Access and into another application. You can cut and paste information from Access directly into other applications. For example, you can export Access tables into Excel, where they are treated as spreadsheets.

Expression Builder   A tool for building mathematic formulas and other expressions that can be placed in form and report controls.

external data   Information that resides outside Access in another format. Access is capable of importing external data that is stored in Excel and Lotus spreadsheets.

field   A particular piece of information, such as a name or address, found in a data record.

field property   A control parameter that dictates how information in a field is stored, handled, or displayed.

filter   To view certain records in a datasheet. You can filter by selection, by selecting an example of a field parameter you want to view by, or you can filter by form, by typing a filter parameter into a specific field.

folder   What used to be called a *directory*; it contains data and software files.

footer   The area at the bottom of a printed page. It is also the bottom area in the form and report Design views. Items placed in the page footer area repeat on every page of the form or report.

form   An object that supplies a record-by-record view of your database records. Forms are excellent for data input and editing.

freeze   To immobilize a particular column in a datasheet so that it remains in view when you scroll to the extreme edges of the data area.

glossary term   In the Help system, a highlighted term and definition of a word or topic that appears in a glossary box.

group   1. An area of a report where certain information is grouped together, such as a subtotal for a set of selected fields. 2. A set of users that have been placed in the same security level for a database.

header   The area at the top of a printed page. In form and report Design views, the header area is at the top of the design area. Items placed in the page header area repeat on every page of the form or report. You can also have section headers and group headers in reports; they are used to place information at the top of a summary group or report section.

home page   The main page that is displayed when you connect to a Web site.

HTML (Hypertext Markup Language)   The set of tagging codes that is used to publish material electronically for the World Wide Web. HTML tells a Web browser such as Internet Explorer how to display the text and graphics contained in the Web document or home page.

hyperlink   In Access, a field type that enables you to jump to another document or item. Placing a URL in a hyperlink field allows you to connect to Web sites on the WWW by clicking on the field.

import   To take data that resides outside Access and place it in a new or existing Access table.

input mask   A defined pattern for all the data entered in a particular field. Input masks are assigned to fields during table design.

insertion point   The blinking, vertical line that points to where you are in a text box, field, or other text area. In former days, this thing was called the *cursor*.

Internet   A global system of linked computers. This mega-network began as an experimental project that enabled universities and military computers to maintain contact during times of national emergencies. The Internet is now a resource for people such as you and me and enables the exchange of email, the transfer of files, and the browsing of Web sites. The World Wide Web is one incarnation of the Internet, and Internet resources are navigated using an Internet Web browser. The Web is really the interface, and the Internet is the underlying backbone.

Internet Explorer   Microsoft's Web browser, which is an integral part of the software tools found in Microsoft Office 97.

join   A link created between two tables (or more, if needed) in the Query Design window. Joins link tables together by a like field. Joins are basically the same thing as a relationship between the tables; however, the join is created for the purpose of the query and is saved with the query. An actual relationship between the tables would have to be created in the Relationship window.

join table   A table that is used to join two tables in a many-to-many relationship. The join table consists of two fields only: the primary keys from each of the tables involved in the relationship. Each table has a one-to-many relationship with the join table, which in effect creates a many-to-many relationship between the two tables.

label   The tag for a control in a form or a report. The label usually contains the name of the field that the control is associated with.

landscape   A page that is oriented with the width greater than the length. This would be 11 by 8 1/2 inches for a typical piece of paper.

list box   A box that provides a drop-down list of choices in a table, form, or report.

local drive   The Windows way of referring to the hard drive on your computer. You can have more than one local drive; it depends on how many fixed disks have been physically installed on your computer.

macro   A set of actions that you put together to automate repetitive tasks. Macros can be built to open specific tables or forms or to open a form, wait for data entry, and then print the form.

mail merge   A process that involves creating a word processing document such as a form letter and exporting data from Access to provide the address information for the letters. Mail merges can be used to create letters, mailing labels, and envelopes, as well as other document types. A mail merge, which is handled by the Mail Merge Wizard, requires that you have Microsoft Word installed on your computer.

mailing label report   A special kind of database report that creates mailing labels for you. A specific wizard exists for the creation of mailing labels.

main form   The parent form that a subform (also known as a *child form*) is placed on. The main form displays record fields that are related to the field shown in the subform. A main form can be any form in Access on which you place a subform in the form Design window.

many-to-many relationship   A relationship between tables in which each record in the first table has many possible matches in the second table, and the records in the second table have many potential matches in the first table.

menu bar   A pull-down system that gives you access to software commands and features.

module   A miniprogram built with Visual Basic code. Modules require programming; they can be used to automate tasks and radically alter the user interface for a particular database.

normalization   The act of taking a table that has fields in which data is repeated and breaking it into smaller related tables. Access has automated the normalization process via the Table Analyzer.

object   An item that originates in a source or server application and is linked to or embedded into a destination application. An object can be a spreadsheet, graph, graphic image, or just about anything that can be created in an application. An object can also be a database item, such as a table, form, or report.

OfficeLinks   A set of commands that make it easy for you to export data from Access to other Microsoft products. You can use OfficeLinks to export tables to Excel or create a mail merge, using Access data in a Microsoft Word form letter.

OLE (object linking and embedding)   A process by which information is placed in an application that has originated in another application. Linking ties outside information to an object such as a table, but the linked file resides outside the database table. Embedded information, such as a graph or a graphic, becomes part of the database file that it is placed in, thus increasing its size.

OLE field   A field that is placed in an Access table that uses linked or embedded objects as its source. For instance, an OLE field in a table can hold embedded photos.

one-to-many relationship   A relationship between tables in which a record in the first table can be matched to more than one record in the second table.

one-to-one relationship   A relationship between tables in which each record in the first table can be matched to only one record in the second table.

optimization   The process of making a database object as efficient as possible. The Performance Analyzer can be used to optimize any of your database objects; it provides tips—recommendations, suggestions, and ideas—and strategies for increasing object performance.

option   A parameter associated with the Access application window. Options can dictate a wide array of things, ranging from whether the status bar is shown to the default size of fields in datasheets or forms.

Page Setup   A menu command that gives you the ability to determine the orientation (portrait or landscape) and the margins of the pages you want to print. Page Setup can be accessed via the Print dialog box or set in the Options dialog box.

password   A security device that makes you the owner of a particular database. You must type in the password every time you open the database.

pivot table   A flexible crosstab-formatted spreadsheet that allows you to drag the columns and rows to new locations, pivoting the data. This enables you to group and summarize the data in the spreadsheet in various ways. You can export an Access database into Excel and then create a pivot table, or you can create a pivot table in Access.

portrait   A page that is oriented with the length greater than the width. This would be 8 1/2 by 11 inches for a typical piece of paper.

primary key   A field that uniquely identifies each record in a table. The table is indexed automatically by the primary key field.

print properties   Global settings that affect all your print jobs. The Print Property dialog box has three tabs: Paper, Graphics, and Device. Remember that when you set print properties, you are affecting all the print jobs from all your software packages.

property   An attribute of controls in forms and reports. The properties of a control dictate the source of the control, such as a particular field. An input mask is also a property of a control in a form.

query   A way to ask a table or tables certain questions. A select query lists the records that satisfy a certain question or parameter. An action query actually does something to a table, such as deleting records that satisfy a certain request. Queries can also be used to return totals or the answers to other mathematic expressions.

record   A collection of data pertaining to a particular person, place, or thing. Appears as a row in a datasheet.

relational database   A database that groups information in discrete tables. Relationships exist between the tables in this type of database. An example is a small business database in which the customer information, product information, supplier information, and employee information all reside in separate tables, but can be tied together by queries, forms, and reports.

Repair   A command that can be used to fix database files that are corrupted or damaged. Because this process entails some risk to your data, make sure to create a copy or to back up the database file before beginning the process.

report   An object that pulls together data from a table or a number of tables and presents the information in a readable, well-designed format.

section   An area that you can add to a report. For instance, you can add a group section that provides a subtotal for certain information or provides some other type of summary information.

sort   To re-order table records numerically or alphanumerically in either ascending or descending order.

Start button   Used to start your applications; it gives you access to all your program groups and application icons.

status bar   An area of the application window that gives you specific information about what's going on with the software.

Static HTML   Database objects saved as .html files that provide you with an object that can be viewed on the World Wide Web. The object is nothing more than a photo of the current Access object. Static HTML objects cannot be updated directly—only viewed.

subform   A form that you can place in a control on an already existing form. It enables you to see data from two different tables as you work with the form.

subreport   A previously created report that can be placed in a control on a second report. Subreports are excellent vehicles for placing a short summary report on a longer, more detailed main report.

table   An object, consisting of information in rows and columns, that is used for data input and editing in your database.

taskbar   A bar that resides at the bottom of the Windows desktop and shows which applications are currently open. You click an application on the taskbar to restore it to the desktop.

template   A blueprint or foundation for a database that can include ready-made tables, forms, reports, and other database components.

title bar   A band that tells you the name of your application and can be used to move the software window on the desktop.

toolbar   A quick-access mechanism that provides a one-click method of invoking a variety of the software's features and commands.

Toolbox toolbar   A group of design tools used to create forms and reports in their respective Design views.

URL (uniform resource locator)   An address that you use to locate a Web site on the World Wide Web.

user level   A degree of access to a database's objects. User levels are assigned to user groups. The group that you belong to dictates your level of access to the objects.

Visual Basic   A Windows programming language. Visual Basic for Applications is a common language used by Microsoft programs such as Access and Excel.

wizard   An interactive feature that walks you through the steps involved in a particular process, such as creating a form. Wizards use a series of dialog boxes to get answers to specific questions and then create a particular object or complete a particular task, based on those answers.

World Wide Web (WWW)   An electronic patchwork of interconnected HTML documents residing on various computers hooked to the Internet. The Web is navigated via a Web browser, which enables you to view the various pages present.

zoom   To increase or decrease the degree of detail that you can see on an object displayed in the Print Preview window. You can zoom out to see the design of the entire page or zoom in to view specific data.

Index

When You're **Smart** Enough to **Know** That **You** Don't Know It All!

For all the ups and downs you're sure to encounter in life,
The Complete Idiot's Guides give you
down-to-earth answers and practical solutions.

Complete Idiot's Guide to Microsoft Office 2000
Joe Kraynak
ISBN: 0-7897-1848-0
$16.99/$25.95

Complete Idiot's Guide to Microsoft Word 2000
Dan Bobola
ISBN: 0-7897-1860-X
$16.99/$25.95

Complete Idiot's Guide to Microsoft Excel 2000
Sherry Kinkoph
ISBN: 0-7897-1868-5
$16.99/$25.95

Complete Idiot's Guide to Visual Basic 6
Clayton Walnum
ISBN: 0-7897-1812-X
$19.99/$29.95

Complete Idiot's Guide to Microsoft PowerPoint 2000
Nat Gertler
ISBN: 0-7897-1866-9
$16.99/$25.95

Complete Idiot's Guide to Microsoft FrontPage 2000
Elisabeth Parker
ISBN: 0-7897-1806-5
$16.99/$25.95

Complete Idiot's Guide to PalmPilot and PalmIII
Preston Gralla
ISBN: 0-7897-1967-3
$16.99/$25.95

Complete Idiot's Guide to Microsoft Outlook 2000
Bob Temple
ISBN: 0-7897-1981-9
$16.99/$25.95

Complete Idiot's Guide to Networking Your Home
Mark Thompson
ISBN: 0-7897-1963-0
$16.99/$25.95

Complete Idiot's Guide to QuickBooks and QuickBooks Pro 99
Gail Perry
ISBN: 0-7897-1966-5
$16.99/$25.95

Other Related Titles

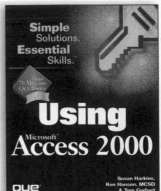

Using Microsoft Access 2000
Harkins, Hansen, and Gerhart
ISBN: 0-7897-1604-6
$29.99/$44.95

Special Edition Using Microsoft Word 2000
Bill Camarda
ISBN: 0-7897-1852-9
$39.99/$59.95

Special Edition Using Microsoft PowerPoint 2000
Patrice Rutledge
ISBN: 0-7897-1904-5
$39.99/$59.95

Special Edition Using Microsoft Outlook 2000
Gordon Padwick
ISBN: 0-7897-1909-6
$39.99/$59.95

Special Edition Using Microsoft FrontPage 2000
Dennis Jones
ISBN: 0-7897-1910-X
$39.99/$59.95

Woody Leonhard Teaches Office 2000
Woody Leonhard
ISBN: 0-7897-1871-5
$19.99/$29.95

Special Edition Using Microsoft Publisher 2000
Roger Parker
ISBN: 0-7897-1970-3
$39.99/$59.95

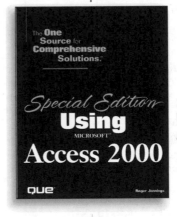

Special Edition Using Microsoft Access 2000
Roger Jennings
ISBN: 0-7897-1606-2
$39.99/$59.95

Special Edition Using Microsoft Office 2000
Ed Bott
ISBN: 0-7897-1842-1
$39.99/$59.95

www.quecorp.com

All prices are subject to change.